Penguin Handbooks
Caribbean Cooking

Elisabeth Lambert Ortiz was born in London but has lived
and worked as a journalist all over the world, including in
England, the United States, Mexico, the Caribbean, the Far
East (principally Bangkok), South and Central America and
Australia. She is at present living in England with her
husband, Cesar Ortiz-Tinoco, a Mexican journalist-diplomat
and a former high official of the United Nations.

Mrs Ortiz has written numerous cookery books, on Mexico,
the Caribbean, Japan (with Mitsuko Endo), and Latin
America, and has also translated, edited and prepared
recipes for *Masterpieces of French Cuisine*. A principal
consultant for the *Time-Life Foods of the World* series, she
has written five chapters for the *World Atlas of Food* and
has contributed to the *Royal Cookbook*. She has written
innumerable articles on subjects ranging from economics to
cooking and travel. She now writes regularly for the *Gourmet*
magazine. She has written two novels; a scientific book for
children on the sea; several books of verse – her work has
appeared in verse anthologies throughout the
English-speaking world and been published in France and
South America in translation – and has had a verse play
broadcast by the B.B.C.

Caribbean Cooking

Elisabeth Lambert Ortiz

 Penguin Books

Penguin Books Ltd,
Harmondsworth, Middlesex, England
Penguin Books,
625 Madison Avenue, New York, New York 10022, U.S.A.
Penguin Books Australia Ltd,
Ringwood, Victoria, Australia
Penguin Books Canada Ltd,
41 Steelcase Road West, Markham, Ontario, Canada
Penguin Books (N.Z.) Ltd,
182–190 Wairau Road, Auckland 10, New Zealand

First published in the U.S.A. as *The Complete Book of Caribbean Cookery*
by M. Evans & Co. Inc., 1973
This revised edition first published 1975 by André Deutsch Ltd
Published in Penguin Books 1977

Made and printed in Great Britain by
Hazell Watson & Viney Ltd, Aylesbury, Bucks
Set in Monotype Walbaum

contents

foreword

I became interested in Caribbean cooking a long time ago when I was lucky enough to spend several years at school in the West Indies. We left London for Portsmouth by train one grey day in February. It had been snowing, and the trees were lacy black skeletons against the white fields. The sky was pale blue, with a faint yellow winter sun. Coming by ship into Kingston Harbour in Jamaica, with everything a blaze of colour, all reds and yellows and deep vivid greens, a sun like fire in a deep blue sky, and the sea – the beautiful Caribbean sea – ranging from jade at the shore, through turquoise to indigo, it was almost more than I could believe.

The market was a sheer delight. The vendors were mostly women, handsome in their full, printed skirts with white blouses. We often saw them coming into the market walking with immense grace, their baskets of produce balanced on their heads. And the produce! Great piles of yellow oranges and green limes, and pale yellow grapefruit, papayas ranging from green to orange, scarlet, yellow and black ackees, green and black avocados, mangoes as vivid as a sunset, great green-skinned, yellow-fleshed pumpkins cut to show their quality to the buyer, and huge yams, and little yams, and tiny green okras. Of course, we had most of them in London markets but there they were imported, exotic, and sold in a setting less vivid than the market at Half-Way Tree, or Cross Roads.

It was my first journey away from home, and like the rest of the family, I loved it. Mother adopted a number of Jamaican dishes into the family repertoire, and brief excursions taught me that, just as every island has its own character, so do their kitchens. Though I managed a few more island trips later, it was not until 1966 that I was able to settle down to a proper study of the cooking which had earlier captured my imagination as a schoolgirl.

The Caribbean kitchen is above all eclectic, gathering its ingredients and cooking methods from Europe, Asia and Africa, and joining them in happy association with its own native foods. Christopher Columbus in 1492 discovered the West Indies, that chain of islands which runs from Florida in the north to Venezuela in the south, and includes the Greater Antilles, Cuba, Jamaica, Hispaniola (Haiti–Dominican Republic), and Puerto Rico, as well as the smaller islands that make up the Lesser Antilles, the Leeward and Windward Islands and the Virgin Islands. Africa, Spain, Britain, France, the Netherlands, Denmark and the USA, as well as Indian and Chinese settlers, not to mention the Caribs and Arawaks, have all played their part in the development of a cuisine where a Dominican sancocho, a Trinidadian curry and a keshy yena from Curaçao are perfectly at home with a Danish-inspired asparagus pudding. Though each island has its specialities, they will be met in other islands as welcome resident aliens, and many dishes, such as the banana and coconut desserts, are truly island-wide.

When he first arrived in the Caribbean, Columbus is said to have remarked that he saw so many islands he hardly knew to which he should go first. I felt rather the same way when I began serious island-hopping. I solved the problem by dividing the islands into language, or national groups – the Dutch Islands, the French-speaking, the English-speaking, and the Spanish-speaking islands. It worked very well as this way I could much more easily trace the origins of the dishes I encountered; later on I had a great deal of fun tracing a single dish in its migration, for dishes in the Caribbean tend to island-hop as much as tourists do. Nevertheless, there is a permanent French stamp on the foods of the French islands, a recognizable Spanish stamp on the foods of the Spanish-speaking islands, and so on. I was also extraordinarily lucky to have friends throughout the islands who helped me by letting me into their kitchens. And later island friends here at home who checked my findings. I am deeply in the debt of all and more grateful than I can say. Yet, after almost seven years of intermittent island visiting, I must in all honesty confess that there are still islands whose culinary treasures I have not yet unearthed: Bequia, Barbuda, unvisited.

I have cooked and tested all the recipes in this book, at home, in New York in my own kitchen with ingredients obtained locally, and without any great difficulty. The local ingredients work very well.

I love the Caribbean, and I love Caribbean food. I hope that readers will feel the same, especially about the food, since this book has very much been a labour of love.

New York – 1966–1972   E.L.O.

acknowledgements

I would like to thank the friends, old and new, who have given me such generous help with this book. I shall be forever in their debt, and if I have, by some accident, left anyone out, I ask forgiveness in advance.

For help with the cooking of the Netherlands Antilles, Mrs Evert M. (Bep) Newton, Mr van Gign, and Mr Sixto Felida; for the Cuban kitchen, Mrs Mirtha Stengel, Mr and Mrs Roberto Rendueles, and Venezuelan diplomat Dr Raul Nass of the O.A.S., Washington, D.C.; for the Guadeloupe kitchen, Mr Roger Fortuné, Mr Mario Petreluzzi, Mr H. Bade and Mrs Jean-Noël Villahaut Ces François; in Jamaica, Mrs Roy A. Lyons, Mr Richard Lyons, Miss Mary R. Olson, Dr Alex D. Hawkes, and Mr Peter Finch; for the Martinique kitchen, Mrs Yveline de Lucy de Fossarieu, Mr Elie Ducros, Mr Jean-Claude Fays, Mr Henry Joseph, Mr Jacques Guannel, Miss Verrey, Mrs Mireille de Lépine, and Mr Gérard R. de Campeau; for the Puerto Rican kitchen, Mrs Tere de Lomba, Miss Josefina de Román and Mr Roberto Ramos Rodriguez; for the cooking of St Kitts and other Leeward Islands, Nevis, St Martin, Montserrat and Anguilla, Mr Arthur Leaman of the *Golden Lemon*, St Kitts, Mrs Aimie Osborne, and Mrs Lilian Johnston; for the cooking of the Dominican Republic, Mrs Amanda Ornés de Perelló; for the cooking of Trinidad, Tobago, Barbados and the Windward Islands, Miss Nonée Osborne, Mr and Mrs Raymond Roopchand, Miss Lilian Fraser, Miss Ivy Walke, Mr and Mrs Leo Byam; for the cooking of Haiti, Mrs Nicole Scott and Mrs Lyonelle Singer.

My special thanks to Olive and Wilma, who refused to give me their full names on the grounds that they weren't really doing anything when they let me work with them in their kitchens, giving me in fact most precious help.

My thanks also go to Miss Barbara Sue Ting Len, not only for secretarial help, but for putting at my disposal her knowledge of the influence of the Guyanese kitchen on Trinidad and other islands, and to Miss Sonia Lecca and Miss Yvonne Wong for secretarial help.

weights and measures

Conversion Table

LIQUID MEASURES

BRITISH

1 quart	=	2 pints	=	40 fl. oz.
1 pint	=	4 gills	=	20 fl. oz.
½ pint	=	2 gills		
		or one cup	=	10 fl. oz.
¼ pint	=	8 tablespoons	=	5 fl. oz.
		1 tablespoon	=	just over ½ fl. oz.
		1 dessertspoon	=	⅓ fl. oz.
		1 teaspoon	=	⅙ fl. oz.

METRIC

1 litre = 10 decilitres (dl.) = 100 centilitres (cl.) = 1000 millilitres (ml.)

AMERICAN

1 quart	=	2 pints	=	32 fl. oz.
1 pint	=	2 cups	=	16 fl. oz.
		1 cup	=	8 fl. oz.
		1 tablespoon	=	⅓ fl. oz.
		1 teaspoon	=	⅙ fl. oz.

Approx. equivalents

BRITISH	METRIC
1 quart	1·1 litre
1 pint	6 dl.
½ pint	3 dl.
¼ pint (1 gill)	1·5 dl.
1 tablespoon	15 ml.
1 dessertspoon	10 ml.
1 teaspoon	5 ml.

METRIC	BRITISH
1 litre	35 fl. oz.
½ litre (5 dl.)	18 fl. oz.
¼ litre (2·5 dl.)	9 fl. oz.
1 dl.	3½ fl. oz.

BRITISH	AMERICAN
1 quart	2½ pints
1 pint	1¼ pints
½ pint	10 fl. oz. (1¼ cups)
¼ pint (1 gill)	5 fl. oz.
1 tablespoon	1½ tablespoons
1 dessertspoon	1 tablespoon
1 teaspoon	⅓ fl. oz.

AMERICAN	BRITISH
1 quart	1½ pints+3 tbs (32 fl. oz.)
1 pint	¾ pint+2 tbs (16 fl. oz.)
1 cup	½ pint−2 tbs (8 fl. oz.)

SOLID MEASURES

BRITISH
16 oz. = 1 lb.

METRIC
1000 grammes = 1 kilogramme

Approx. equivalents

BRITISH	METRIC
1 lb. (16 oz.)	400 grammes
½ lb. (8 oz.)	200 g.
¼ lb. (4 oz.)	100 g.
1 oz.	25 g.

METRIC	BRITISH
1 kilo (1000g.)	2 lb. 3 oz.
½ kilo (500g.)	1 lb. 2 oz.
¼ kilo (250g.)	9 oz.
100g.	3½ oz.

PROPOSED TABLE OF TEMPERATURE EQUIVALENTS FOR OVEN THERMOSTAT MARKINGS

Present Scale Fahrenheit	Gas	Recommended Conversion to Centigrade Scale
225°F	Mark ¼	110°C
250°F	½	130°C
275°F	1	140°C
300°F	2	150°C
325°F	3	170°C
350°F	4	180°C
375°F	5	190°C
400°F	6	200°C
425°F	7	220°C
450°F	8	230°C
475°F	9	240°C

techniques of caribbean cooking

Certain techniques used in Caribbean cooking are what give their characteristic flavours to many of the dishes of the region. In the Spanish-speaking islands sofrito, a highly seasoned tomato–sweet pepper sauce, adapted from the original Spanish 'version, is widely used, so is lard or oil flavoured with achiote (annatto). Dry or wet massala (curry powder or paste) and ghee (clarified butter) are used in Trinidad, where the Indian influence is strong. An important Amerindian contribution is cassareep, a liquid seasoning made from grated cassava roots. Originally from Guyana on the South American mainland, its use has spread to Trinidad, to Barbados in the Windward Islands, to St Kitts in the Leeward Islands, and over to Jamaica in the Greater Antilles. A strong French influence can be seen in the use of seasonings, especially on islands which changed hands between Britain and France innumerable times, persisting even when the island ended up English.

The islanders themselves travel widely, so that one meets gifted cooks who have introduced the specialities of their island to another island quite far from home base. Our cook, Annie, was, I think, originally from Trinidad, Wilma, in Trinidad, was from St Lucia, Olive, in St Kitts, was from Dominica and called her casserole a daubing pot – an historical footnote to the fact that the island was more than once French. It is this internal migration that gives an overall quality to Caribbean cooking, though what are called in the islands nationality dishes – colombo in Martinique and Guadeloupe, saltfish and ackee in Jamaica, asopao in Puerto Rico, sancochos in the Dominican Republic, coo-coo, jug-jug and pudding and souse in Barbados, callaloo and accra and floats in Trinidad, and carne mechada in Cuba – are still very much alive in their original homelands.

No special cooking equipment is needed except that pots should be of good, heavy quality and not flimsily made. I find enamelled cast-iron ware very satisfactory for most Caribbean dishes, as it is both oven- and flame-proof. Puerto Rico has a special cooking pot, the caldero (literally a cauldron), which is a heavy cast-aluminium or iron casserole, round or oval, with a tight-fitting lid. Such diverse dishes as fillet of beef and arroz con pollo (chicken with rice) can be cooked with great success in this. Occasionally an earthenware casserole is advised, in which case make sure it is heavy enough not to crack over direct heat. Use one or more asbestos mats under it if necessary.

Any reasonably well-equipped kitchen will have a blender, wire whisks, kitchen scales, measuring cups and spoons, and so on; in fact all that is needed for these recipes.

For the recipes in the Drinks section the usual home bar equipment is all that is needed. This should include a variety of glasses, a shaker and mixing glass set with a strainer, a corkscrew, tin and bottle opener, a long stirring spoon, or a glass stirring rod, and a jigger measure with an accurate scale of $\frac{1}{2}$ and $\frac{1}{4}$ ounces. I find particularly useful the double-ended measure whose bowls are $\frac{3}{4}$ ounce at one end and 1 ounce at the other. These double measures come in a variety of sizes: $\frac{3}{4}$ and $1\frac{1}{4}$ ounces, $\frac{3}{4}$ and $1\frac{1}{2}$ ounces, 1 and $1\frac{1}{2}$ ounces, and 1 and 2 ounces.

There are no unusual techniques for preparing foods for cooking. Fruits and vegetables are washed and peeled in the usual way. Meats, poultry, fish and shellfish require no more than ordinary methods of handling and storage.

There are few difficulties facing a determined shopper planning to cook Caribbean. Meats and poultry are the same, except that goat and kid are used more than here. Fish and shellfish vary very little, and where a specific tropical fish is not available a similar fish is given as an alternative. The fruits, vegetables, herbs and spices for the recipes in this book can all be found without much effort. The Glossary explains them, and oriental, West Indian and Middle Eastern food shops carry the more exotic ones, though nowadays much that was once regarded as exotic has become commonplace, and available in supermarkets.

When a recipe calls for rum, you will always get a better result if you use the rum of the island, instead of relying on an all-purpose rum. The Drinks section can be consulted for using up any leftovers.

Recipes for these fundamentals of the Caribbean kitchen, and notes on island seasonings, are grouped here for convenience in the immediately following directions. They will, I think, be helpful for any cooks unfamiliar with the cooking approach of this region, and should be read before starting to cook the various island dishes.

cassareep

4 lb. cassava (yuca) roots

good ⅓ pint cold water

½ teaspoon ground cinnamon

½ teaspoon ground cloves

4 teaspoons dark brown sugar

Peel the cassava roots under cold running water. Dry on paper towels. Grate on the second finest side of the grater, or cut up coarsely and grate bit by bit in an electric blender. Add the water to the grated roots and stir to mix well. Squeeze about a cupful at a time through a dampened cloth, twisting the cloth to extract as much liquid as possible. When all is squeezed, put the cassava meal in a plastic bag and store it in the refrigerator for use in recipes calling for cassava meal.

Combine the liquid which has been squeezed out in a saucepan with the cinnamon, cloves and sugar. Bring to the boil, reduce the heat and simmer slowly, stirring from time to time, until the liquid is thick and syrupy. If the cassareep is not dark enough some cooks add caramel or a bottled commercial browning liquid for gravy. Use as directed in the recipe for Pepperpot. Keep refrigerated. Makes about 1 cup.

chicharrones de puerco   *spanish islands*

Pork Cracklings

I have made these with varying degrees of success. The secret lies, I am certain, in the age of the pig. Skin from the back of a young pig is what one needs. Fortunately, ready-made packaged chicharrones are available in shops in some West Indian neighbourhoods.

Have the butcher cut the skin from the back of a young pig, leaving about ¾ inch of fat on it. Carefully score the fat in a crisscross pattern without cutting through to the skin itself. Soak in cold water for 2 or 3 hours, drain and pat dry. Put the pork pieces in a heavy saucepan with a little melted lard, and cook, uncovered, very, very slowly for about 4 hours. When the skin looks transparent, increase the heat a little and cook for about 30 minutes longer until the skins puff up. Drain. Sprinkle with a little cold water, or Seville orange juice, and cook for a few minutes longer. Lift out and season with salt.

coconut milk and cream

Coconut milk and coconut cream are used a great deal in all the islands. If fresh coconut is not available, try to find packaged coconut cream. Failing this, use dried coconut, available packaged in supermarkets and from health-food stores. Health-food stores also carry tinned coconut milk, sometimes called coconut juice. The liquid inside the fresh coconut is called coconut water.

Pierce 2 of the 3 eyes of a coconut and drain out the water.

Strain and set aside. Put the coconut, eyes down, on a very hard surface and whack at it with a hammer. It will crack into enough small pieces to make it easy to remove the meat with a knife, levering the pieces out. Do not bother to remove the brown skin from the pieces to make milk or cream. However, if grated coconut is to be used in a recipe, it is necessary to peel this off.

Grate the coconut as fine as possible, or put into a blender with the reserved coconut water. For a very rich coconut milk, squeeze the grated coconut through a damp cloth, twisting the cloth to extract as much liquid as possible. For ordinary use, however, pour one cup of boiling water over the grated coconut and let it stand for one hour. Squeeze through a cloth. This process may be repeated with a second cup of boiling water if abundant, not very rich coconut milk is needed.

For coconut cream, allow the coconut milk to stand until the cream rises to the top. This is very thick and rich and is wonderful with desserts.

As packaged shredded coconut, and tinned moist grated coconut, may not be as rich as fresh coconut, hot milk or single cream may be used instead of water to make coconut milk or cream.

Packaged coconut cream should be mixed to the desired consistency with hot water.

The average coconut weighs about 1 ½ lb., and yields between 3 and 4 cups of grated meat. If mixed with the coconut water and hot water, this should yield about 3 cups of coconut milk. The amount will vary with the freshness and quality of the coconut.

ghee   *trinidad*

1 lb. unsalted butter

Cut the butter into 4 or 6 pieces and put it into a heavy saucepan over medium heat. Melt the butter, stirring from time to time, then increase the heat to bring the butter to the boil. Let it boil for about 1 minute. Reduce the heat to the lowest point possible, using 2 or 3 asbestos mats if necessary. Cook the butter, without stirring, for 45 minutes, by which time it will be golden and the milk solids in the bottom of the pan will be brown.

Wring a piece of cheesecloth out in hot water and, using it folded into 4 layers, line a sieve. Carefully pour the butter through the cheesecloth. Pour the sieved butter, now ghee, into a jar and store in the refrigerator. It will keep indefinitely. It will keep at room temperature for 2 or 3 months. Makes about 1 ½ cups.

massala   *trinidad*

Ground Spice Mixture

This mixture of ground spices and hot pepper was brought to Trinidad by migrant Hindu workers. When ground dry it is curry powder. When wet, because of the addition of fresh hot peppers or a liquid, it is curry paste. Commercial curry powder may be used, but since massala is easy to make, and all the ingredients readily available, it is worth the extra effort. Massala may be used in any island recipe calling for curry powder.

WET MASSALA

1 teaspoon saffron threads, or
    ground turmeric
4 tablespoons coriander seeds
2 teaspoons anise seeds
2 teaspoons whole cloves
2 teaspoons cumin seeds
2 teaspoons fenugreek seeds

3 teaspoons black peppercorns
2 teaspoons mustard seeds
1 large onion, finely chopped
4 cloves garlic, chopped
Fresh hot red peppers to
    taste

Soak the saffron threads in a little water and, using a mortar and pestle, grind into a paste. Grind all the remaining ingredients using a mortar and pestle, or combine in an electric blender, a little at a time, to make a heavy paste. Remove the seeds from the hot peppers unless a very hot curry paste is wanted. Use as directed in recipes, or to taste. Keep refrigerated in jars, but use within a day or so. Makes about 2 cups. Also see curry powder I and II.

DRY MASSALA

Grind the saffron threads dry, or use turmeric. Omit the onion and garlic, and substitute dried red peppers for the fresh ones. Store in airtight glass jars at room temperature. Dry massala will keep for 6 months. Makes about 1 cup.

salt beef and pork   *all islands*

Salt beef and salt pork are widely used in the West Indies, largely because in the old days there was no refrigeration, and in the hot climate meat spoiled easily. Now that refrigeration has altered the situation, people still use salted meat because they have acquired a taste for it. Fresh meats, poultry, fish and shell-fish are, of course, also eaten. But certain dishes still call for salt meat. The meat may be either pickled in brine or dry corned.

PICKLING SOLUTION FOR ABOUT 5 POUNDS OF MEAT

¾ lb. coarse salt   1 tablespoon allspice berries
2 teaspoons saltpetre   1 tablespoon dry mustard
4 oz. dark brown sugar   6 pints water
4-inch piece stick cinnamon

Combine all the ingredients in a large enamelware or stainless steel saucepan. Bring to the boil and boil for 5 minutes. Skim.

Allow to cool. Pour into a stoneware crock, or a stainless steel or enamel container with a tight-fitting lid. Add the meat together with 1 teaspoon thyme, 2 or 3 sliced spring onions, 1 sliced onion, and 1 or 2 fresh hot red peppers. Store in a cool place for 7 to 10 days, turning the meat daily. Keep refrigerated until needed. Meat should be in one piece. For beef, brisket is the best cut. Rump and chuck can also be used. For pork, use belly or shoulder.

TO DRY CORN BEEF AND PORK

3 lb. boneless meat	1 teaspoon saltpetre
¾ lb. coarse salt	2 teaspoons brown sugar

Mix the salt, saltpetre and sugar together in a large glass or china bowl or stoneware crock. Rub mixture well into the meat. Sprinkle a little more dry salt over the meat to cover it well. Each day for 3 days pour away any liquid that collects. The first day there will be a great deal, the other two days hardly any. Sprinkle a little more salt on the meat after draining it, and turn it daily. Refrigerate for 7 to 10 days, turning the meat daily.

To use, wash meat thoroughly. Drain, cover with fresh water and simmer for about 20 minutes to the pound. Keep refrigerated until needed.

seasoning for
various dishes　　　　*dominican republic*

Sazón Preparado

This is a variation of sofrito, and comes from the Dominican Republic, where it is used to flavour stews, beans, rice and vegetables. It is easy to make and is useful to have on hand, especially for the cook in a hurry.

3 medium onions, chopped
1 green bell pepper, seeded
and chopped
1 red bell pepper, seeded and
chopped, or 2 tinned
pimentos, chopped
4 large cloves garlic, peeled
and chopped
1 tablespoon orégano
1 bunch chopped spring
onions using green part as
well as white

3 tablespoons coarsely
chopped parsley
3 tablespoons chopped fresh
green coriander leaves
1 teaspoon Tabasco, or hot
pepper sauce
1 tablespoon sweet paprika
1 teacup tomato paste
1 teacup olive, or vegetable oil
6 tablespoons vinegar,
preferably cane or white
distilled
Salt to taste

Combine all the ingredients and blend, bit by bit, to a purée in an electric blender. Pour into a saucepan and simmer, stirring constantly, for 5 minutes. Cool and bottle. Makes about 6 cups.

marinade

'*Seasoning-up*' *Meats and Poultry*

Just as sofrito and achiote lard or oil are essential to the cooking of the Spanish-speaking islands, so is the technique of 'seasoning-up' meats and poultry essential to the cooking of the English-speaking islands.

The great inventiveness of island cooks makes it difficult to give precise recipes. On returning to the islands, I kept catching echoes of the flavours our family cook, Annie, produced daily. Since my own mother was a very good cook and incorporated a lot of island approaches into her own repertoire, I grew up in a very well-flavoured world and my memory of island cooking was kept intact.

Rather than lay down hard and fast rules, I would prefer to give a fairly standard marinade (seasoning-up). My own experience is that if one stays within the limits imposed by these seasoning rules, one can do much as one pleases, always with admirable results.

The herbs and vegetables most commonly used are onion, garlic, chives, spring onions, shallots, thyme, marjoram, parsley, (preferably flatleaved parsley), celery leaves, bay leaves, basil, sage, rosemary, tarragon, orégano, ginger and fresh hot peppers. Among the spices, cloves, cinnamon, nutmeg, mace, allspice, and both black and white pepper are used, as are curry powder, cayenne pepper, Spanish (hot) paprika, sweet paprika, soy sauce, Worcestershire sauce, Seville orange juice, lime juice, oil, vinegar, and wines such as sherry, Madeira, and red and white table wines. And, of course, rum. It is a formidable list, and gives a great deal of leeway to the creative cook.

In a number of islands the term 'herb' refers to the local chives available there. Garlic used sparingly with spring onions, chives and shallots gives the authentic flavour of island chives, and is much to be preferred to our more usual onion–garlic mixture.

Island cooks are fussy about the appearance of the finished dish, and dislike the use of thyme in a marinade as the leaves tend to leave dark specks in a sauce or gravy. For this reason such herbs as thyme and marjoram are usually tied in a piece of cheesecloth, and added to the pot in which the meat is cooked rather than directly to the marinade. Hot peppers, whole and with the stem on, are added to the pot so that they can be retrieved at the end of cooking, having lent more flavour than heat to the dish. Peppers may also be tied in a square of cheesecloth and removed before serving.

The marinating technique almost certainly goes back to 16th-century France and Britain, when meat was often tough, and in the summer months might well be tainted. Spices and herbs not only tenderized and flavoured meat, but also preserved it.

The following is a fairly standard marinade and can be used for any meat or poultry which can then be stewed, braised, broiled or roasted. This is sufficient for about 3 lb. of meat.

1 medium onion, grated
1 clove garlic, crushed
4 blades chive, chopped coarsely, or 1 spring onion coarsely chopped
1 sprig celery leaves, coarsely chopped

2 tablespoons cane or malt vinegar
2 tablespoons dry sherry or rum
1 tablespoon soy sauce
1 teaspoon cayenne pepper or Spanish (hot) paprika

Mix all together. Rub well into the meat or poultry and allow to stand at room temperature for at least 1 hour, turning once or twice. Or use as suggested in recipes.

If the meat is to be stewed it can go straight into the stew pot with water or stock to cover, and all of the marinade. If it is to be braised the marinade should be scraped off and reserved, and the meat patted dry before braising. Two teaspoons of brown sugar should be rubbed into the meat and it should then be sautéed in a little butter or oil or fat from the meat. Put it into a casserole with the marinade and stock or water, as well as sliced onions, carrots and so on according to the meat recipe. For boiling or roasting, the marinade should be scraped off and reserved for making a sauce or gravy when the meat is done.

marinade variations

Olive, a very gifted cook in St Kitts, has a slightly different technique, which produces a very subtle flavour. It is given in detail in the recipe for Olive's Seasoned-up Pot Roast. The same technique can be used for pork with the addition of a little sage, while the addition of finely grated fresh ginger root, or ground Jamaica ginger, is pleasant with chicken.

Some cooks prefer to crush the stems of fresh herbs, such as parsley, instead of chopping them coarsely; all the island cooks prefer to use fresh herbs rather than dried ones.

CARAMEL COLOURING

Island cooks usually make their own caramel colouring from local brown sugar, or rub sugar direct into the meat before searing.

To make the caramel:

1 lb. island sugar, or use granulated sugar

2 tablespoons water

Combine the sugar and water in a heavy saucepan and cook over medium heat until the sugar is dark brown, stirring from time to time. Add ¾ pint cold water, bring to the boil, stir and simmer until the caramel has the consistency of syrup. Cool and bottle. Be careful not to let the caramel burn as it will develop an acrid taste.

Undercooked caramel will give a sweet taste to food. If properly made, caramel will colour without sweetening.

seasoning mixture   *barbados*

2 medium onions, very finely chopped

2 tablespoons finely chopped chives

3 cloves garlic, crushed

1 fresh hot red pepper, seeded and mashed

1 teaspoon orégano

½ teaspoon ground cloves

1 teaspoon salt

1 tablespoon lime juice

Mix all ingredients together thoroughly. Rub well into the inside of a suckling pig prepared for roasting. Makes about 1 cup, enough for a 10–12 lb. pig.

To season whole cleaned fish, gash two or three times on each side of the backbone, and stuff the seasoning into the incisions. Any fish, or meat, may be seasoned with the mixture. Cook as directed in recipes.

sofrito   *puerto rico*

½ lb. salt pork, diced
4 medium onions, finely
  chopped
12 cloves garlic, finely
  chopped
2 medium green bell peppers,
  seeded and chopped
½ lb. ham, diced

1 lb. tomatoes, peeled and
  chopped, or 2 cups drained
  canned tomatoes, coarsely
  chopped
1 tablespoon finely chopped
  fresh green coriander
1 teaspoon dried orégano
Salt, freshly ground pepper

Fry the salt pork dice in a heavy frying pan over medium heat, stirring from time to time, until they have given up all their fat and are crisp and brown. Lift out of the fat with a slotted spoon and reserve.

Add the onions, garlic and green peppers and sauté until the onion is tender but not browned. Add the ham, tomatoes, coriander, orégano, reserved salt pork dice, and pepper to taste. Simmer over low heat for 30 minutes, stirring from time to time. Season to taste with salt. Cool and pour into glass jars, cover tightly and refrigerate until needed. Use as directed in recipes. Makes about 2 cups.

ackee patties   *jamaica*

4 oz. salt codfish
2 tablespoons vegetable oil
1 small onion, finely chopped
1 fresh hot red pepper,
  seeded and chopped, or
  use hot pepper sauce

Freshly ground pepper
1 tablespoon parsley, chopped
1 cup drained canned ackees
1 recipe Flaky Pastry (as for
  Meat Patties) (see Index)
1 egg white, lightly beaten

Soak the fish overnight. Drain, rinse, and put on to cook with fresh cold water to cover. Cook until tender, about 15 minutes. Drain. Remove any bones and skin and flake fish finely. Heat the oil in a frying pan and sauté the onion until tender, but not browned. Add the fish, hot pepper, pepper to taste, parsley and ackees, and cook for a few minutes, stirring with a wooden spoon. Crush the ackees into the mixture, which should be fairly smooth but not a purée.

Roll out the pastry about ⅛ inch thick on a lightly floured board and cut into about twelve 5-inch circles. Add the fillings, damp the edges of the pastry with water and fold over each into a crescent. Seal the edges by pinching together with the fingers, or crimping with a fork. Brush with egg white and prick the tops to let the steam escape.

Bake on an ungreased baking sheet in a 425°F (gas 7) oven for 20 to 30 minutes, or until lightly browned. Serve for lunch with a vegetable or a salad, or as a snack or first course.

For cocktails, put 1 teaspoon of the mixture on 2-inch pastry circles, fold as described and bake 15 to 20 minutes.

accra   *trinidad*

Salt Fish Cakes

This is a member of the same family as Barbados Codfish Cakes,
Jamaica's Stamp and Go, Puerto Rico's Bacalaitos, Martinique's
and Guadeloupe's Acrats de Morue, and Haiti's Marinades, and
illustrates how the same dish changes from island to island.
Accra are traditionally served with Floats.

2 teaspoons active dry yeast
6 tablespoons warm water
½ lb. salt codfish
4 oz. plain flour
1 teaspoon sugar
1 onion, finely chopped
1 clove garlic, finely chopped

1 tablespoon fresh hot peppers,
  seeded and finely chopped
1 tablespoon finely chopped
  chives
Salt, freshly ground pepper
Vegetable oil for deep frying

Soak the fish for several hours, or overnight. Sprinkle the yeast
on the warm water and let stand for 10 minutes. Pour boiling
water over the codfish, and allow to cool. Rinse in cold water,
remove any skin and bones, and shred fish very fine. Mix fish
with the flour, sugar, onion, garlic, peppers, chives, salt if
necessary and a generous amount of pepper. Add the yeast and
beat until smooth. Allow to rise for 1½ to 2 hours in a warm
draught-free place.

Drop by tablespoon into hot oil (370°F on frying thermometer)
and fry until golden brown. Drain on paper towels and serve
hot with hot Floats (see Index). Makes about 24.

akkra   *jamaica*

Bean Fritters

These fritters are known as calas in Curaçao, and in that island
are made only from black-eyed peas. Sweet rice fritters made

with yeast, called calas, were once very popular in the French Quarter of New Orleans. How the name reached Curaçao or who has the best right to it, no one knows.

½ lb. black-eyed peas, or soy   2 teaspoons salt
  beans   Oil for frying
2 fresh hot red peppers,
  seeded and chopped

Soak the beans overnight in cold water. Drain, rub off and discard the skins, cover beans again with cold water and soak for 2 or 3 hours longer. Drain, rinse, and put through a meat grinder, using the finest blade, or reduce bit by bit in an electric blender. Grind the peppers. Add the salt and peppers to the beans and beat with a wooden spoon until they are light and fluffy and considerably increased in bulk. Heat the oil in a heavy frying pan and fry the mixture by tablespoonfuls until golden brown on both sides. Drain on paper towels. Serve hot as an accompaniment to drinks. Makes about 24 fritters.

tostones de plátano   *puerto rico*

Green Plantain Chips

1 large, green plantain, peeled   Salted water
  and cut into diagonal slices   Vegetable oil for frying
  ½ inch thick   Salt

Soak the plantain slices for at least 30 minutes in the salted water. Drain and pat dry with paper towels. Heat 2 or 3 tablespoons of oil in a heavy frying pan and sauté the plantain pieces until tender, but do not let them get crusty on the outside. Drain on paper towels.

Lay a sheet of waxed paper over the plantain slices and flatten evenly by pressing until about half as thick as before. Dip the pressed plantain in salted water and fry until crusty and golden brown on both sides. Drain on paper towels, salt lightly and serve with meat or fish dishes, or as an accompaniment to drinks. Makes about 15 Tostones.

In the French islands this is known as Banane Pesé. In Haiti it is a traditional accompaniment to Griots de Porc.

buljol   *trinidad*

Salt Codfish Salad

8 oz. salt codfish
1 medium onion, finely
  chopped
2 medium tomatoes, peeled,
  seeded and chopped
1 fresh, hot red pepper,
  seeded and chopped

Freshly ground black pepper
3 tablespoons olive, or
  vegetable, oil
1 tablespoon lime, or lemon,
  juice
Lettuce leaves
1 medium avocado (optional)

Place the fish in a bowl and cover with boiling water. Allow to cool. Drain. Remove any skin, and bones, and shred the fish. Pour boiling water over a second time. When cool, drain and press out all the water. Mix the onion, tomatoes and hot pepper with the fish. Season with pepper, oil and lime or lemon juice. Serve on lettuce leaves. Garnish with slices of peeled avocado, if liked. Serves 3 to 4 as a first course.

In Trinidad this is often served for breakfast.

cassava chips   *jamaica*

Cassava root   Salt
Oil for deep frying

Peel the cassava root and slice, crosswise, as thinly as possible.
Steep in iced water for 30 minutes, drain and dry on paper towels.
    Fry until delicately browned and crisp in deep oil heated to
370°F on a frying thermometer. Drain on paper towels, sprinkle
with salt, and serve as an accompaniment to drinks.

VARIATIONS: For Platanutri (Plantain Crisps) use peeled green,
or half ripe plantains instead of cassava root. In St Kitts green
bananas are used. For Sweet Potato Crisps, St Vincent, use white
(boniato) sweet potatoes.

chiquetaille de morue   *haiti*

Salt Codfish Salad

1 lb. dried salt codfish   1 clove garlic, crushed
generous ⅓ pint salad, or   2 carrots, scraped and finely
    olive oil   diced
6 tablespoons vinegar   2–3 oz. raw green beans,
2 shallots, chopped   finely diced
1 onion, finely chopped   1 tablespoon parsley, chopped
1 leek, well washed and   Freshly ground pepper
    chopped fine   Hot pepper sauce

Put the codfish in a large bowl and pour boiling water over it.
Allow to cool. Drain, remove the bones and skin and shred the
fish. Pour boiling water over the fish a second time, and allow to
cool. Drain and press out all the water. Return fish to the bowl
and mix with all the remaining ingredients, seasoning to taste
with pepper and hot pepper sauce. Allow to stand for 2 hours at
room temperature for the flavour to develop.

Serve as a spread on canapés, or in sandwiches, as an accompaniment to drinks. Makes about 4 cups.

féroce d'avocat   *martinique–guadeloupe*

This could be translated as 'a fierceness of avocado' which, while picturesque, would give an unfair impression since féroce simply refers to how much hot fresh pepper has been used in the dish. Traditionally this is highly seasoned but ultimately one pleases oneself and adds hot pepper to taste.

4 oz. salt codfish
1 medium-sized avocado, peeled, seeded and cut into ½-inch cubes
⅓ pint vegetable oil
3 tablespoons lime, or lemon, juice
½ medium onion, finely chopped
1 clove garlic, crushed
1 tablespoon chopped parsley

1, or more, fresh hot red or green peppers, seeded and chopped
Salt and freshly ground pepper to taste
⅛ teaspoon sugar
4 oz. farine de manioc (cassava meal)
6 tablespoons coconut milk, or milk.

Soak the cod overnight in cold water. Drain thoroughly, refresh with cold water, pat dry and grill until lightly coloured on both sides. When cool enough to handle, remove bones and skin and shred as finely as possible. Place fish in a bowl with the avocado. Mix together the oil and lime or lemon juice, add the onion, garlic, hot pepper, parsley, salt and pepper to taste, and the sugar. Be careful not to over-salt, as the cod will still be salty. Pour mixture over the cod and avocado.

Mix the cassava meal with the coconut milk to barely moisten it. Add to the cod and avocado and mix all together thoroughly with a wooden spoon to a smooth heavy paste. Serve as an appetizer, or on canapés to accompany drinks.

marinades   *haiti*

Fritters

4 oz. plain flour
1½ teaspoons baking powder
1 teaspoon salt
4 eggs

2 teaspoons unsalted butter,
   melted and cooled
2 teaspoons vegetable oil
2 teaspoons rum

Sift the flour with the baking powder and salt into a bowl. Make
a well in the centre and add the eggs, butter, oil and rum. Beat
thoroughly until the batter is smooth. Let the batter stand 1 or 2
hours before using.

To make the fritters, mix the batter with 4 oz. salt codfish,
soaked, shredded and drained, with any skin and bones removed;
or use 4 oz. cooked chicken, cut into dice; or add chopped shallots,
parsley and hot pepper to the batter; or cooked shrimps, or in
fact anything on hand.

For sweet fritters, reduce the salt to ½ teaspoon, add a tablespoon
of sugar, and add ¼ lb. mashed or sliced bananas, or any suitable
fruit.

Heat vegetable oil in deep pan (to 370°F on a frying thermometer). Drop fritter mixture by tablespoonfuls into the hot
fat. Fry until golden brown on both sides. Drain on paper towels.
Makes about 24.

mero en escabeche   *puerto rico*

Soused or Pickled Red Grouper

Mero, or red grouper, is a tropical sea bass. Mediterranean
grouper is sometimes available in England, but sea bass, striped
bass, haddock or mackerel are all suitable for this dish.

3 lb. fillets of red grouper, or
   other suitable fish

2 whole cloves garlic
2 bay leaves

Salt
¾ pint olive oil
2 medium onions, thinly
  sliced

¼ teaspoon peppercorns
generous ⅓ pint vinegar
½ lb. small pitted green
  olives

Cut the fish fillets into 1½-inch pieces and season with salt. Heat 2 or 3 tablespoons of the olive oil in a frying pan and fry the pieces of fish. Lift out and place in a deep glass or porcelain bowl.

Combine the onions, garlic, bay leaves, peppercorns and vinegar in a saucepan and simmer until the onion is tender. Cool. Add the remaining olive oil and the olives and pour over the fish. Cover the bowl and refrigerate for at least 24 hours before serving.

Serve cold, garnished with lettuce leaves. Serves 6 to 8.

pastelillos de carne de cerdo   *puerto rico*

Little Pork Pies

FOR THE PASTRY

½ lb. plain flour
1 teaspoon salt
½ teaspoon baking soda

2 oz. unsalted butter
1 egg, lightly beaten
6 tablespoons water, about

Sift the flour, salt and baking soda into a large bowl. Rub the butter into the flour with the fingertips until it has the consistency of a coarse meal. Make a well in the centre. Mix the egg with the water and pour gradually into the flour, mixing with a wooden spoon until the dough is smooth. Gather the dough into a ball, wrap in waxed paper and refrigerate for 1 hour.

FOR THE FILLING

3 tablespoons vegetable oil
or lard
½ lb. lean pork, minced
2 oz. ham, minced
Salt, freshly ground pepper
1 cup sofrito (see Index)

2 teaspoons distilled white
vinegar
2 teaspoons capers
2 tablespoons seedless raisins
2 oz. small, pitted green olives
1 hard-boiled egg, coarsely
chopped

Heat the oil or lard in a heavy frying pan and add the pork, ham, and salt and pepper to taste. Cook, stirring for about 5 minutes, or until there is no trace of pink in the pork. Add the sofrito and vinegar, stir to mix well, cover and cook over low heat for 30 minutes. Add the capers, raisins, olives and egg and cook for a minute or two longer. Allow to cool.

Cut the dough into 3 pieces. Roll each of the pieces out on a lightly floured board, one at a time, to ⅛ inch thickness or less. Cut into circles about 4 inches in diameter. There will be about 18 circles in all. Place a tablespoon of the meat mixture in the center of each circle of dough, moisten the edges with cold water and fold the circle in half, pressing the edges down with the tines of a fork to seal them securely.

Fry in deep oil at a temperature of 350°F on a frying thermo-meter. When the pastelillos rise to the top of the oil, spoon a little of the hot oil over them to make them puff up, then turn to brown a little more. Drain on paper towels and serve hot, or at room temperature, as a first course.

For pastelillos to serve as an accompaniment to drinks, cut the pastry circles 2½ inches in diameter and use 1 teaspoon of filling on each. Makes about 4 dozen of the smaller size.

VARIATION: For Pastelillos de Queso (Cheese Turnovers) use 6 oz. grated cheddar, Edam or similar cheese in place of the meat filling to stuff the pastelillos.

pâté de harengs saurs   *haiti*

Pâté of Smoked Herring

Smoked herrings   Freshly ground pepper
Milk, or water   Hot pepper sauce
Unsalted butter

Soak the herrings in milk or water for several hours to remove
the salt. Drain and remove the fillets, discard bones and skin.
Put the fillets into a heavy frying pan with a little milk and
butter and cook for about 8 to 10 minutes. Season to taste with
freshly ground pepper and hot pepper sauce. Using a mortar and
pestle, reduce the herring to a smooth paste, using some of the
pan juices and more butter. Spread on fingers of fresh, hot toast
and serve as an appetizer, or as an accompaniment to drinks.

picklises   *haiti*

Green beans, cut French-style   Tender young green peas
Cabbage, very finely shredded   Radishes, thinly sliced
Cauliflower, separated into   Celery, sliced
    flowerets   3 fresh hot red peppers,
Carrots, scraped and thinly   pricked in 2 or 3 places
    sliced   with a fork
Onion, thinly sliced   Vinegar

Prepare equal amounts of the vegetables and place in a large
crock or jar. Cover with vinegar and allow to stand in a cool place
for 1 week. Serve as a relish with steak or any roast meat, or with
crackers and cheese as an accompaniment to drinks. Store in the
refrigerator, if the picklises last long enough to store (which they
seldom do).

phulouri   *trinidad*

Split Pea Fritters

½ lb. split peas   Salt, freshly ground pepper
1 medium onion, chopped   Oil for deep frying
1 clove garlic, chopped

Soak the split peas overnight in cold water to cover. Drain
thoroughly. Put through the fine blade of a food mill with the
onion and garlic, or reduce to a purée in an electric blender.
Season highly with salt and pepper. Beat with a wooden spoon
until light and fluffy, or use an electric beater.

Heat the oil in a deep fryer or saucepan (370°F on a frying
thermometer). Form the mixture, a tablespoonful at a time, into
balls and drop into the hot oil, about 6 at a time. Fry until
brown all over. Drain on paper towels. Serve hot, each stuck
with a toothpick, as an appetizer. Makes about 24.

If liked, a tablespoon of curry powder may be added to the
split peas when they are ground. A hot pepper sauce is often
served as a dip for the Phulouri.

run down   *jamaica*

Fish and Tomatoes

1 lb. mackerel fillets   1 lb. tomatoes, peeled and
3 tablespoons lime, or lemon   chopped
  juice   Salt, freshly ground pepper
3 cups coconut milk (see   ¼ teaspoon thyme
  Index)   1 tablespoon vinegar,
1 large onion, finely chopped   preferably malt or cane
2 cloves garlic
1 tablespoon finely chopped
  fresh hot pepper,
  preferably red

Pour the lime juice over the fish and set aside. Cook the coconut milk in a heavy frying pan until it is oily. Add the onion, garlic, and cook until the onion is tender. Add the hot pepper, the tomatoes, salt, pepper, thyme and vinegar, and stir and cook very gently for 10 minutes. Drain the fish, add to the other ingredients and cook until the fish is tender, about 10 minutes. Serve hot with boiled bananas.* Serves 4 as an appetizer, 2 as a main course. Run Down can also be used as a stuffing for breadfruit.

Salt codfish or rock lobster tails can be used instead of mackerel.

souscaille   *martinique*

Fresh Mango Appetizer

This is derived from the fresh mango chutneys of the Hindu agricultural workers who migrated to the north of Martinique in the 19th century. It makes an unusual and refreshing appetizer, or an accompaniment to drinks. The mango used in Martinique is usually the mango vert, a rather stringy mango, not considered to be one of the fine dessert mangoes, known as mangue. Other mangoes are used in Martinique, and as our choice of mangoes is not very wide, any type will do so long as it is green, that is, underripe. The mango is peeled and cut into slices and marinated in the hot sauce for at least 10 minutes – longer if desired – then eaten by hand.

*For cooking instructions for green bananas see Banane Jaune avec Sauce Blanche (Green Bananas with White Sauce).

SAUCE PIQUANTE

⅓ pint cold water
2 cloves garlic, crushed
½ teaspoon salt
Freshly ground pepper

1 or more fresh hot green
    peppers, finely chopped
3 tablespoons lime juice

Mix all the ingredients together. Add sliced green mangoes and
marinate for at least 10 minutes. Eat by hand.

stamp and go   *jamaica*

Codfish Cakes

½ lb. salt codfish
4 oz. plain flour
1 teaspoon baking powder
½ teaspoon salt
1 egg, lightly beaten
⅓ pint milk

1 tablespoon butter, melted
1 onion, finely chopped
1 fresh hot pepper, chopped
Vegetable oil or lard for deep
    frying

Put the codfish in a bowl, cover with warm water and soak for
2 hours or longer, according to the saltiness and hardness of the
fish. Drain, rinse and place in a saucepan with boiling water to
cover. Simmer gently, covered, until the fish is tender, about 15
minutes. Drain fish, remove its bones and skin, and shred it
finely.

Sift the flour, baking powder and salt together. Combine the
egg, milk and butter and stir into the dry ingredients. Add the
fish, onion and pepper and mix well. Drop by the tablespoonful
into hot oil (370°F on a frying thermometer) and fry until
golden brown. Drain on paper towels and serve hot. Makes
about 24.

VARIATIONS: For Bacalaitos (Salt Codfish Fritters), Puerto Rico, use ½ lb. flour and 2 teaspoons of baking powder. Add a clove of garlic, crushed, and ⅜ pint water. Omit the egg, milk, butter and hot pepper. For Acrats de Morue (Codfish Fritters), Martinique and Guadeloupe, use 6 oz. flour, 2 medium eggs, 1½ oz. butter and ⅜ pint milk. Instead of onion, use 2 spring onions, finely chopped, and add 1 clove garlic crushed, 1 tablespoon chopped parsley, ½ teaspoon thyme, freshly ground pepper, and 1 melegueta peppercorn, or 1 allspice berry, ground.

ackee soup

Our cook, Annie, used to make a wonderful ackee soup, which I have never come across anywhere but in her kitchen. I suspect she invented it, using broken ackees left over from the salt fish and ackee that characterized our Fridays. Annie's salt fish and ackee was of an elegance, largely I think to beat down our resistance to salt fish, since, being English, we were devoted to the fresh-caught article, or failing that, finnan haddie. Since canned ackees tend to have a number of broken pieces of the vegetable, they are ideal for ackee soup.

1 tin ackees (19 oz.), about 4 cups
¾ pint chicken stock
2 medium tomatoes, peeled and chopped
2 shallots, chopped

Salt, freshly ground pepper to taste
Pickapeppa hot pepper sauce or Tabasco, to taste
6 tablespoons double cream

Put the ackees together with the liquid from the tin into a saucepan with the chicken stock, tomatoes, shallots, salt and pepper to taste, cover and simmer gently until the shallots are tender. Purée in an electric blender. Return to the saucepan, season to taste with hot pepper sauce, stir in the cream and heat through. The soup is also very good served chilled. Serves 6.

The soup may be garnished with chopped chives or chopped parsley, or with sweet paprika.

bouillon   *haiti*

Modestly called bouillon, this is really a pot-au-feu.

1 stewing chicken weighing
    4–5 lb.
2 lb. shin of beef, cut into
    2-inch cubes
1 calf's foot, split
6½ pints water
2 carrots, scraped and sliced
2 stalks celery, sliced
1 large onion, chopped
2 cloves
3 medium tomatoes, peeled,
    seeded and chopped
1 bay leaf

2 or 3 sprigs parsley
½ teaspoon thyme
1 lb. sweet potatoes,
    preferably white type,
    peeled and sliced
1 lb. potatoes, peeled and
    sliced
2 ripe plantains, or 3 under-
    ripe bananas, peeled and
    cut into 2-inch slices
2 medium potatoes, peeled
    and left whole
Salt, freshly ground pepper

Put the fowl, with its giblets, the beef and the calf's foot into a
large saucepan. Add the water and bring to the boil. At the end
of 10 minutes skim the surface thoroughly. Reduce to a simmer,
cover and cook for 2 hours. Add the vegetables and seasonings,
bring back to a simmer, cover, and cook for 1 hour longer. Lift
out the two whole potatoes and mash. Stir into the soup. Remove
the bay leaf, cloves, and parsley sprigs.

Cut the chicken into serving pieces. Take out and discard the
bones in the calf's foot. Cut the meat into serving pieces.

Serve the hot bouillon in large, rimmed soup plates making
sure each one gets some of the chicken, meat, and vegetables.
Or arrange the hot meats and vegetables on a warmed platter
and pour the soup into a warmed tureen. Serve meat, vegetables
and soup in soup plates. Serves 8 to 10.

bisque de cribiches   *martinique*

Freshwater Crayfish Bisque

Ecrevisses – freshwater crayfish – abound in both Martinique
and Guadeloupe. Unfortunately they are rarely found in fish-
mongers in Britain, but you might perhaps catch your own. In
most of the English-speaking islands 'crayfish' have become
'crawfish'. In Martinique and Guadeloupe 'écrevisses' have
been transformed into 'cribiches'.

2 oz. unsalted butter
2 lb. crayfish, cleaned and
   shelled
1 onion, finely chopped
2 cloves garlic, chopped
Sprig fennel (optional)

1 small, fresh hot pepper,
   left whole
1½ pints water
⅓ pint coconut milk
2 egg yolks, or 1 tablespoon
   arrowroot
Salt

Heat the butter in a heavy saucepan and add the crayfish, onion
and garlic. Sauté over medium heat until the crayfish have
changed colour, about 5 minutes. Add the fennel, hot pepper and
water. Cover and cook at a gentle simmer for 30 minutes.
Remove and discard the fennel and the hot pepper. Remove the
crayfish, pound in a mortar and push through a fine sieve, or
reduce to a purée in an electric blender with a little of the stock.
Return the puréed crayfish to the saucepan. Add the coconut
milk and heat through. Beat the egg yolks with a little of the
soup and stir into the saucepan. Cook over low heat, stirring
constantly, until the soup is lightly thickened. Or mix the
arrowroot with a little water, add to the soup, and stir over low
heat until thickened. Serves 6.

I like to simmer the crayfish shells for about 15 minutes to
make a stock instead of using plain water, as this gives a richer
flavour.

breadfruit vichyssoise   *grenada*

1 oz. unsalted butter
2 medium onions, finely
  chopped
1 clove garlic, chopped
½ lb. fresh breadfruit, or
  ⅓ can (26 oz.) breadfruit
  (see Glossary)

1 ½ pints chicken stock
½ pint single cream
Salt, freshly ground white
  pepper to taste
Chopped chives

Heat the butter in a heavy saucepan and sauté the onions and garlic until tender but not browned. If using fresh breadfruit, peel the breadfruit, remove core and dice. If using tinned breadfruit, chop coarsely. Add to the onions and garlic with the chicken stock and cook, covered, at a gentle simmer until the breadfruit is tender. Cool. Put into an electric blender and blend until smooth, adding the cream while blending. Season with salt and pepper. Chill thoroughly. If the soup is too thick, thin it with a little milk. Serve soup sprinkled with chopped chives. Serves 6.

cream of pumpkin soup   *jamaica*

2 oz. unsalted butter
2 large onions, finely chopped
2 lb. West Indian pumpkin
  (calabaza)
2 pints chicken stock

½ pint single cream
Salt, freshly ground pepper
Dash of Pickapeppa hot
  pepper sauce or Tabasco
Freshly ground nutmeg, if
  liked

Heat the butter in a large, heavy saucepan and sauté the onions until tender but not browned. Pare the pumpkin, remove any seeds and strings, and cut into 1-inch cubes. Add the pumpkin and chicken stock, cover and simmer until the pumpkin is disintegrating, about 45 minutes. Cool slightly and put through sieve, or purée quickly in an electric blender. Be careful not to overblend. Return to saucepan, season to taste with salt and pepper, add the cream and the hot pepper sauce and reheat gently. Pour into a warmed soup tureen and sprinkle with nutmeg. Serves 6.

VARIATION: Trident Pumpkin Soup, Jamaica. For this very elegant version of pumpkin soup created by John Macy, at Trident Villas and Hotel, Port Antonio, cook as for Cream of Pumpkin soup but do not sieve or purée. Crush the pumpkin pieces with a wooden spoon against the sides of the saucepan so that the texture is nice and lumpy. Add double, instead of single cream, together with ½ pint shelled oysters and their liquor, and 4 tablespoons dry sherry. Cook just long enough for the edges of the oysters to curl, and to heat the soup. Prawns, diced lobster, or crab meat can be used instead of oysters.

VARIATION: Pumpkin Soup, Trinidad. Put the pumpkin on to cook with ½ green bell pepper, seeded and chopped, 1 onion, chopped, clove garlic, chopped, *bouquet garni* of ½ teaspoon each thyme and marjoram, sprig celery with leaves, 2 or 3 sprigs parsley, bay leaf, and 4 blades of chive, tied in a square of cheesecloth, 1 medium tomato, peeled, seeded and chopped, salt and pepper to taste, and 2 pints chicken stock. Cover and simmer until pumpkin begins to disintegrate. Remove and discard *bouquet garni*, and purée soup quickly in an electric blender, or put through a sieve. Return soup to saucepan, stir in ⅓ pint double cream and heat through. Add a dash of Pepper Wine to each serving.

callaloo

This is perhaps the most famous of all the creole soups and there are even more versions of it than there are ways of spelling its name. It turns up as Calaloo, Callilu and Callaloo. Trinidad is most generally credited with it, but it also turns up in other islands – Jamaica, Grenada, Haiti, Martinique, Guadeloupe, to name a few.

Essential to the dish is callaloo, which is a name given the young leaves of certain aroids, such as taro. And here one really runs into trouble with names, since this refers to a diverse group of tropical plants with edible tubers, and sometimes edible leaves.

Everyone knows this family's inedible members: the anthuriums, philodendrons, and calla lilies. Leaves of the edible plants are variously known as dasheen, dachine, eddoe, taro, elephant ear, tannia, taniers and yautía. Various members of the family are carefully distinguished one from the other but really it makes very little difference what either leaf or tuber is called, as they taste much the same. One further complication: Chinese spinach, which can often be found in Chinese shops, under that name in English, or as hon-toi-moi or yin-choi, is also called callaloo or bhaji in some of the islands. It can be bought tinned in shops that sell Caribbean foods, and fresh in Chinese markets. Since taro leaves are seldom, if ever, available, it is useful to have authentic substitutes, and I have found that fresh garden spinach and Swiss chard have much the same flavour and texture. No one needs to go without Callaloo for want of the right ingredients.

le calalou   *guadeloupe*

This is a much more elaborate version of callaloo soup. It is served with Riz Créole (rice) and Chiquetaille de Morue (codfish salad), as a complete meal.

3 lb. callaloo leaves, or
    spinach, Chinese spinach,
    or Swiss chard
½ lb. okra, sliced

1 lb. aubergine, peeled and
    coarsely chopped
4 tablespoons vegetable oil

4 oz. lean salt pork, cut into ½-inch cubes

3 green (unripe) bananas, peeled and chopped

2 onions, finely chopped

2 cloves garlic, minced

½ teaspoon thyme

¼ teaspoon ground cloves

2 tablespoons chopped chives

1 fresh hot pepper, seeded and chopped

1 tablespoon white vinegar

Salt, pepper to taste

⅓ pint coconut milk

Wash, drain and coarsely chop the greens. Place in a large, heavy saucepan with the okra and aubergine and 1½ pints of water. Cover and cook until the vegetables are very tender. Set aside.

In a heavy casserole heat the oil and fry the salt pork lightly. Add the bananas, onions and garlic. Cover and cook gently until the bananas and onions are tender. Add all the rest of the ingredients and cook for a few minutes longer. Take out the cubes of salt pork and reserve. Rub mixture through a sieve. Add the cooked vegetable mixture and beat thoroughly with a *lélé*, if you have one, or with an electric mixer or any beater, until you have a light purée. If the mixture is very thick, add a little chicken stock or water. Return the cubes of pork to the casserole and heat through. The soup should be a thick, smooth purée. Serves 6.

callaloo   *trinidad*

1 lb. callaloo leaves or spinach, Chinese spinach, or Swiss chard

2½ pints chicken stock

1 onion, finely chopped

1 clove garlic, chopped

2 or 3 spring onions, chopped, using green and white parts

¼ teaspoon thyme

4 oz. lean salt pork, cut into ½-inch cubes

½ lb. fresh, tinned or frozen crab meat

6 tablespoons coconut milk

½ lb. young okras, or 10 oz. package frozen okra, sliced

Salt, freshly ground pepper
to taste

Pickapeppa hot pepper sauce,
Tabasco or any similar
sauce, to taste

Wash greens and chop coarsely. Put greens into a large heavy saucepan with the chicken stock, onion, garlic, spring onions, thyme and salt pork. Cover and cook at a gentle simmer until the pork is tender. Add the crab meat, coconut milk, and okras and cook until the okras are done, about 10 minutes. Season to taste with salt, pepper and hot pepper sauce. Serves 6.

Serve with Foo-foo (see Index).

VARIATION: Le Calalou, Martinique. Use 2 lb. callaloo and $1\frac{1}{2}$ pints water instead of chicken stock. Omit onion. Use $\frac{1}{2}$ lb. piece of ham instead of salt pork, and omit crab meat and coconut milk. Add 1 tablespoon chopped parsley, and 1 fresh hot green pepper, seeded and chopped instead of hot pepper sauce, if possible. When soup is cooked, remove ham, chop and reserve. Beat soup to a purée and add ham, or purée with ham in a blender. Serve as soup or as a meal, accompanied by Riz Créole (white rice) and Morue Grillé (Grilled Salt Codfish).

VARIATION: Le Calalou, Haiti. Render 2 oz. salt pork, cut into $\frac{1}{2}$-inch cubes, with 3 rashers of bacon. When bacon is crisp, drain, crumble and reserve. In fat, fry $\frac{1}{2}$ lb. fillets any white fish cut into 1-inch pieces. Transfer fish and salt pork pieces to a large saucepan and add ingredients as for Trinidad Callaloo, omitting lean salt pork, crab meat and coconut milk. Serve sprinkled with crumbled bacon.

VARIATION: Callau, St Lucia. Add a 4-oz. slice of corned pork, stalk of celery with leaves, chopped, 4 spring onions, chopped, using white and green parts. Use water instead of stock, if liked. Before serving slice the meats and place some in each soup plate. Omit hot pepper sauce. A fresh hot pepper may be cooked with soup if liked, and removed before serving.

consommé à l'orange   *haiti*

Orange Consommé

This is a good example of how the same idea results in different
recipes from island to island. This was certainly the original
orange soup, which turns up in Grenada transformed into
Jellied Orange Consommé.

1¾ pints rich chicken stock,   2 cloves
    clarified and well seasoned   1 orange, thinly sliced
¾ pint strained orange juice

Combine the chicken stock, orange juice and cloves in a saucepan,
cover and bring to a simmer over very low heat. Simmer for 2
or 3 minutes. Strain into bouillon cups and garnish with the
orange slices. Serves 6. The soup may be served chilled.

VARIATION: Jellied Orange Consommé, Grenada. Increase the
orange juice to 1¼ pints and use 6 tablespoons of it to soften
2 tablespoons (2 envelopes) unflavoured gelatine. Combine with
all the other ingredients, except the sliced orange, in a saucepan
and simmer, stirring, until the gelatine is dissolved. Take out
and discard the cloves. Refrigerate until set. Serve in chilled
bouillon cups, breaking up the jelly before serving. Garnish with
orange slices. Serves 6.

crème de navets   *northern martinique*

Cream of Turnip Soup

This recipe is from the family collection of Charles and Yveline
de Lucy de Fossarieu, who have recently restored the De Leyritz
Plantation as an inn, at Basse Pointe in the north of Martinique.
I was amused when Mme de Fossarieu explained that it was a
Northern dish. I realized I was being arrogant. An island of

50-by-19 miles is as entitled to a regional kitchen as anywhere else. The colombos, curries brought in by Indian plantation workers, are also considered Northern dishes, developed and modified by the genius of France in the kitchen.

1 lb. white turnips	2½ pints rich milk
¾ oz. unsalted butter	Salt
	White pepper

Peel the turnips and slice thinly. Heat ½ oz. of the butter in a saucepan large enough to hold all the ingredients, and toss the turnips in the butter for 2 or 3 minutes. Add the milk, salt and pepper to taste and cook, partially covered, stirring from time to time, and taking care not to let the milk boil over. The turnips will be tender in about 20 to 25 minutes. Purée in an electric blender, or push through a sieve or the fine blade of a food mill. Adjust the seasoning and heat through. Serves 6.

cream of crab soup   *barbados*

1 oz. unsalted butter	1 pint milk
2 tablespoons plain flour	¼ pint single cream
2 hard-boiled eggs	½ lb. crab meat, flaked
Juice and finely grated rind	Salt, freshly ground pepper
1 lime, or lemon	Dash Angostura bitters
1¼ pints fish stock	3 tablespoons dry sherry

Melt the butter in a saucepan and add the flour. Cook, stirring, for a minute or two. Remove from the heat and add the eggs, mashing them to a smooth paste. Add the juice and rind of the lime, the fish stock, milk, cream and crab meat. Return the saucepan to the heat and simmer gently, stirring from time to time, for 10 minutes. Season with salt and pepper, add the bitters and sherry and reheat gently. Serves 6.

chilled cream of cucumber soup   *barbados*

3 medium cucumbers, about
  1½ lb., peeled and
  chopped
1 medium onion, finely
  chopped

2 pints chicken stock
Salt and white pepper to taste
2 teaspoons arrowroot
⅓ pint double cream
1 tablespoon chopped chives

Put the cucumbers, onion and stock into a heavy saucepan, cover and simmer gently for 15 minutes. Cool a little, then pour into an electric blender and reduce to a purée. Strain and return to the saucepan. Season to taste with salt and pepper. Mix the arrowroot with 1 tablespoon of water and stir into the soup, simmer, until lightly thickened, but do not boil. Stir the cream into the soup. Chill and serve garnished with the chives. Serves 6.

aubergine soup   *nevis*

2 aubergines, each weighing
  about 1 lb.
4 oz. unsalted butter
1 medium onion, finely
  chopped

2 spring onions, sliced, using
  both green and white parts
1½ pints chicken stock
¼ teaspoon dried thyme
Salt, freshly ground pepper
⅓ pint double cream

Peel the aubergines and cut into ¼-inch slices. Cut enough aubergine into ¼-inch cubes to make 2 cups and set aside. Heat half of the butter in a saucepan large enough to hold all the ingredients and sauté the onion and spring onions until tender, but not browned. Add the sliced aubergine, the stock and the thyme. Season to taste with salt and pepper, cover and simmer until the aubergine is tender, about 15 minutes. Purée in an electric blender, or put through the fine blade of a good mill. Return to the saucepan and adjust the seasoning. Stir in the cream and heat the soup through.

Meanwhile, heat the remaining butter in a heavy frying pan and sauté the 2 cups of aubergine cubes, stirring frequently, until they are browned all over. Add to the hot soup and serve immediately. Serves 6.

groundnut soup   *st kitts*

Peanuts are often called groundnuts in the English-speaking islands.

4 oz. peeled and roasted
  peanuts
2 pints chicken stock
Salt, freshly ground pepper
Pickapeppa hot pepper sauce,
  or Tabasco

⅓ pint double cream, or
  evaporated milk
1 tablespoon Angostura bitters
Dry sherry, or dry vermouth
  (optional)
Croûtons, or chopped chives

Put the peanuts and enough chicken stock to cover in an electric blender and blend on high speed to a smooth paste. Pour into a heavy saucepan, add the rest of the stock, season to taste with salt and pepper and hot pepper sauce. Cook over low heat, stirring from time to time, for about 15 minutes. Stir in the cream and cook, stirring, until heated through. Stir in the Angostura bitters.

A tablespoon of dry sherry, or dry vermouth, may be added to each serving. Garnish with croûtons and serve hot. Or chill and serve sprinkled with chives. Serves 6.

lobster chowder with foo-foo   *jamaica*

Botanist, columnist and cookbook author, Dr Alex D. Hawkes, a friend who now lives and works in Jamaica, was kind enough to let me have his favourite Jamaican Lobster Chowder recipe.

The lobsters are, of course, Jamaican crawfish or crayfish, better known here as rock or spiny lobsters.

4 1-lb. rock lobsters, or lobsters, or use frozen rock lobster tails
6 tablespoons coconut, or vegetable, oil
2½ pints rich fish stock
6 chopped spring onions using green and white parts
2 medium scraped and chopped carrots
2 tablespoons finely chopped parsley
2 teaspoons sweet paprika
3 tablespoons tomato paste
Salt
6 whole peppercorns
4 tablespoons brandy
1 oz. unsalted butter
2 tablespoons plain flour
½ pint coconut cream (see Index)
3 tablespoons Madeira
Foo-Foo Balls (see Index) for garnish

Cut the lobsters in halves, lengthwise. Heat the oil in a large saucepan and add the lobster halves. Sauté, stirring constantly, until the shells turn red. Drain off and discard the oil. Add the fish stock, spring onions, carrots, parsley, paprika, tomato paste, salt to taste, and peppercorns.

Cover and simmer gently for 10 minutes. Remove the lobsters, and, when they are cool enough to handle, take the meat from the shells and cut it into bite-size pieces. Set aside.

Pound the shells, using a mortar and pestle, until they are reduced to a fine powder. Place in a small, heavy saucepan. Warm the brandy and pour over the shells, and ignite. When the flames die down, add to the chowder. Stir to mix, cover, and simmer for 30 minutes. Strain, rinse the saucepan and return the chowder to it.

In a small, heavy saucepan, melt the butter, stir in the flour, and cook, stirring constantly for 1 or 2 minutes. Gradually stir in the coconut cream, and cook, stirring constantly, until the mixture has thickened. Add the Madeira, then pour into the chowder. Add the reserved lobster meat and heat through. Adjust the seasoning and serve in soup bowls, garnished with the Foo-Foo balls – one or more according to taste. Serves 6 to 8.

jigote

cuba

Chicken Consommé

Traditionally served at elegant parties and receptions in Cuba, this rich consommé, in bouillon cups, was handed to guests at midnight, and indicated that refreshments, usually a lavish buffet, were about to be served. The custom, though no longer wide-spread, still lingers on, and I have met it in several countries of Latin America.

1 stewing chicken, weighing
    4–5 lb.
3 lb. shin of beef, cut into
    2-inch cubes
2 or 3 veal bones
6½ pints water
2 carrots, scraped and sliced
2 small white turnips, peeled
    and sliced
1 stalk celery, with leaves

1 large onion, peeled and
    stuck with 2 cloves
4 medium tomatoes, sliced
1 clove garlic
1 bay leaf
2 or 3 sprigs parsley
Salt, freshly ground pepper
½ teaspoon allspice
½ pint dry sherry

Put the fowl, with its giblets, the beef and veal bones into a large saucepan. Add the water and bring to the boil. At the end of 10 minutes skim the surface thoroughly.

Reduce to a simmer, cover and cook for 3 hours. Add the vegetables and seasonings, bring back to a simmer, cover, and cook for 2 hours more. The broth should by now be reduced to about 5 pints. Strain, cool, and refrigerate.

Remove the fat from the surface, then strain the consommé through a sieve lined with a dampened linen napkin to remove any remaining traces of fat. Return the consommé to the saucepan, add the sherry and heat through.

Mince the tender parts of the cooked gizzard, liver, and chicken breast together. Put a teaspoonful of this in the bottom of each bouillon cup in which the soup is to be served, and add the hot consommé. Serves 12.

red pea soup   *jamaica*

The red peas in this soup are not the red kidney bean, though this may be used. They are a close relative, slightly smaller, and marketed under a variety of names, sometimes as California pink beans, sometimes as Mexican chili beans. This is one of the most famous of the Jamaican soups.

1 lb. red beans
3 pints water
¼ lb. salt pork, diced
1 medium onion, finely
  chopped
2 or 3 sprigs parsley
½ teaspoon dried thyme

Small stalk celery with leaves
1 fresh hot red pepper,
  seeded and chopped, or
  Pickapeppa hot pepper
  sauce
Salt

Wash the beans thoroughly, drain and put on to cook with 3 pints water, salt pork, onion, parsley, thyme, celery and fresh hot pepper. Cover, and simmer until the beans are very tender, about 2½ to 3 hours. Remove the parsley, and celery. Purée the bean soup quickly in an electric blender, or put through the coarse blade of a food mill. The purée should retain some texture.

Return the soup to the saucepan and season to taste with salt. If using Pickapeppa hot pepper sauce, add to taste at this point. Heat through and serve. If the soup is too thick, thin with a little hot water. Serves 6.

pepperpot soup   *jamaica*

This soup should not be confused with the pepperpot stew, containing cassareep, which comes originally from Guyana and has spread to Trinidad, Barbados and beyond. A very similar soup is popular in Antigua.

1 lb. shin of beef, cubed
½ lb. corned beef or salt
    pork, cubed
3 pints water
1 lb. kale, chopped
1 lb. callaloo, or spinach, or
    Chinese spinach, chopped
1 onion, chopped
1 clove garlic, chopped
4 spring onions, chopped,
    using green and white parts

½ teaspoon dried thyme
1 fresh hot green pepper,
    chopped
½ lb. yam, peeled and sliced
½ lb. coco (taro) peeled and
    sliced
Salt, freshly ground pepper
1 dozen okras
½ oz. unsalted butter
4 oz. cooked shrimps
⅓ pint coconut milk

Put the meats on to cook in a large saucepan with 2¼ pints of water. Simmer, covered, for 1 hour. Put the kale and callaloo with ¾ pint of water into another saucepan and cook until tender – about 30 minutes. Rub the kale and calaloo through a sieve, or purée in an electric blender. Then add, with all the liquid, to the meats, together with the onion, garlic, spring onions, thyme, pepper, yam, coco, and salt and pepper to taste. Cover, and simmer until the meats are tender and the coco and yam are done.

Slice the okras. Heat the butter in a small frying pan and sauté the okras until lightly browned. Add to the soup. Add the shrimps and the coconut milk and simmer for 5 minutes longer. Dumplins (see Index) may be added to the soup in the last 15 minutes of cooking. Serves 6 to 8.

sopa de camarones   *cuba*

Shrimp Soup

1 lb. shrimps or prawns
1½ oz. unsalted butter
1 medium onion, finely
    chopped

1 clove garlic, minced
3 large tomatoes, peeled,
    seeded and coarsely
    chopped

Bay leaf
2 cloves
6 new potatoes, scraped and
  halved
1½ pints milk

2 ears sweet corn, each cut
  into 6 slices
2 egg yolks
6 poached eggs (optional)

Shell the shrimps and set aside. Heat ½ oz. of the butter in a small frying pan and sauté the shrimp shells for 2 or 3 minutes. Transfer to a small saucepan, add ¾ pint water and boil until reduced to half. Strain and set the stock aside. Discard shells.

Heat the remaining 1 oz. of butter in a larger pan and sauté the onion and garlic until the onion is tender but not browned. Add the tomatoes, bay leaf, cloves and shrimp shell stock. Cover and cook for 15 minutes. Strain. Return to the saucepan and add the potatoes. Cover and simmer until the potatoes are almost done – about 15 minutes. Add the milk, shrimps, and corn. Cook, covered, for 5 minutes.

Beat the egg yolks lightly. Beat 3 or 4 tablespoons of the hot soup into the yolks, then stir the egg mixture into the soup over low heat until it thickens slightly. Serve in rimmed soup plates with a potato, 2 slices of corn and some shrimps in each plate.

A poached egg may be added if liked, in which case poach the eggs during the last few minutes of cooking the soup, as overcooking will toughen the shrimps. Serves 6.

This soup makes an admirable lunch if followed by a green salad, cheese and fruit.

sopa de frijol negro   *cuba*

Black Bean Soup

1 lb. black beans
1 cup sofrito (see Index)
½ teaspoon ground cumin
1½ pints, about, of beef or
  chicken stock

Salt, freshly ground pepper
Finely chopped white onion
  for garnish
Pepper Wine (see Index)

Wash the beans thoroughly, drain and put into a large saucepan with the sofrito, cumin, and enough water to cover by about 2 inches. Bring to the boil, lower the heat, cover, and simmer for 2 to 3 hours, or until the beans are very tender. If necessary add a little hot water from time to time.

Drain the cooked beans. Measure the liquid and add enough stock to bring the quantity up to 2½ pints. Purée the beans in an electric blender with some of the liquid, or put through a food mill or sieve. Return the beans and liquid to the saucepan, taste for seasoning adding salt and pepper to taste. Simmer gently for 15 minutes longer. Serve in soup bowls with a little chopped white onion as garnish. Pepper Wine may be added at table as liked. Serves 6 to 8.

VARIATION: Sopa de Habichuelas Negras (Black Bean Soup), Puerto Rico. Put the beans on to cook with the sofrito and 3 pints of chicken stock. Simmer gently, covered, for 2½ to 3 hours. Season to taste with salt and freshly ground pepper, and serve. The soup should be quite thick, the beans still whole but on the point of disintegrating. If the beans absorb so much liquid during cooking that the soup is drying out, add hot stock or water.

VARIATION: Black Bean Soup, Trinidad. Soak 1 lb. beans overnight, drain, rinse and put on to cook with ½ lb. piece corned beef, or a pig's tail, 1 medium chopped onion, 2 cloves garlic, chopped, 2 sprigs parsley, sprig thyme, 2 small stalks celery with leaves, chopped, 3 spring onions, using green and white parts, chopped, 1 bay leaf, 2½ pints beef or chicken stock, salt and pepper to taste. Simmer gently, covered, until tender, about 2 hours. Discard bay leaf and parsley sprigs. Take out beef, or pig's tail. If using pig's tail, discard. Purée soup in an electric blender, or put through a sieve or food mill. Return to saucepan to heat through, adding the corned beef, chopped, if liked. Pepper Wine may be added to each serving.

sopa de gandules   *puerto rico*

Green Pigeon Pea Soup

1 lb. green pigeon (gunga)   pumpkin (calabaza), peeled
  peas, fresh or tinned   and cut into 1-inch cubes
2½ pints chicken stock   1 cup sofrito (see Index)
1 lb. West Indian   Salt, freshly ground pepper

Combine the pigeon peas, stock, pumpkin and sofrito in a large
saucepan, cover and simmer gently until the pigeon peas are
tender and the pumpkin has disintegrated and thickened the
soup, about 20 minutes. Season to taste with salt and pepper if
necessary. Serves 6.

If fresh pigeon peas are not available, use dried peas which
you have soaked and cooked in advance.

sopito   *curaçao*

Fish and Coconut Soup

½ lb. corned beef   2 bay leaves
1½ lb. whole fish, such as   2 leaves fresh basil, or 1
  bass or bream, cleaned and   teaspoon dried
  scaled   3 cloves
2 medium onions, finely   ¼ teaspoon ground cumin
  chopped   Salt
2 tablespoons chopped shallots   3 tablespoons yellow corn
2 stalks celery, chopped   meal
1 green bell pepper, peeled,   ⅓ pint coconut cream
  seeded and chopped

Cover beef with boiling water and let it stand until cold. In a
large saucepan bring 3 pints of water to the boil with 1 of the
onions. 1 tablespoon of the shallots, 1 of the stalks of celery, the
green pepper, bay leaves, basil, cloves, cumin and a little salt.

Simmer, covered, for 20 minutes. Add the fish and poach until it flakes easily with a fork. Strain, reserving the fish and other solids. Remove and discard the cloves and bay leaves. Reserve the fish stock.

Drain the beef and rinse with fresh cold water. Cut into ½-inch cubes, and put into the pan with the strained fish stock, and the remaining onion, shallots and celery. Cook, covered, until the meat is tender, about 1½ hours. Sprinkle the corn meal over the soup and stir for a minute or two. Stir in the coconut cream.

Bone the fish, and cut it into 1½-inch pieces. Return it and the other strained out solids to the soup, taste for seasoning, and heat through, but do not let it boil. Serve with Funchi (see Index). Serves 6.

soppi mondongo   *curaçao*

Tripe Soup

2 lb. tripe
3 tablespoons lime juice
2 pig's feet, split and cleaned
 for cooking
Salt
½ lb. corned beef
1 onion, coarsely chopped
3 chopped shallots
1 stalk celery, coarsely
 chopped
1 lb. West Indian pumpkin
 (calabaza), peeled and cut
 into 1-inch cubes

1 sweet potato, preferably
 white type, peeled and
 cubed
3 potatoes, peeled and cubed
6 pitted green olives
1 tablespoon capers
1 tablespoon seedless raisins
1 green bell pepper, seeded
 and coarsely chopped
1 fresh hot green pepper,
 seeded and chopped
Freshly ground pepper
¼ teaspoon grated nutmeg
¼ teaspoon ground cloves

Wash and drain the tripe. Pour the lime juice over it and let it stand for 10 minutes. Transfer the tripe to a large saucepan. Add the pig's feet and 5 pints salted water. Cook until tender, about 2½ to 3 hours. Meanwhile, pour boiling water over the corned beef, and allow to stand for ¾ hour. Drain, rinse and add to the cooking tripe. When the meats are tender, let cool. Cut the tripe into strips about ¾-inch wide, and the corned beef into ½-inch cubes. Remove the meat from the pig's feet and discard the bones. Put all the vegetables into the stock, with the meats, and seasonings. Simmer gently until the vegetables are tender. About 30 minutes.

Cooks in Curaçao say the soup should be left to cool and stand for 3 hours or so after it is cooked, then reheated, as this improves the flavour. They often add a tablespoon of dry sherry or brandy to each soup plate. Serve with crusty French bread. Serves 10 to 12.

soupe au poisson *martinique–guadeloupe*

Fish Soup

Fish soup is popular in both islands and, though there is a standard recipe, each cook adds his or her special touch. M. Mario Petreluzzi, the moving spirit of La Pergola Restaurant at Gosier, in Guadeloupe, used to add a dash of Ricard to his soup. And the cooks at the Bakoua Hotel at Trois Ilets in Martinique, add croûtons and grated Gruyère cheese to theirs. In both cases with admirable results.

3 tablespoons olive oil or unsalted butter
2 medium onions, finely chopped
4 spring onions, chopped, using green and white parts

1 lb. tomatoes, peeled, seeded and chopped
⅛ teaspoon ground saffron if using plain oil or butter, otherwise omit
½ teaspoon ground ginger
4 pints water

3 lb. whole fish, such as
  bream, bass or other white
  fish, cleaned and scaled
2 fresh hot red peppers, left
  whole
2 cloves garlic, crushed

2 cloves
2 melegueta pepper berries
  or 2 allspice berries
1 bay leaf
1 lb. potatoes, peeled and
  sliced

Heat the oil or butter in a large saucepan and sauté the onions
and spring onions until the onions are golden. Add the tomatoes
and cook, stirring, for 1 or 2 minutes. Add the remaining ingredients, bring to the boil, lower the heat and cook, uncovered,
at a brisk simmer for 30 minutes.

Lift out the fish, remove and discard the bones and set the
fish aside. Put the soup through a sieve, pressing down to extract
all the juices. Return the fish and soup to the saucepan and heat
through. If preferred, the fish may be pressed through the sieve.
Serves 6 to 8.

fish and shellfish

arroz con camarones
dominican republic

Prawns and Rice

4 tablespoons oil
1 large onion, finely chopped
2 cloves garlic, minced
2 cups long grain rice
4 cups chicken stock
2 medium tomatoes, peeled, seeded and chopped
1 bay leaf

1 tablespoon fresh coriander, chopped
Salt, freshly ground pepper
Oil or butter
1 lb. raw prawns, peeled, deveined and cut into ½-inch pieces if large

Heat the oil in a heavy 10- to 12-inch covered frying pan. Sauté the onion and garlic until the onion is tender but not browned. Add the rice, stir and cook until the rice has absorbed all the oil, taking care not to let it brown. Add the chicken stock, tomatoes, coriander, bay leaf, and salt and pepper to taste. Cover, and simmer until the rice is tender and all the liquid absorbed.

Heat a little oil or butter in a frying pan and toss the prawns in the fat over fairly high heat until they are pink, 3 or 4 minutes. Add them to the rice, mixing gently and cook, covered, for a minute or so longer. It is important not to overcook the prawns, as this toughens them. Serve with a fresh hot pepper sauce. I like to shell the prawns and set them aside, then make a stock from the shells. Used in place of the chicken stock, this gives the rice a very rich flavour. Serves 4.

TO MAKE PRAWN STOCK

In a small saucepan, heat 1 tablespoon of oil or butter and toss the shells in this until they turn pink. Add a sprig of parsley, a leaf of basil, ⅛ teaspoon orégano or marjoram, ⅛ teaspoon thyme, a clove of garlic, sprig of celery leaves, 1 or 2 cloves of allspice, and salt and pepper to taste, add 2 pints of water, bring to the boil, reduce the heat and simmer, covered, for 30 minutes. Strain and measure, making up the quantity to 4 cups with water.

ackee and prawns   *jamaica*

1 lb. raw prawns
1 tin ackee (10 oz.), or 1 lb.
  fresh ackees
1 oz. butter
1 onion, finely chopped
1 clove garlic, minced
½ teaspoon marjoram
2 tablespoons golden rum
⅜ pint ackee–prawn stock

1 tablespoon mixed mustard,
  preferably Dijon
1 teaspoon Pickapeppa hot
  pepper sauce, or Tabasco
3 oz. tomato purée
Salt, freshly ground pepper
  to taste
2 teaspoons arrowroot

Shell and devein the prawns. Drain the ackees and add water to make the liquid up to ¾ pint. Put the shells and the ackee liquid on to cook. Simmer until liquid is reduced by half. Strain and set stock aside.

Heat the butter in a heavy frying pan and sauté the onion, garlic and marjoram until the onion is tender but not browned. Add the prawns and cook for 2 or 3 minutes. Heat the rum, pour over the prawns, light and let the flame burn out. Add the ackee–prawn stock, the ackees, the mustard mixed with the hot pepper sauce, the tomato purée, and salt and pepper to taste. Simmer gently until heated through. Mix the arrowroot with 1 tablespoon of water, stir into the prawn mixture and cook until lightly thickened. Pile hot mixture in the centre of a warmed platter. Surround with plain boiled white rice. Serves 4 to 6.

bombas de camarones y papas
dominican republic

Shrimp and Potato Balls

2 lb. potatoes
3 oz. unsalted butter
2 egg yolks
4 oz. Muenster cheese, grated
1 tablespoon chopped parsley
Salt, white pepper
1 medium onion, finely
chopped

2 lb. cooked shrimps, or
prawns, shelled and coarsely
chopped
Flour
1 egg, lightly beaten
3 oz. bread crumbs
Vegetable oil for deep frying
Lemon slices for garnish

Peel and cook the potatoes until tender in salted water. Drain thoroughly, then mash with 2 oz. of the butter, the egg yolks, grated cheese, parsley, and salt and white pepper to taste. Set aside.

Heat the remaining butter in a frying pan and sauté the onion until tender, but not browned. Cool slightly and stir in the shrimps, mixing well. Form the potato mixture into balls about the size of a small egg then stuff each with about 1 tablespoon of the shrimp mixture. Roll each lightly in flour, dip in beaten egg and then in bread crumbs. Place on a piece of waxed paper and refrigerate for at least 20 minutes.

Deep fry balls in hot oil (375°F on a frying thermometer) 3 or 4 at a time, until all are golden brown all over. Drain on paper towels and keep warm until all the bombas are done. Makes about 30.

Serve garnished with lemon slices and a Salsa Tártara or Tomato Sauce (see Index) as luncheon dish, for 6. Or as a first course for 12.

The bombas, made smaller and served on toothpicks, with the sauces for dipping are an excellent accompaniment to drinks.

baked lobster   *jamaica*

When we lived in Jamaica, this was our cook Annie's great dish
for entertaining. It was always served as a fish course. When we
had visitors, Annie insisted on the formalities, and nothing less
than four courses was acceptable. However, it makes an excellent
main course for either lunch or dinner. Lobsters in Jamaica are
really crayfish (crawfish), delectable creatures with the best flesh
in the tail rather than in the claws. It makes no great matter
which is used, and I have found crab meat a splendid variation.

1¾ lb. fresh lobster, cut into
  1-inch chunks, or 2 14-oz.
  tins lobster
Juice 2 large limes, about 6
  tablespoons
5 oz. unsalted butter
2 medium onions, finely
  chopped
2 cloves garlic, finely
  chopped

1 tablespoon fresh hot red or
  green peppers, seeded and
  chopped
3 oz. freshly made bread
  crumbs
Salt, freshly ground pepper
2 teaspoons Worcestershire
  sauce
Lime wedges

Mix the lobster with the lime juice and leave for 15 minutes.
Heat all but 1 oz. of the butter in a heavy 10-inch frying pan and
sauté the onions lightly with the garlic and peppers until the
onions are tender but not browned. Add 2 oz. of the bread crumbs
and cook, stirring from time to time, until the bread crumbs are
golden. Add the lobster and lime juice, season to taste with salt,
pepper and Worcestershire sauce and turn into a buttered 1½
pint soufflé dish. Top with remaining bread crumbs and dot with
remaining butter.

Bake in a preheated 350°F (gas 4) oven for half an hour, or
until the top is golden.

Serve with lime wedges. Serves 4 to 6 according to appetite.

asopao de langosta y camarones   *puerto rico*

Rice, Lobster and Prawn Stew

Asopao is Puerto Rico's special contribution to the Caribbean kitchen. It can be made with various shellfish or chicken, and the finished product is slightly soupy, which is what asopao means.

1 lb. long grain rice	1 lb. green peas, shelled, or
2 cups sofrito (see Index)	10 oz. package frozen peas
1 lb. raw prawns, shelled,	2½ pints chicken stock
deveined and cut into	1 tablespoon capers
½-inch pieces if large	3 oz. small pitted green olives
1 lb. rock lobster tails, or	2 pimentos, cut in strips
lobster meat, cut into	
½-inch chunks	

Put the rice to soak for 30 minutes in ¾ pint cold water. Heat the sofrito in a heavy casserole, stir in the prawns and lobster and cook, stirring from time to time, for 5 minutes. Drain the rice and add to the casserole with the peas and chicken stock, stir and cook, covered, at a gentle simmer until the rice is tender, about 20 minutes. If using frozen peas, add according to package directions. Stir in the capers, olives and pimentos and cook just long enough to heat through. Serves 6.

If liked, the Asopao may be garnished with asparagus tips.

For Asopao de Mariscos (Shellfish Stew) use a mixture of shellfish such as prawns, crab, lobster, and mussels and finish it with 6 tablespoons dry sherry stirred in just before serving.

For Asopao de Calamares, use squids, cleaned and cut into 1-inch pieces.

Asopao de Jueyes is made with land crabs. Use lump crab meat instead.

camarones rellenos   *dominican republic*

Stuffed Prawns

24 Pacific prawns, or Scampi
4 tablespoons anchovy paste
2 oz. unsalted butter,
  creamed
2 oz. freshly made bread
  crumbs
2 tablespoons lime, or lemon,
  juice
2 tablespoons onion juice

½ teaspoon freshly ground
  pepper
4 oz. plain flour
Oil for deep frying
Freshly grated Parmesan
  cheese
Salsa Tártara (Tartare
  Sauce) (see Index)

BATTER

4 oz. plain flour
1 teaspoon salt

½ oz. unsalted butter, melted
⅓ pint flat beer*
1 egg, separated

Peel and devein the prawns, making an extra deep and long incision to serve as a pocket for the stuffing. Combine the anchovy paste, butter, bread crumbs, lime juice, onion juice and pepper. Refrigerate for 30 minutes.

To make the batter, sift the flour and salt into a bowl. Make a well in the centre and add the butter, beer, and the yolk of the egg. Mix quickly and thoroughly, and set aside in a warm place.

Stuff each prawn with about 1 teaspoon of the anchovy stuffing, and dust lightly with flour. Beat the egg white until stiff and fold into the batter. Dip the stuffed prawns into the batter and fry in deep hot oil, 350°F on a frying thermometer, two or three at a time. Drain on paper towels and keep warm. When all the prawns have been fried, sprinkle them with grated cheese and serve immediately with Salsa Tártara (Tartare Sauce) served separately. Serves 4 to 6.

*Beer gives a lighter batter, but milk or water may be used.

court bouillon de poisson
martinique–guadeloupe

Fish Poached in Tomato Sauce

The name court bouillon should not mislead. It does not mean court bouillon in the sense of a poaching liquid; here it means fish cooked in a special sauce. With Poisson en Blaff this is probably the most characteristic dish of the French islands.

7 tablespoons lime juice
1 fresh hot red pepper, pounded
3 cloves garlic, crushed
1 tablespoon salt
¾ pint cold water, about
2 1-lb. white-fleshed fish, cleaned but with heads left on
3 tablespoons oil
5 shallots, finely chopped
4 spring onions, finely chopped

2 teaspoons finely chopped garlic
3 medium tomatoes, peeled and chopped
Salt, freshly ground pepper
1 fresh hot red pepper, left whole
2 sprigs parsley
1 bay leaf
1 sprig thyme
½ pint dry white wine, or ¼ pint wine, ¼ pint water
2 tablespoons olive oil

In a large shallow dish combine 6 tablespoons of the lime juice, the pounded pepper, crushed garlic, salt and water. Add the fish and a little more water, if necessary, to cover. Marinate for 1 hour. Drain, discard the marinade, and cut each fish in half, crosswise.

In a heavy frying pan, large enough to hold the fish comfortably, heat the oil, add the shallots, spring onions and 1 teaspoon of the chopped garlic. Sauté until the shallots are tender, but not browned. Add the tomatoes, salt and pepper to taste and cook for a few minutes longer. Add the fish and cook for two minutes, turning once. Add the whole pepper, parsley, bay leaf and thyme, all tied in a square of cheese-cloth, and the wine. Simmer uncovered for 10 to 15 minutes, or until the fish is done.

Remove and discard the *bouquet garni*. Mix the olive oil with the remaining tablespoon of lime juice and teaspoon of garlic, beating well with a fork. Pour over the fish and serve immediately. Serves 2.

Serve with Riz Créole (Rice Creole-style) or with two or three local vegetables, plainly cooked, such as breadfruit, plantains or bananas, yams, West Indian pumpkin, and sweet potatoes, served separately.

crab pilau   *tobago*

1 lb. fresh, tinned or frozen crab meat, picked over to remove any cartilage
3 tablespoons lime juice
2 tablespoons vegetable oil
1 oz. unsalted butter
2 medium onions, finely chopped

1 clove garlic, chopped
1 fresh hot pepper, seeded and chopped
2 tablespoons curry powder
1 lb. raw long-grain rice
1½ pints coconut milk
Salt, freshly ground pepper
1 tablespoon chopped chives

Put the crab meat into a bowl, add the lime juice and set aside. In a heavy casserole, heat the oil and butter and sauté the onions, garlic and hot pepper until the onions are tender but not browned. Add the curry powder and cook, stirring for 3 or 4 minutes, being careful not to let the curry powder burn. Stir in the rice and cook for about a minute longer, just to coat the grains. Add the coconut milk, season to taste with salt and pepper, stir, and cook, covered, over low heat until the rice is almost done, about 15 minutes. Fold in the crab meat and any liquid, and the chives. Cover and cook for about 5 minutes longer, or until the liquid is all absorbed and the crab heated through. Serves 6.

crabes farcis   *martinique–guadeloupe*

Stuffed Crabs

Land crabs are used for this dish in the islands.

6 small, hard-shelled crabs
3 oz. freshly made bread
  crumbs
1 fresh hot pepper, seeded
  and chopped fine, or hot
  pepper sauce to taste
3 tablespoons chives, chopped
2 tablespoons parsley, chopped
2 cloves garlic, crushed

1 tablespoon lime juice
Salt, freshly ground pepper
¼ teaspoon allspice
3 tablespoons Madeira, or
  dark rum, preferably
  Martinique or Guadeloupe
  rhum vieux
Butter

Plunge the crabs into boiling water and boil for 8 to 10 minutes. Remove and cool. Carefully take out the meat from the shells and claws, and chop fine. Discard spongy fibre. Scrub the empty shells if small and reserve.

Mash 2 oz. of the bread crumbs into the crab meat until the mixture is quite smooth. Add the hot pepper, chives, parsley, garlic, lime juice, salt, pepper, allspice, and Madeira or rum, mixing thoroughly. Stuff the reserved crab shells with the mixture. If using three or four larger crabs, use the meat to stuff six scallop shells or put in ramekins. Sprinkle with the remaining bread crumbs and dot with butter. Bake in a 350°F (gas 4) oven for 30 minutes, or until lightly browned. Serves 6 as an appetizer, 2 to 3 for lunch.

If live crabs are not available, buy 1 lb. fresh, frozen, or tinned crab meat and stuff scallop shells, or buy plain boiled crabs.

crapaud   *dominica and montserrat*

Fried Frogs' Legs

Crapauds, also called mountain chickens, are a special type of frog found in Dominica and Montserrat. They are much larger than the usual type of frog and have a very delicate flavour. They are worth a trip to the islands, especially to Dominica which produces the most remarkable limes, whose juice, mixed with the local rum, makes a memorable punch for sipping while waiting for one's crapauds.

1 medium onion, grated	12 pairs medium sized frogs'
3 cloves garlic, crushed	legs, defrosted if frozen,
½ teaspoon ground cloves	and split in half
1 teaspoon salt	⅓ pint vegetable oil
¼ teaspoon white pepper	4 oz. flour
1 tablespoon malt vinegar	Lime wedges

Mix together the onion, garlic, cloves, salt, pepper, and vinegar in a large mixing bowl. Add the frogs' legs and allow to stand for at least 1 hour, turning the frogs' legs from time to time.

Heat the oil in a heavy frying pan. Pat the frogs' legs dry with paper towels and dip in flour. Fry half a dozen or so at a time, for about 5 minutes on each side. Drain on paper towels and serve with lime wedges on the side. Serves 6.

daube de poisson   *martinique–guadeloupe*

Fish Stew

8 tablespoons lime, or lemon,	1 tablespoon salt
juice	¾ pint cold water, about
1 fresh hot red pepper,	3 lb. fresh tuna, or similar
pounded	fish, cut into 6 steaks
3 cloves garlic, crushed	Plain flour

4 tablespoons olive oil
1 onion, finely chopped
4 spring onions, chopped,
   using green and white parts
2 medium tomatoes, peeled
   and chopped

Salt, freshly ground pepper
Bay leaf
$\frac{1}{4}$ teaspoon thyme
1 tablespoon olive oil

In large bowl mix together 6 tablespoons of the lime juice, the hot pepper, 2 cloves of the garlic, the salt and water. Add the fish and, if necessary, a little more water to cover. Allow to stand for 1 hour. Drain thoroughly and discard the marinade.

Pat the fish dry with paper towels and dust lightly with flour. Heat the 4 tablespoons of oil in a heavy frying pan and sauté the fish lightly until golden on both sides.Lift out and keep warm.

In the oil remaining in the frying pan, adding a little more if necessary, sauté the onion and spring onions until the onion is tender but not browned. Add the tomatoes, salt and pepper to taste, the bay leaf and thyme and cook, stirring occasionally for 5 minutes.

Add the fish and enough water barely to cover. Cover and cook for 10 to 15 minutes, or until the fish is tender. Discard the bay leaf. Just before serving beat together the remaining clove of garlic, the remaining 2 tablespoons of lime juice and the 1 tablespoon of olive oil and pour over the fish. Serves 6.

escovitch or caveached fish *jamaica*

This is the Jamaican version of the Pescado en Escabeche of the Spanish islands.

3 green bell peppers, seeded
   and sliced
2 medium onions, thinlysliced
3 carrots, scraped and thinly
   sliced

Bay leaf
$\frac{1}{2}$-inch slice fresh ginger
   root, finely chopped
6 peppercorns
$\frac{1}{8}$ teaspoon mace

Salt
¾ pint water
2 tablespoons olive oil
6 tablespoons vinegar,
   preferably malt or cane

3 tablespoons olive oil for
   frying
2 lb. white fish fillets
Olives and pimentos for
   garnish

Combine the peppers, onions, carrots, bay leaf, ginger, pepper-corns, mace and salt with the water. Cover and simmer for 30 minutes. Add the olive oil and vinegar and simmer for a minute or two longer. Strain.

Heat the 3 tablespoons of olive oil in a large, heavy frying pan and sauté the fish fillets until lightly browned on both sides; be careful not to overcook. Drain the fish and arrange in a warmed serving dish. Pour the hot sauce over the dish and serve hot. Or chill the fish in its sauce and serve cold, garnished with olives and pimentos.

Serves 4 as a main course, 8 as a first course.

flying fish pie   *barbados*

Unhappily flying fish are not a routine item in fish shops or supermarkets here, but rather than lose this attractive dish altogether, substitute fillets of any white fish. Be careful to get real yams, not the sweet potatoes known as Louisiana yams.

12 flying fish, or 1½ lb.
   white fish fillets
Salt, freshly ground pepper
2 oz. unsalted butter
2 lb. yams

1 large onion, very finely
   sliced
1 large tomato, peeled and
   thinly sliced
2 hard-boiled eggs, sliced

FOR THE SAUCE

2 egg yolks
2 tablespoons vegetable oil
1 oz. unsalted butter, melted

1 tablespoon Worcestershire
sauce
6 tablespoons dry sherry

Season the fish with salt and pepper. Heat 1 oz. of the butter in a frying pan and sauté the fish lightly on both sides. Cut in halves. Peel the yams and cook in salted water until tender. Cool and slice thinly. Butter a deep dish, or soufflé dish. Arrange half the fish fillets in one layer. Make a layer of half the onion, tomato, and 1 of the eggs. Cover with a layer of yams, using half. Then the rest of the fish, the rest of the onion, tomato and the egg. Top with the other half of the sliced yams. Dot with the remaining butter.

Beat the egg yolks, then thoroughly mix in the oil, melted butter, Worcestershire sauce and sherry. Pour over contents of the baking dish. Bake in a 350°F (gas 4) oven until the top of the pie is golden brown and heated through, about 30 minutes. Serves 4 to 6.

fricassée d'escargots 1755 *northern martinique*

Fricassee of Snails, 1755

This snail dish was created in the kitchens of the de Leyritz Plantation in 1755 to celebrate a domestic event connected with the building of a *petit chateau bordelais,* the main house of the plantation, built near Basse Pointe, in the north of Martinique, by Michel de Leyritz at the beginning of the 18th century. It is still in the repertoire of the restored plantation, now a restaurant and small hotel, and is another example of the good cooking of the north of the island.

2 oz. unsalted butter
1 medium onion, finely
  chopped
1 clove garlic, chopped
1 tablespoon parsley, chopped
¼ lb. sliced mushrooms

Salt, freshly ground pepper
Dash of hot pepper sauce
  (optional)
8 oz. can (4 oz. drained
  weight) escargots (snails)
6 tablespoons double cream

Heat the butter in a heavy, medium-sized frying pan and sauté
the onion, garlic, parsley, and mushrooms until the onion is
tender and the mushrooms cooked. Season to taste with salt and
pepper, and a dash of hot pepper sauce, if liked.

If the snails are very large, cut them into halves or quarters.
Add the snails to the mushroom mixture and cook over low heat
for 5 to 8 minutes. Stir in the cream and cook for a minute or
two longer.

Serve with Riz Créole (see Index), or with any plainly cooked
starchy vegetable such as potatoes, sweet potatoes, breadfruit,
yams, etc. The recipe may be successfully doubled, or trebled.
Serves 2.

keshy yena coe cabaron   *curaçao*

Stuffed Cheese with Shrimp Filling

4 lb. Edam cheese
1½ lb. cooked shrimps,
  shelled
1 oz. unsalted butter
1 large onion, finely chopped
1 lb. tomatoes, peeled, seeded
  and chopped
Salt, freshly ground pepper
  to taste

⅛ teaspoon cayenne pepper
2 oz. freshly made bread
  crumbs
3 tablespoons seedless raisins
2 tablespoons finely chopped
  sweet pickles
4 tablespoons chopped black
  olives
2 eggs, well beaten

Peel the red wax covering from the cheese, cut a 1-inch slice
from the top, hollow out and reserve for use as a lid. Scoop out

the cheese, leaving a shell about ½ inch thick. Cover the shell and lid with cold water and soak for an hour. Grate the scooped out cheese and reserve ½ lb. Store the remaining cheese for another use.

Heat the butter in a frying pan and sauté the onion until tender. Add the tomatoes, salt and pepper and cayenne pepper and cook until the mixture is smooth and fairly thick. Add the bread crumbs, raisins, pickles, olives, grated cheese, and the shrimps. Fold the eggs gently but thoroughly into the shrimp mixture.

Remove the cheese shell and lid from the water and pat dry. Stuff with the shrimp mixture. Replace top of cheese. Put the stuffed cheese into a greased 4-pint casserole and bake in a 350°F (gas 4) oven for 30 minutes. Do not overcook as the cheese becomes tough, instead of soft and bubbly. Slide the cheese out of the casserole onto a warmed serving dish. Cut into wedges and serve immediately. Serves 6 to 8.

VARIATION: For Keshy Yena coe Pisca (Stuffed Cheese with Fish Filling) prepare the cheese in the same way, and stuff with the following filling.

1 lb. white fish fillets
1 oz. unsalted butter
1 large onion, finely chopped
2 medium tomatoes, peeled and chopped
Salt, freshly ground pepper to taste
⅛ teaspoon cayenne pepper

2 oz. freshly made bread crumbs
3 tablespoons seedless raisins
2 tablespoons finely chopped sweet pickles
10 small pimento-stuffed green olives, chopped
2 eggs, well beaten

Place the fish fillets in a frying pan, cover with cold water, bring to a simmer, cover and cook for about 6 minutes, or until the fish flakes easily with a fork. Cool in the stock, remove and flake. Set aside. Discard the stock, rinse out and dry the pan.

Heat the butter in the pan and sauté the onion until tender but not browned. Add the tomatoes, salt and pepper and cayenne pepper and cook, stirring, until the mixture is smooth and fairly thick. Add the bread crumbs, raisins, pickles, olives, fish and grated cheese. Fold the eggs gently but thoroughly into the fish mixture. Stuff the cheese and bake as above.

herring gundy   *u.s. virgin islands*

This dish obviously derives from the period, before 1917, when the islands, St Thomas, St Croix and St John, were Danish. The name is a corruption of salmagundi, a word of unknown origin used as early as 1674 to describe a dish of chopped meat, anchovies, eggs, onions, oil and seasonings. A similar term, salmigondis, is used in the French kitchen to describe a ragout of several meats, reheated.

2 lb. salt herring
2 lb. potatoes
2 medium onions, finely chopped
1 green bell pepper, seeded and chopped
1 teaspoon finely chopped hot red or green pepper
3 oz. small pitted green olives, chopped

4 medium diced, cooked beetroot
4 medium freshly grated carrots
4 hard-boiled eggs
8 fl. oz. salad oil
3 tablespoons vinegar, preferably cane or malt
Freshly ground pepper
Parsley sprigs
Lettuce leaves

Wash the herrings, drain and soak overnight in cold water to cover. Drain, pat dry with paper towels, remove the skin and bones, and put the fish through the coarse blade of a food mill. Peel the potatoes and cook until tender in salted water, Drain, mash and combine with the herring. Add the onions, bell pepper, hot pepper, olives, ⅓ of the beetroot, ¼ of the carrot and 1 of the eggs, finely chopped. Add the oil, vinegar and a generous amount of freshly ground pepper. Mix well. Chill, if liked.

Mound on a serving platter and surround with small heaps of diced beets, grated carrot and chopped egg. Garnish with parsley sprigs and lettuce leaves. Serves 6 as a main course, 12 as a first course.

langosta enchilada   *cuba*

Lobster in Pepper Sauce

The lobsters of the Caribbean are really salt-water crayfish, spiny or rock lobsters. Frozen lobster tails, or lobsters may equally be used.

2 2-lb. lobsters, uncooked	1 tablespoon lime juice
2 tablespoons oil	6 slices bread
2 cups sofrito (see Index)	Oil or butter for frying

Set aside the tomalley or coral (if any). Remove all the meat from the lobsters and set aside. Heat 2 tablespoons of oil in a heavy frying pan and sauté the lobster shells over high heat, turning them constantly, until they turn pink. Transfer the lobster shells to a large saucepan and pour in ¾ pint of water. Bring to the boil and cook, covered, until the liquid is reduced by half. Pour off most of the oil from the frying pan, add the lobster meat, the sofrito, and the stock from the shells. Cook, covered, for 20 minutes. Stir in the lime juice, and the tomalley and coral, rubbed through a sieve. Cook the mixture for a minute or two longer.

In the meantime, cut the slices of bread into triangles and fry in oil or butter until browned on both sides. Transfer the lobster and sauce to a warmed platter with the triangles of fried bread arranged as a decorative border. Serves 4 to 6.

VARIATION: A similar dish, Cangrejos Enchilados (Crabs in Pepper Sauce), is made in the Dominican Republic. The sofrito is made with olive oil, the ham is left out, and 3 tablespoons of tomato purée are added. One pound of crabmeat, picked over to remove any cartilage or shell, is heated through in the sofrito to which 1 tablespoon lime or lemon juice, and 6 tablespoons dry sherry are added at the last minute. The finished dish, sprinkled with parsley, is served with white rice. Serves 4 to 6.

matoutou de crabes   *martinique*

This is the Carib word for a dish that was originally made with cassava meal but is now more often cooked with rice. In Guadeloupe the dish with rice is called matété, with cassava meal, matoutou.

2 lb. crab meat, fresh, tinned or frozen, picked over to remove any shell or cartilage	¼ teaspoon thyme
	1 bay leaf
	1 tablespoon chopped parsley
	3 tablespoons lime juice
4 tablespoons olive oil	Salt, freshly ground pepper
3 shallots, chopped	1 teaspoon fresh hot red pepper, seeded and chopped
4 cloves garlic, crushed	
2 tablespoons chopped chives	2 cups rice

Heat the oil in a heavy casserole, add the crab meat, and cook for a few minutes, stirring from time to time. Add all the ingredients, except the rice, and sauté for a minute or two longer. Add the rice and 4 cups of water, cover and cook over low heat until the rice is tender and all the liquid absorbed. Serves 6.

pargo asado

Baked Sea Bream

5–6 lb. bream, cleaned and
  scaled
6 tablespoons lime juice
Salt, freshly ground pepper
6 tablespoons olive oil
1 large onion, finely sliced
½ teaspoon thyme
½ teaspoon orégano
1 bay leaf, crumbled

1 medium onion, finely
  chopped
2 cloves garlic, chopped
1 fresh hot red or green
  pepper, seeded and
  chopped
1 tablespoon chopped parsley
2 oz. toasted almonds, ground

Cut the head off the fish and use to make ½ pint stock.

Mix the lime juice with salt and pepper to taste and rub into
the fish, inside and out. Set aside. Pour 4 tablespoons of the
olive oil into a baking dish large enough to hold the fish comfortably. Arrange the sliced onion on the bottom of the dish and
sprinkle with the thyme, orégano and bayleaf. Season with salt
and pepper. Drain the fish and pour the marinade over the
onions together with all but 6 tablespoons of the fish stock. Place
the fish in the baking dish.

Make the following dressing. Heat the remaining 2 tablespoons of oil in a frying pan and sauté the chopped onion and
garlic until the onion is tender but not browned. Add the hot
pepper, parsley and almonds and the remaining fish stock.
Spread the dressing over the top and sides of the fish. Bake,
uncovered, in a 400°F (gas 6) oven for 40 to 45 minutes. Serves 6.

Striped bass may also be used.

TO MAKE FISH STOCK

Put the fish head into a saucepan with 1 pint of water, or half
water, and half white wine. Add a small onion, coarsely chopped,
some parsley stalks and simmer, uncovered, for about 20 minutes,
or until the liquid is reduced to half. Strain and season to taste
with salt.

pargo asado con salsa esmeralda   *cuba*

Baked Sea Bream with Green Sauce

2 teaspoons salt
¼ teaspoon freshly ground
   pepper
4 cloves garlic, crushed
¼ teaspoon orégano
¼ teaspoon ground cumin
6 tablespoons lime juice

5–6lb. bream
   cleaned and scaled, but
   with head and tail left on
Butter
2 lb. potatoes, peeled and cut
   into ½-inch slices
8 fl. oz. olive oil
4 tablespoons parsley, chopped
2 pimentos, cut into strips

Mix together the salt, pepper, garlic, orégano, cumin and lime juice and rub into the fish inside and out. Set aside for half an hour. Butter an oven-proof dish large enough to hold the fish comfortably. Arrange the potatoes on the bottom of the dish, place the fish on top, pouring the marinade over the fish. Pour the oil over fish and potatoes. Cook in a 400°F (gas 6) oven for 40 to 45 minutes. Decorate with parsley and pimentos and serve with the Salsa Esmeralda. Serves 6. Striped bass may also be used.

SALSA ESMERALDA

Green Sauce

3 cloves garlic, crushed
2 tablespoons chopped capers,
   preferably Spanish
Yolks of 4 hard-boiled eggs,
   mashed
1 teaspoon salt

¼ teaspoon white pepper
2 tablespoons chopped parsley
2 oz. toasted almonds, ground
¼ pint olive oil
3 tablespoons distilled white
   vinegar

In a mortar mash together the garlic, capers, egg yolks, salt, pepper, parsley and almonds. Beat in the oil little by little and at the last minute add the vinegar. Makes about 1½ cups.

pargo con salsa de aguacate　　　　*cuba*

Sea Bream with Avocado Sauce

1 onion, sliced
1 clove garlic, crushed
1 bay leaf
½ teaspoon thyme
½ teaspoon orégano
Sprig celery leaves

2 or 3 sprigs parsley
6 peppercorns, bruised
6 tablespoons lime juice
5–6 lb. bream, cleaned and
　scaled but with head and
　tail left on

Place all the ingredients, except the fish, in a large saucepan. Add 6 pints of water, bring to the boil and simmer, partially covered, for half an hour. Cool. Wash the fish, drain and wrap in a long, double-thick piece of cheesecloth. Lay the fish in a roasting pan or fish poacher large enough to hold it comfortably, with the ends of the cheesecloth hanging over the two ends of the pan. If the pan has handles, tie the cheesecloth ends to the handles. Pour in the poaching liquid, which should cover the fish by at least an inch. If necessary add a little water. Bring the liquid to a bare simmer, cover tightly, flipping ends of cheesecloth, if untied, on top of the lid, and cook for 30 to 40 minutes, or until the thickest part of the fish feels firm when pressed with a finger.

When done, using the ends of the cheesecloth, lift the fish onto a large board. Open the cheesecloth and gently peel off the fish skin in strips. Using the cheesecloth, carefully turn the fish onto a serving platter. Discard cheesecloth. Remove the skin from the up-turned side.

The fish may be eaten hot or cold. If it is to be eaten hot, the sauce should be served separately. If served cold, the fish should be masked with some of the sauce, and the rest served separately. The cold platter should be garnished with olives, both green and black, cherry tomatoes, radishes, parsley sprigs, tiny lettuce leaves and wedges of lime. Serves 6. Striped bass may also be used.

SALSA DE AGUACATE

Avocado Sauce

2 large avocados
1 tablespoon lime juice
3 tablespoons vegetable oil

1 teaspoon salt
Freshly ground black pepper
  to taste

Peel, pit and mash the avocados with a fork. Add the lime juice
oil, salt and pepper and beat until the sauce has the consistency
of mayonnaise.

pescado con salsa de coco   *dominican republic*

Fish with Coconut milk Sauce

3 cloves garlic
2 teaspoons salt
3 tablespoons lime juice
1 teaspoon orégano
⅛ teaspoon freshly ground
  pepper
2½ lb. white fish fillets
Flour

6 tablespoons peanut oil
1 onion, finely chopped
1 fresh hot green pepper,
  sliced
Bay leaf
¾ pint coconut milk
3 tablespoons tomato paste

Crush 1 of the garlic cloves with the salt, add 2 tablespoons of the
lime juice, ½ teaspoon of the orégano, and the freshly ground
pepper. Mix well, allow to stand for about 30 minutes, strain
and pour over the fish fillets. Allow to stand for 1 hour. Dry the
fish and dust with flour. Heat the oil in a frying pan and fry the
fish until tender and golden brown. Keep warm.

Chop the remaining 2 cloves of garlic and sauté with the
onion and hot pepper in the oil remaining in the frying pan, until the onion is tender. Add the bay leaf, remaining ½ teaspoon
orégano, coconut milk, and tomato paste. Cook, stirring, for 3
minutes. Add the remaining 1 tablespoon of lime juice and cook
for 2 minutes longer. Pour over fish. Serves 6.

revuelto de cangrejo   *dominican republic*

Crab and Cod with Scrambled Eggs

This translates literally as 'scrambled of crab'. Hence the more descriptive English name.

1 lb. salt codfish
3 tablespoons olive oil
2 lb. lump crab meat, picked
  over to remove any cartilage

4 cloves garlic, finely chopped
2 tablespoons chopped parsley
Salt, freshly ground pepper
6 eggs, lightly beaten

Soak the cod in cold water, the time depending on the hardness and saltiness of the fish. Drain, rinse in fresh water and put on to cook in cold water. Simmer gently for 15 minutes, or until the fish is tender. Drain thoroughly, remove any bones and skin and shred.

Heat the oil in a large, heavy frying pan. Add the shredded cod, the crab meat, and the garlic and cook, stirring from time to time, for 5 minutes. Add the parsley. Season to taste with salt and pepper. Fold in the eggs and cook, stirring as for scrambled eggs, until the eggs are lightly set. Serves 6.

Lobster may be used instead of crab.

poisson en blaff   *martinique–guadeloupe*

Poached Fish

One theory of the term blaff is that when a freshly caught fish is thrown into the poaching liquid it makes the sound 'blaff'. Unprovable as a linguistic theory, but very plausible. This is one of the most characteristic dishes of the French islands.

7 tablespoons lime juice
1 fresh hot red pepper,
  pounded

3 cloves garlic, crushed
1 tablespoon salt
¾ pint cold water, about

2 1-lb. white-fleshed fish,
1 of them a bream, if
possible, cleaned and scaled,
with heads and tails left on
½ pint dry white wine
1 medium onion, finely
chopped, or 2 to 3 spring
onions, sliced, using the
green and white parts

1 clove garlic, crushed
2 whole cloves
1 fresh hot red pepper, left
whole
2 melegueta peppercorns
(see Glossary) or use 2
allspice berries
2 melegueta leaves, or use
bay leaves

In a large, shallow dish combine 6 tablespoons of the lime juice, the pounded pepper, 3 cloves of crushed garlic, salt, and water. Add the fish and a little more water, if necessary, to cover. Marinate for 1 hour. Drain, discard the marinade, and cut each fish in half, crosswise.

Pour the wine and ¼ pint of water with the remaining tablespoon of lime juice into a heavy frying pan, large enough to hold the fish comfortably. Add the onion or spring onions, garlic, cloves, whole pepper, and melegueta peppercorns and leaves, or allspice and bay leaves. Bring to the boil, and simmer for 5 minutes. Add the fish and simmer, uncovered, until it is done, about 10 minutes. Serve in individual deep oval dishes, dividing the fish so that each dish contains one head, and one tail portion. Pour the poaching liquid over the fish. The bream makes an attractive contrast with the other fish.

Serve with Riz Créole (Creole Style rice), Pois et Riz (Rice and Beans), or fried ripe plantains or bananas. Serves 2.

salt fish and ackee   *jamaica*

1 lb. salt cod
2 dozen ackees or 18 oz. tin
ackees
4 oz. salt pork, diced fine

2 medium onions, finely
chopped
1 green bell pepper, seeded
and chopped (optional)

1 teaspoon finely chopped
  fresh hot pepper, seeded
4 spring onions, chopped using
  the green and white parts
¼ teaspoon thyme

4 medium tomatoes
Freshly ground pepper
6 slices bacon, fried crisp
Parsley sprigs, or watercress
  for garnish (optional)

Soak the salt cod in cold water. The length of time will depend
on the hardness and saltiness of the fish. Drain, and cook in fresh
cold water. Simmer until tender, adding the fresh ackees 15
minutes before the fish is done. Drain and set the ackees aside.
Remove any bones and skin from the fish, flake and add to the
ackees.

In a heavy frying pan fry the salt pork until it has given up
all its fat and the dice are crisp and brown. Lift out the brown
pieces with a slotted spoon and set aside with the fish and ackees.
Sauté the onions and bell pepper in the fat until they are tender
and very lightly browned. Add hot pepper, the spring onions,
thyme, and 3 of the tomatoes, peeled and coarsely chopped and
sauté for about 5 minutes. Add the flaked cod, ackees and salt
pork dice and heat through. If using tinned ackees, drain and
add at this point.

Transfer to a heated serving dish, season with freshly ground
pepper, and garnish with the crisp bacon slices, the remaining
tomato cut into 8 wedges, and if liked, parsley sprigs or watercress. Serves 4.

salt fish in chemise   *dominica*

1 ½ lb. salt codfish
3 oz. unsalted butter
2 medium onions, finely
  chopped
2 cloves garlic, chopped
2 tablespoons finely chopped
  chives

3 tomatoes, peeled and chopped
½ teaspoon thyme
1 teaspoon fresh hot red or
  green pepper, seeded and
  chopped
Salt, freshly ground pepper
6 eggs

Put the salt fish in a bowl, cover with warm water and soak for 2 hours or longer, according to the saltiness and hardness of the fish. Drain, rinse and pat dry. Remove any skin and bones, and shred the fish. Heat the butter in a frying pan and sauté the onions and garlic until the onions are tender but not browned. Add the chives, tomatoes, thyme, hot pepper, salt, if necessary, and pepper to taste. Add the shredded fish, and a little water if the mixture is too dry to cook the fish. Simmer, covered, for 15 minutes

Butter a casserole and pour in the mixture, or divide among 6 individual casseroles. Break the eggs over the fish mixture and place in a large frying pan with about an inch of water. Cover and steam until the eggs are done. Serves 6.

prawn curry   *trinidad*

1 ½ teaspoons coriander seeds
1 ½ teaspoons cumin seeds
1 ½ teaspoons brown mustard seeds
1 ½ teaspoons whole black peppercorns
½ teaspoon crushed hot red pepper
2 bay leaves
3 tablespoons vegetable oil
1 ½ oz. unsalted butter
2 large onions finely chopped
2 cloves garlic, crushed

1 tablespoon fresh ginger root, finely chopped
4 medium tomatoes, peeled and chopped, or 1 medium tin tomatoes, chopped, drained
2 tablespoons lime juice
1 tablespoon chopped lime pickle (optional)
Salt
2 lb. large raw prawns, peeled and deveined

In a mortar, or in an electric blender, pulverize the coriander, cumin, and mustard seeds with the peppercorns, hot pepper and bay leaves. Set aside. Heat the oil and butter in a large, heavy skillet and sauté the onions until very lightly browned. Add the garlic, ginger root and the ground spices and cook, stirring for

2 or 3 minutes longer. Add the tomatoes, lime juice, and lime pickle, if liked. This is very hot. Season to taste with salt, cover and cook for 30 minutes over very low heat, stirring from time to time. If necessary add a little stock or water. The sauce should be quite thick. Add the prawns, and cook, covered, for 5 minutes, or until the prawns are firm and pink. Be careful not to overcook. Serves 4. Serve with boiled rice and mango chutney, and roti (see Index).

For an informal lunch for six, divide the mixture equally among 6 hot roti, fold the roti over to make a neat package and serve as one would a sandwich.

annie's creole rabbit   *jamaica*

This was a speciality of Annie, our brilliant and gifted Jamaican cook, but whether one can call it pure Jamaican is another matter. There seems to be considerable Spanish influence here, which isn't surprising with Cuba next door, as it were.

2 2 lb. rabbits, cleaned, ready to cook, and cut into serving pieces
4 oz. salt pork, cut into cubes
1 onion, finely chopped
2 cloves garlic, chopped
2 tablespoons brandy
¼ pint dry sherry
½ lb. peeled and chopped tomatoes or 1 small tin Italian plum tomatoes

1 tinned pimento, chopped, and 1 tablespoon juice from tin
1 fresh hot green pepper, seeded and chopped
1 bay leaf
⅛ teaspoon orégano
½ pint chicken or rabbit stock, about
Salt, freshly ground pepper to taste

In a heavy frying pan render the salt pork. Sauté the rabbit pieces in the fat until browned all over. Transfer to a heavy, covered casserole. Fry onion and garlic until browned, and add to the casserole. Pour the brandy into the pan, stir and scrape up all the brown bits. Pour over the casserole contents and ignite. Add all the other ingredients, using enough stock to cover the rabbit pieces. Cover the casserole and cook in a 350°F (gas 4) oven for about 2½ hours, or until the rabbit is tender. Serves 6.

annie's holiday tripe   *jamaica*

3 lb. tripe
4 tablespoons oil
3 carrots, scraped and finely sliced
1 green bell pepper, seeded and coarsely chopped
2 spring onions, chopped, using green and white parts
3 coarsely chopped shallots
1 lb. raw rice
2 tablespoons light rum
1 tablespoon chopped chives
12 pimento-stuffed green olives, halved

1 tablespoon chopped capers, preferably Spanish
1 teaspoon vinegar from capers
1 pimento, coarsely chopped
½ lb. peeled and coarsely chopped tomatoes
1 teaspoon tomato paste
1 teaspoon Pickapeppa hot pepper sauce or Tabasco
Salt, freshly ground pepper to taste
Grated Parmesan cheese

Place the tripe in a large saucepan, cover with cold water, bring to the boil and simmer, covered, until tender, about 2 hours. Drain the tripe and reserve the stock. Cut tripe into 1-inch squares. Heat the oil in a heavy frying pan and sauté the pieces of tripe until golden. Lift out with a slotted spoon into a heavy, covered casserole. In the oil remaining in the pan sauté the carrots, bell pepper, spring onions and shallots. Lift out and add to casserole. In the oil remaining, adding a little more if necessary, sauté the rice until it has absorbed the oil, being careful not to let it burn. Add to casserole.

Stir the rum into the pan, scraping up all brown bits. Add to the casserole together with the chives, olives, capers, vinegar, pimento, tomatoes, tomato paste, hot pepper sauce or Tabasco, salt and pepper and about 1 ½ pints of the tripe stock. Simmer gently for 30 minutes.

Serve in rimmed soup bowls with crusty bread, and cheese separately. Serves 6.

arroz con carne de cerdo   *dominican republic*

Rice with Pork

3 cloves garlic, crushed
1 medium onion, finely
chopped
1 fresh hot red or green
pepper, seeded and
chopped
1 bay leaf, crumbled
1 tablespoon chopped
parsley, preferably flat
Italian type
2 tablespoons distilled white
vinegar
Salt to taste

1 lb. lean boneless pork, cut
into 1-inch cubes
2 slices bacon, coarsely
chopped
1 oz. boiled ham, coarsely
chopped
4 tablespoons lard
3 tablespoons tomato purée,
freshly made or tinned
2 cups raw long-grain rice
1 tablespoon capers,
preferably Spanish type
12 small pimento-stuffed
green olives, halved

Mix together the garlic, onion, pepper, bay leaf, parsley, vinegar, salt, pork, ham and bacon and marinate for about an hour.

In a heavy saucepan heat the lard and sauté the marinated mixture for 2 or 3 minutes. Add the tomato purée, the rice, capers and olives and add 4 cups cold water. Stir to mix, bring to the boil, cover and cook over very low heat until the rice is tender and has absorbed all the liquid. Serves 4 as a main course.

beef curry   *trinidad*

4 tablespoons vegetable oil
3 lb. chuck steak, cut into
1-inch cubes
2 onions, finely chopped
2 cloves garlic, finely chopped

1 tablespoon finely chopped
chives
1 tablespoon finely chopped
fresh ginger root

1 small fresh hot pepper,
  seeded and chopped
2 tablespoons curry powder

¾ pint coconut milk
Salt

Heat the oil in a heavy casserole and add the onions, garlic, chives, ginger root, pepper and curry powder and cook, stirring constantly over medium heat for about 5 minutes, being careful not to let the curry powder burn. Add the beef cubes and cook, stirring, for a few minutes longer. Add the coconut milk, cover the casserole and simmer gently until the meat is tender, about 1½ hours. Season to taste with salt. Serve with boiled white rice and side dishes of grated coconut, mango chutney, raisins, chopped cucumber, chopped tomato, peanuts, and sliced bananas. Serves 6.

bisté à la criolla   *cuba*

Beefsteak, Creole Style

6 tournedos (slices of fillet of
  beef cut from a section
  near the end, 1½ inches
  thick)
1 onion, finely chopped
2 cloves garlic, minced

1 heaping tablespoon
  chopped parsley
Juice 1 lemon
1 teaspoon salt
Several grinds of black pepper
3 oz. clarified unsalted butter

Mix the onion, garlic, parsley, lemon juice, salt and pepper and marinate the tournedos in the mixture for one hour. Remove the steaks and pat them dry with paper towels. Reserve the marinade.

Using a heavy frying pan large enough to hold the meat comfortably, heat the butter, which should cover the bottom of the pan generously. Brown the meat over high heat for 2 to 4 minutes on each side, depending on the degree of doneness desired. Remove to a warmed serving platter. Cook the reserved marinade in the butter remaining in the pan, for 2 or 3 minutes. Pour over the steaks and serve. Serves 6.

bistec en cazuela   *puerto rico*

Casseroled Beefsteak

It is worth going to some trouble to find Seville oranges for this
dish. The juice gives an unusual and delicate flavour which
substitutes cannot reproduce.

6 small steaks, such as rump
  or round, each weighing
  about 8 oz.
Salt, freshly ground pepper
½ pint Seville orange juice
4 tablespoons lard, or
  vegetable oil

3 medium onions, finely
  chopped
2 cloves garlic, chopped
½ teaspoon orégano
3 tablespoons beef stock

Have the butcher flatten the steaks, or do it yourself with a meat
cleaver. Season to taste with salt and pepper on both sides. Place
in a bowl and pour in the orange juice. Cover, and refrigerate
overnight, turning once or twice.

Lift the steaks out of the adobo (marinade) and pat dry.
Reserve the adobo. Heat the lard or oil in a heavy frying pan
and sauté the onions and garlic with the orégano. When the
onions are tender, but not browned, push them to one side and
sauté the steaks until lightly browned on both sides. Add the
adobo and beef stock. Cover and cook until the steaks are tender.
Serves 6.

bisté en cazuela a la criolla   *cuba*

Casseroled Beefsteak, Creole Style

6 small steaks such as rump,
  round or sirloin, each
  weighing about 8 oz.
2 teaspoons salt

½ teaspoon freshly ground
  pepper
2 cloves garlic, crushed

3 tablespoons lime or lemon
juice
3 tablespoons lard, or
vegetable oil
1 onion, finely sliced
1 green bell pepper, seeded
and chopped
1 fresh hot pepper, left whole

6 medium tomatoes, peeled
seeded and pushed through
a sieve
Bay leaf
Sprig fresh coriander
3 tablespoons dry red wine,
or red wine vinegar
½ pint beef stock

Season the steaks with the salt, pepper, garlic and lime juice and allow to stand for an hour or two. At the end of that time, lift out of the seasonings, pat dry and reserve any juices.

Heat the lard or oil in a heavy frying pan and sauté the steaks, one by one, on both sides until lightly browned. Transfer to a casserole, preferably earthenware*. In the fat remaining in the pan, adding a little more if necessary, sauté the onion and bell pepper. Add to the steaks together with the seasoning juices, the hot pepper, tomatoes, bay leaf and coriander. Add the wine or vinegar to the pan, stir and scrape up any brown bits and add to the casserole. Add the beef stock, cover and simmer gently until the steaks are tender, about 1 ¼ hours. Transfer the steaks to a serving platter and keep them warm. Reduce the sauce if necessary and pour over the steaks. Serve with a purée of boniato (white sweet potato), or other puréed root vegetable. Serves 6.

bisté en rollo   *cuba*

Rolled Steak

2½ lb. flank or rump steak,
in a piece
Salt, freshly ground pepper

3 tablespoons lime, or lemon
juice
1 clove garlic, crushed
4 oz. ham, cut into strips

*If using earthenware make sure it is heavy enough not to crack over direct heat. Use one or more asbestos mats if necessary.

1 carrot, scraped and thinly
  sliced
1 teaspoon sugar
½ oz. unsalted butter
1 tablespoon red wine
  vinegar
3 tablespoons dry red wine
3 tablespoons vegetable oil

1 bay leaf
1 large onion, thinly sliced
1 green bell pepper, seeded
  and chopped
½ teaspoon orégano
4 medium tomatoes, peeled,
  seeded and chopped
1 pimento, chopped

Rub one side of the steak with salt and pepper to taste, 1 table-spoon of the lime juice, and the garlic. Cover the steak with a layer of ham strips. Pour the remaining lime juice over the carrot slices and leave for a minute or two. Drain and arrange the carrot slices over the ham. Sprinkle with the sugar and dot with the butter. Roll the steak with the grain, fasten with tooth-picks, then tie with kitchen string at both ends and in the middle. Pour the vinegar and wine over the steak and let it stand for half an hour.

Lift the steak out of the marinade and pat dry with paper towels. Heat the oil in a heavy casserole and brown the steak all over. Add the bay leaf, onion, bell pepper, orégano, tomatoes, pimento and the marinade. Cover and cook over low heat until the steak is tender, about 2½ hours, and most of the liquid has evaporated leaving a thick but not abundant sauce. Serve the steak with the sauce poured over it. Serve with mashed potatoes, or any boiled and mashed root vegetable. Serves 4 to 6.

carne de cerdo mechada *dominican republic*

Stuffed Leg of Pork

5–6 lb. leg of pork
4 oz. raw ham, coarsely
  chopped

1 medium onion, finely
  chopped

20 small, pitted green olives, chopped

2 tablespoons capers

6 slices bacon, coarsely chopped

Salt, freshly ground pepper

4 cloves garlic, crushed

2 tablespoons white vinegar

3 tablespoons lard, or vegetable oil

1 fresh, hot pepper, seeded and chopped

½ pint dry white wine

2 teaspoons arrowroot, or potato flour

With a steel, or with a sharp, narrow knife make evenly spaced holes in the meat, about the thickness of one's little finger, almost to the centre of the leg. Stuff each hole with a little of the ham, onion, green olives, capers and bacon. Season the meat with salt and pepper, garlic and vinegar and leave for about an hour.

Heat the lard or oil in a casserole large enough to hold the meat comfortably. Brown the meat all over. Add the pepper and the wine, and any of the marinade. Cover and cook over low heat until the meat is tender, about 2½ to 3 hours.

Remove the meat to a serving platter and keep warm. Dissolve the arrowroot in a little water and stir into the liquid in the casserole. Cook over low heat until lightly thickened. Adjust the seasoning and serve in a sauce bowl. Serve with rice, or a starchy vegetable. Serves 6 to 8.

carne fiambre   *dominican republic*

Cold Beef, Ham and Prawn Sausage

This is a traditional dish for a día del campo (picnic) or for an outdoor Sunday buffet luncheon. It is served with pickled cucumbers and pimento-stuffed olives, and lettuce and tomatoes with an oil and vinegar dressing.

1 lb. lean minced beef
4 oz. lean, boneless ham,
  coarsely chopped
½ lb. large raw prawns,
  shelled, deveined and
  coarsely chopped
1 medium onion, coarsely
  chopped
1 clove garlic, coarsely
  chopped

1 fresh hot red or green
  pepper, seeded and
  chopped
Salt, freshly ground pepper
2 eggs
Saltine crackers
3 oz. tiny frozen peas,
  defrosted
1 egg, well beaten, for coating
1 onion, sliced
Bay leaf

Put the minced beef, ham, prawns, onion, garlic and hot pepper through the finest blade of a mincer. Or, chop everything as fine as possible and combine. Season to taste with salt and pepper. Add the 2 eggs, one at a time, mixing thoroughly. Coarsely crumble enough saltine crackers to make about 1½ cups, then crush with a rolling pin. Beat the crackers, half a cup at a time, into the meat mixture with a wooden spoon, until the texture is smooth. It should not be sloppy, but firm enough to hold its shape. Use only the amount of cracker crumbs necessary. Last of all, fold in the peas as gently as possible. Shape the mixture into a roll about 10 inches long and about 3 inches in diameter.

Cover a piece of waxed paper generously with more cracker crumbs. Roll the sausage in the crumbs so that it is thickly coated all over. Roll it in the beaten egg, then roll it again in more cracker crumbs to coat thickly. Centre the sausage on a double thickness of cheesecloth. Wrap the cheesecloth lengthwise over the sausage to enclose it completely. Tie the ends securely with kitchen string. In the old days, the sausage would have been sewn into a kitchen cloth, but cheesecloth does just as well.

Place the sausage in a heavy, covered casserole large enough to hold it comfortably. Add the sliced onion and the bay leaf, and enough water to cover the sausage by about 2 inches. Bring to the boil, reduce the heat to a simmer, cover and cook for about an hour, or until the sausage is firm to the touch. Lift out of the casserole by the cheesecloth ends and allow to cool. Remove the cheesecloth and place the sausage on a large platter. The cracker crumbs and beaten egg will have formed an attractive outside coating. Cut into ½-inch slices to serve. Serves 6 to 8.

carne mechada   *cuba*

Stuffed Meat

3 lb. boliche,* or any boneless beef roast such as rump or topside

¼ lb. chorizo sausage, skinned and chopped

2 slices bacon, chopped

2 oz. boiled ham, chopped

1 hard-boiled egg, chopped

2 oz. Cheddar cheese cut in small cubes

12 pimento-stuffed green olives, halved

18 seedless raisins

4 pitted prunes, soaked to soften, quartered

2 teaspoons large Spanish capers, chopped

6 tablespoons olive oil

8 fl. oz. dry sherry

1 onion, chopped

2 cloves garlic, chopped

1 green bell pepper, seeded and chopped

1 carrot, scraped and thinly sliced

¼ teaspoon ground cumin

½ teaspoon orégano, crumbled

1 bay leaf

Sprig parsley

Salt, freshly ground pepper

8 fl. oz. Seville orange juice

¾ pint beef stock

With a steel, or with a sharp narrow knife make six evenly spaced holes about the thickness of one's thumb in the roast, almost to the centre of the meat. Divide the sausage, bacon, ham, egg, cheese, olives, raisins, prunes and capers into six equal

*Boliche, or bola, is a Latin American cut of meat from the thigh.

heaps and stuff into the holes with the fingers, ending with the bacon.

In a heavy casserole big enough to hold the meat comfortably, heat 3 tablespoons of the oil and brown the stuffed meat on all sides. Remove the meat to a platter, discard the oil. Stir the sherry into the pot scraping the sides. Set this liquid aside. Rinse and dry the pot. In it heat the remaining 3 tablespoons of the oil. Sauté the onion, garlic, pepper and carrot until the onion is tender, but not browned. Add the meat, cumin, orégano, bay leaf, parsley, salt and pepper, orange juice, reserved sherry and the beef stock. Bring to the boil, reduce heat to a bare simmer. Cover and cook until the meat is tender, about 2 hours. Remove the meat to a warmed platter and slice.

Strain the sauce and push the solids through a sieve or reduce them to a purée in an electric blender. Stir this into the sauce and heat it through. It should be thickened lightly. Pour some of the sauce over the meat. Serve the remaining sauce separately. Serves 6.

VARIATION: In the Dominican Republic the meat is stuffed with ham, capers, carrots, onion, bell pepper, garlic, parsley and orégano, ending with the ham. It is browned in oil, seasoned with salt and pepper and is cooked in 1 ½ pints beef stock with 1 tablespoon Worcestershire sauce, 3 tablespoons tomato purée and 1 tablespoon cider vinegar.

carne rellena   *dominican republic*

Stuffed Flank Steak

2 ½ lb. flank steak,
  in a piece
3 cloves garlic, crushed
1 ½ teaspoons salt

⅛ teaspoon freshly ground
  pepper
1 teaspoon orégano
4 oz. cooked ham

1 large carrot

1 fresh hot, red or green
   pepper, seeded and chopped

1 large onion, finely chopped

2 hard-boiled eggs, sliced

3 tablespoons vegetable oil

4 tablespoons tomato paste

1 tablespoon Worcestershire
   sauce

1 tablespoon vinegar

1 pint beef stock

1 bay leaf

Spread the steak with a mixture of garlic, salt, pepper and orégano, stopping about ¼ inch from the edges of the steak. Cut the ham into thin strips and arrange in a layer on top of the garlic mixture. Scrape the carrot and cut into very thin slices with a vegetable peeler and arrange over the ham. Mix the hot pepper and onion together, spread on top of the carrot. Arrange the slices of egg down the centre of the steak. Carefully roll the steak up. Fasten with toothpicks and tie firmly with string.

In a heavy covered casserole large enough to hold the steak comfortably, heat the oil. Brown the steak all over, then add the tomato paste, Worcestershire sauce, vinegar, the beef stock, and the bay leaf. Cover and simmer for 2 to 2½ hours, or until the steak is tender, turning it once or twice during the cooking.

Lift out of the casserole onto a warmed serving platter. Remove the toothpicks and string, cut into slices about an inch thick, and serve with the sauce poured over it. Check during the cooking, and if the sauce seems too thin, cook for the last hour partially covered. Serves 6.

carry de mouton   *martinique–guadeloupe*

It could be argued that it is not really a curry since it contains so few of the curry spices. Whatever it is called it is a beautifully subtle dish.

2½ lb. lean lamb, cut into
  1-inch cubes
2 oz. unsalted butter
1 onion, finely chopped
4 oz. ham, cut in dice
2 medium tomatoes, peeled
  and chopped
½ teaspoon thyme
1 bay leaf
3 cloves garlic, finely chopped
2 whole cloves

⅛ teaspoon nutmeg
⅛ teaspoon cinnamon
Salt, freshly ground pepper
  to taste
8 fl. oz. stock (chicken or
  lamb)
8 fl. oz. coconut milk
6 tablespoons double cream
3 tablespoons lime, or lemon,
  juice

Heat the butter in a heavy covered casserole or baking pan. Add the onion and sauté until tender but not browned. Add the ham, tomatoes, thyme, bay leaf, garlic, cloves, nutmeg, cinnamon, salt and pepper. Stir and cook for 3 or 4 minutes. Add the lamb and cook for about 5 minutes longer, stirring from time to time. Add the stock, coconut milk and cream and simmer, covered, for about 2 hours, or until the lamb is tender. Stir in the lime or lemon juice and cook for a few minutes longer. Serves 6.

Serve with Riz Créole or Pois et Riz.

chou à pomme avec la viande salée

northern martinique

Cabbage with Corned Beef

2 lb. corned brisket of beef
1 medium onion, stuck with
  a clove
2 lb. green cabbage, finely
  shredded
2 finely chopped onions
4 or 5 chopped spring onions,
  using green and white parts

2 cloves garlic, minced
1 or 2 fresh hot red peppers,
  seeded and chopped, or use
  a hot pepper sauce to taste
Salt, freshly ground pepper
3 tablespoons olive oil

Soak the beef in cold water to cover for 30 minutes. Drain and rinse. Cut the meat into 1-inch cubes and put on to cook in fresh cold water with the onion, quartered. Cover and simmer until the meat is tender, about 2 hours.

Cook the cabbage in boiling salted water, covered, until tender, 5 to 8 minutes. Drain very thoroughly.

Drain the meat, reserving 1 cup of the stock. Make a sauce with the stock, chopped onions, spring onions, garlic, hot peppers or pepper sauce, salt, freshly ground pepper and olive oil. Mix thoroughly, stir, heat through and pour over the hot cabbage arranged in a serving dish. Toss lightly. Arrange the beef cubes over the cabbage. Serves 4.

May be accompanied by rice, or any starchy vegetable such as breadfruit, potatoes, yams, etc.

colombo d'agneau   *northern martinique*

Lamb Curry

This curry, given me by Mme Yveline de Lucy de Fossarieu of the de Leyritz Plantation, can be made with kid as well as lamb. It is an old family recipe and perfectly illustrates the Hindu influence in the north of Martinique; the wine represents France, and the vegetables represent the Americas. It is this ability to bring together foods and cooking techniques from very widely scattered parts of the world that is the real genius of Caribbean cooking.

3 tablespoons peanut oil
3 lb. lean, boneless lamb, cut into 2-inch cubes
2 medium onions, finely chopped
2 cloves garlic, crushed

1 tablespoon tamarind pulp (see Glossary)
1 green mango, peeled and chopped
1½ tablespoons curry powder
¾ pint dry white wine

1 lb. potatoes, peeled and
sliced
½ lb. West Indian pumpkin
(calabaza), peeled and
sliced
1 christophene (chayote),
peeled and sliced, or use

½ lb. courgettes, sliced
Salt
1 teaspoon lime juice
2 tablespoons dark rum,
preferably Martinique
rhum vieux

Heat the peanut oil in a large, heavy frying pan and sauté the lamb until it is lightly browned all over. Transfer to a casserole, earthenware* if possible. In the oil remaining in the pan, sauté the onions until golden. Add the garlic, tamarind pulp, mango, and curry powder. Cook, stirring from time to time, for 3 to 4 minutes. Add to the casserole with the wine. Cover and simmer gently for 1½ hours. Add the potatoes, West Indian pumpkin, christophene, and salt to taste. Cover and simmer for 30 minutes longer, or until the lamb is tender and the vegetables done. Stir in the lime juice and rum, and cook for 3 or 4 minutes longer.

The gravy should not be very abundant, but if the dish seems to be drying out when the vegetables are added, pour in a little water. Serves 6.

Serve with Riz Créole, or with Pois et Riz (see Index), and fried ripe plantains or bananas.

curried kid   *jamaica*

The Jamaicans in a fine frenzy of honesty call this curried goat, which is enough to put anyone off what is an excellent dish. It is best to use kid. Lamb is sometimes substituted, but in my view this is one step too far from the original.

*If using earthenware make sure it is heavy enough not to crack over direct heat. Use one or more asbestos mats if necessary.

2 tablespoons vegetable
  shortening
3 lb. kid, cut into small
  serving pieces
2 large onions finely chopped
3 tablespoons curry powder
1 fresh hot red pepper,
  chopped

Bay leaf
½ teaspoon allspice
8 fl. oz. coconut milk
Beef or chicken stock
Salt, freshly ground pepper
  to taste
Juice ½ lime

Melt the shortening in a skillet and brown the meat all over. Remove meat to a covered heavy casserole. Sauté the onions in the fat remaining in the skillet until transparent. Add the curry powder and hot pepper and sauté, stirring, for a few minutes. Add to the casserole with the bay leaf, allspice, coconut milk, and enough stock to cover the meat. Season with salt and pepper, cover and simmer gently until meat is tender, about 2 hours. Just before serving, add the lime juice, and cook 2 or 3 minutes longer. Serves 6.

VARIATION: In the Leeward Islands rabbit is curried in much the same way. A 2½ lb. rabbit is cut into serving pieces and cooked as for the kid with the addition of 3 tablespoons of guava jelly. When the rabbit is tender, after about 1½ hours, 1 to 3 tablespoons of lime, or lemon juice are stirred into the stew, according to the sweetness of the guava jelly. The sauce is thickened lightly with 2 teaspoons arrowroot mixed with a little cold water. For a hotter curry a chopped fresh hot pepper is added at the beginning of cooking. Serve with white rice or boiled potatoes and mango chutney. Serves 4 to 6.

VARIATION: Montserrat has a simpler kid dish known as Goat Water in which the kid is put into a large saucepan with 2 large onions, finely chopped, 2 cloves garlic, chopped, 1 tablespoon tomato paste, 3 cloves, 1 teaspoon freshly ground pepper, salt to taste, and enough water to cover. It is simmered, covered, until the meat is tender, about 2 hours. The stew is lightly thickened by stirring into it 2 tablespoons of butter mixed with 2 tablespoons plain flour. It is served with white rice and boiled dasheen leaves. Spinach is an adequate substitute for dasheen. Serves 6.

conejo tapado   *puerto rico*

Smothered Rabbit

2 2 lb. rabbits, ready-to-cook
  and cut into serving pieces
1 average head garlic, peeled
1 large onion
1 lb. tomatoes, peeled,
  seeded and chopped
1 tablespoon olive oil
3 tablespoons capers and 1
  tablespoon vinegar from
  capers

8 fl. oz. dry sherry
1 teaspoon orégano
Salt, freshly ground pepper
  to taste
12 new potatoes, scraped or
  peeled
12 pimento-stuffed olives,
  quartered

Put the rabbit pieces in a heavy, covered casserole. Mince the garlic and the onion and add to the casserole with the tomatoes, oil, capers, caper vinegar, sherry, orégano, salt, and pepper. Cover and simmer gently for about 1½ hours. Add the potatoes and cook for a further 30 minutes.

Young rabbits will cook in about 2 hours; older ones take up to 3 hours, so allow for this when adding potatoes. Just before serving, add the olives. Simmer for a minute or two longer. Serves 6 to 8. (This dish does not have a strong garlic flavour despite the fact that a whole head of garlic is used. Most of it disappears in the cooking.)

deep dish meat pie   *st thomas*

MEAT FILLING

1 pound lean minced beef
1 medium onion, finely
  chopped
1 fresh hot red pepper,
  seeded and finely chopped,
  or 1 teaspoon hot dried
  red pepper, crumbled
1 teaspoon salt
Freshly ground pepper to taste
1 clove garlic, chopped
2 medium tomatoes, peeled
  and chopped
1 oz. unsalted butter

1 tablespoon distilled white
  vinegar
½ teaspoon thyme
1 tablespoon chopped parsley
1 tablespoon green bell
  pepper, seeded and
  chopped
1 tablespoon pimento-
  stuffed green olives,
  chopped
1 tablespoon flour
½ teaspoon dry mustard
3 tablespoons dry sherry

Thoroughly mix together all the ingredients except the flour, mustard and sherry. Pack into a heavy 9-inch frying pan, cover, and cook over low heat for about half an hour. West Indians call this method 'sweating'; actually the meat is steamed.

Mix the flour and mustard with a little water and stir into the meat mixture. Mix the meat thoroughly with its own pan liquid as it separates with this cooking method. Stir over low heat until slightly thickened. Add the sherry. Cool and set aside.

PIE CRUST

10 oz. plain flour
½ teaspoon salt

6 oz. lard, chilled and cut
  into small bits
Cold water

Sift the flour and salt into a large bowl. With the fingertips rub the lard into the flour until the mixture is crumbly. Sprinkle it with enough cold water to form a stiffish dough, 4 to 6 tablespoons. Gather the dough gently into a ball and refrigerate for about 15 minutes. Divide the dough into two parts, one slightly larger than the other. Roll out the larger piece to a circle 13 inches in diameter and about ⅛ inch thick. Drape the dough over the rolling pin and unroll it over a straight-sided 9-inch pie dish that is 1½ inches deep. Gently press the dough into the dish and allow it to overlap all round the outside edge. Trim the overlap to about half an inch all round. Spoon the filling into the lined dish. Moisten the edges of the crust with cold water.

Roll out the smaller ball of dough to a 10-inch circle, and using the rolling pin as before, fit the pastry over the filling in the pie dish. Turn up the edge of the under pastry and press the edges of top and bottom pastry together. Pinch with the fingers or press with the tines of a fork to make sure the edges are completely sealed. Cut three or four slits in the centre of the top pastry to allow the steam to escape during baking.

Bake in an oven preheated to 450°F (gas 8) for 10 minutes, then reduce the heat to 350°F (gas 4) and continue baking for about 45 minutes longer, or until the crust is golden brown. Serve hot or cold directly from the pie dish. Serves 4 to 6.

filete al caldero   *puerto rico*

Beef Fillet Pot Roasted

Pot Roasted is a poor translation to explain the Puerto Rican caldero which is a large, heavy round, or oval cast-iron or aluminium casserole used widely in this island. Enamelled cast-iron is probably the best substitute, but the pot must be a heavy one.

3 lb. fillet of beef, trimmed
9 tablespoons olive oil
6 tablespoons vinegar
2 large cloves garlic, crushed
2 teaspoons salt

Freshly ground pepper
3 medium onions, thinly
  sliced
½ lb. sliced mushrooms

Mix together 6 tablespoons of olive oil, the vinegar, garlic, salt, a generous amount of freshly ground pepper, and one of the onions. Rub this into the fillet of beef and let it marinate overnight in the refrigerator. Take out the beef and pat dry with paper towels. Discard the marinade. Heat the other 3 tablespoons of oil in the caldero and brown the beef all over. Add the remaining 2 onions and the mushrooms. Cover and cook over medium heat on top of the stove for 10 to 15 minutes for rare meat, 18 to 20 minutes for medium rare. Serve with rice and beans, and green peas. Serve the mushrooms and onions with the pan juices as a sauce. Serves 6.

daube de porc aux bélangères   *martinique*

Pork Stew with Aubergine

3 lb. piece lean, boneless pork
3 tablespoons plain flour
2 tablespoons peanut oil
1 oz. lard
½ teaspoon thyme
¼ teaspoon sage

6 corns melegueta pepper
   (see Glossary), or allspice
Salt, freshly ground pepper
   to taste
3 lb. aubergines, peeled and
   cut into 1-inch cubes
½ pint water, about

Dredge the pork with flour. Heat the oil and lard in a heavy covered casserole and sauté the pork until it is golden all over. Add the thyme, sage, melegueta peppercorns, salt, freshly ground pepper and water. Cover and cook over low heat until the pork is almost tender, about 2 hours. Add the aubergine, cover, and cook for 15 minutes longer, or until the aubergine is done. Serves 6.

griots de porc   *haiti*

Glazed Pork Pieces

3 lb. shoulder of pork, cut
   into 2-inch cubes
1 large onion, finely chopped
3 chopped shallots
½ teaspoon dried thyme
½ pint Seville orange juice
1 fresh hot red or green
   pepper, chopped

2 cloves garlic, finely
   chopped (optional)
Salt, freshly ground pepper
   to taste
6 tablespoons vegetable oil or
   lard

Place the pork in a heavy, covered casserole with the onion, shallots, thyme, bitter orange juice, hot pepper, garlic if liked, salt and pepper to taste and allow to stand for 1 hour at room temperature. Some cooks marinate the pork overnight in the refrigerator.

When ready to cook cover with water and simmer, covered, until the pork is tender, about an hour and a half. Drain thoroughly.

Rinse out the casserole, add the oil or lard and fry the pork pieces until they are brown and crusty on the outside. Serve with Sauce Ti-Malice, Banane Pesé (fried plantain slices), and fried sweet potatoes. Serves 6.

VARIATION: A similar dish of garlic pork comes from Trinidad. Cut 4 lb. lean pork into small cubes and pour over the juice of a large lime. Blanch ¼ lb. garlic, peel and chop it and mix with 1 teaspoon chopped fresh thyme, 1 fresh hot red pepper, seeded and chopped, 2 teaspoons salt and some freshly ground black pepper. Stir thoroughly into the meat. Pour on ¾ pint white vinegar, cover and refrigerate for 2 days. Drain and pat dry the pieces of meat and fry in deep fat or oil. Serve hot. Serves 6 to 8 as a main course.

VARIATION: In Nicole Scott's grillots recipe 5 lb. cubed lean pork is put in a marinade of ½ pint vinegar, 1 large onion sliced thinly, 1 bell pepper, seeded and chopped, 2 cloves garlic, chopped, freshly ground pepper, 2 tablespoons chopped parsley and 3 or 4 hot red peppers, seeded and chopped. Leave it in the refrigerator overnight. Then pour the contents of the bowl into a shallow baking tin and bake in a 400°F (gas 6) oven. From time to time pour off and reserve any juices that accumulate in the baking tin. They will be used as a sauce to serve with the grillots. The pork is ready when the pieces are crusty, about 1½ hours. Serves 8 to 10.

To serve, heat the pan juices and pour into a sauceboat. Have Nicole Scott's Ti-Malice Sauce in another sauceboat (see Index). Serve with platters of Banane Pesé (fried plantain slices), and fried sweet potatoes, preferably white sweet potatoes (see Index). All 3 dishes may be served as appetizers, or with drinks.

keshy yena coe carni   *curaçao*

Stuffed Cheese with Beef Filling

4 lb. Edam cheese
4 oz. unsalted butter
2 medium onions, chopped
1½ lb. lean, minced beef
1 green bell pepper, seeded and coarsely chopped
1 fresh hot red or green pepper, seeded and chopped, or dash of Sambal Oelek or Tabasco
2 oz. mushrooms, coarsely chopped
2 tablespoons brandy

2 tomatoes, peeled and coarsely chopped
2 hard-boiled eggs, coarsely chopped
2 tablespoons seedless raisins
2 tablespoons black olives, coarsely chopped
2 tablespoons finely chopped sweet gherkins
1 tablespoon tomato ketchup
6 tablespoons brown sauce
Salt, freshly ground pepper to taste

Heat the butter in a heavy frying pan and sauté the onions until golden brown. Add the beef and sauté lightly. Add the peppers and the mushrooms and sauté for 5 minutes longer, stirring frequently and taking care the mixture does not burn. Heat the brandy, pour over the mixture and ignite, stirring until the flame dies out. Add the rest of the ingredients, season to taste with salt and pepper and simmer for 5 minutes stirring from time to time.

Meanwhile, remove the red wax covering from the cheese. Cut off the top, hollow out this lid and reserve. Scoop out the cheese leaving a shell about ½ inch thick. Cover the shell and lid with cold water and soak for an hour. Then drain and wipe dry. Grate scooped-out cheese and add 4 oz. to the meat mixture. Save the rest of the cheese for another use. Pack the meat mixture into the cheese shell, replace the top, and put the filled cheese into a greased 5-pint casserole. Bake uncovered in a preheated 350°F (gas 4) oven for 30 minutes. Do not overcook as the cheese becomes tough, instead of soft and bubbly. Slide the cheese out of the casserole onto a warmed serving dish, cut in wedges and serve immediately. Serves 6 to 8.

A popular way of cooking this dish is to peel off the outer wax covering of the cheese and cut the cheese into ¼-inch slices. Use the slices to line a greased 5-pint baking dish on bottom and sides, in an overlapping pattern. Pour in the meat mixture and cover with the remaining slices of cheese. Bake for 30 minutes in a preheated 350°F (gas 4) oven. Small individual casseroles may also be used, in which case reduce the cooking time to 15 to 20 minutes.

kebabs   *anguilla*

Broiled, skewered beef with pineapple, tomatoes, peppers and onions.

6 tablespoons unsweetened
  pineapple juice
3 tablespoons distilled white
  vinegar
2 tablespoons molasses
2 teaspoons salt
Freshly ground pepper to taste

2 lb. top sirloin of beef, cut
  into 12 1½-inch cubes
12 small white onions
12 cherry tomatoes
2 medium sized green bell
  peppers, seeded and cut
  into 1½-inch squares
12 1-inch cubes pineapple

Combine the pineapple juice, vinegar, molasses, salt and several grinds of black pepper. Add the cubes of beef and allow to stand in the marinade at room temperature for 1 hour. Drain, reserve marinade to use as a basting sauce.

Meanwhile drop the onions into boiling water and simmer for 5 minutes. Drain, and when cool slip off the skins.

Thread the meat, onions, tomatoes, green peppers and pineapple cubes alternately on four 12-to-14-inch skewers. Brush with marinade.

Using a charcoal or oven grill, both preheated, cook the kebabs 4 inches from the heat, turning every 3 minutes or so, for about 10 minutes, or until the beef is cooked to the required degree of doneness. Baste with marinade each time the kebabs are turned. Serve with plain boiled white rice. Pour any remaining marinade over the kebabs. Serves 4.

lambchi and boonchi   *aruba*

Skewered Lamb with Yard-long Beans

2 tablespoons grated onion
1 tablespoon Spanish (hot)
  paprika
1 tablespoon curry powder
1 tablespoon fresh ginger
  root, grated
2 cloves garlic, crushed

¼ teaspoon freshly ground
  pepper
6 tablespoons lemon juice
3 tablespoons peanut oil
2 lb. lean lamb, cut into
  16 1½-inch cubes

16 small white onions

8 slices bacon, halved

2 green peppers, seeded and
   cut into 16 2-inch squares

16 1-inch cubes pineapple

16 cherry tomatoes

4 young yard-long beans,
   parboiled

In a large bowl combine the onion, paprika, curry powder, ginger, garlic, salt, pepper, lemon juice and oil. Add the lamb cubes, mixing thoroughly. Marinate in the refrigerator overnight.

Drop the onions into boiling water and simmer for 5 minutes. Drain, and when cool slip off the skins. Wrap the bacon pieces round the pieces of pepper. Drain the marinated lamb and seasonings. Thread the meat, onions, pineapple, bacon and pepper squares, and the tomatoes alternately on four 12- to 14-inch skewers. Wrap the beans round the skewers, tying them in place at each end with string. Brush on all sides with the marinade.

Using a charcoal or oven grill, both preheated, cook the lambchi and boonchi* 4 inches from the heat, turning every 3 minutes or so, for about 10 minutes, or until the lamb is done. Untie the boonchi and slide with the meat, vegetables and pineapple off the skewers on to heated plates. Serves 4.

Serve with the following sauce.

SAUCE

2 tablespoons prepared
   mustard

2 tablespoons peanut butter

½ teaspoon ground turmeric

2 tablespoons soy sauce

2 tablespoons Worcestershire
   sauce

Hot pepper sauce (Tabasco)
   to taste

Combine all the ingredients and blend thoroughly.

*Boonchi, sometimes called yard-long beans, Chinese beans, or asparagus beans, are originally from the Asian tropics. The pods have been known to reach 4 feet in length yet only about ½ inch wide. When young they are soft and pliable. They can sometimes be found in Chinese shops.

lengua rellena

dominican republic

Stuffed Tongue

1 fresh beef tongue, 4–5 lb.
2 cloves garlic, finely chopped
1 medium onion, finely
  chopped
2 oz. ham, finely chopped
1 carrot, scraped and finely
  chopped
1 teaspoon salt
¼ teaspoon freshly ground
  pepper
1 tablespoon Spanish capers,
  chopped

1 medium tomato, peeled
  and chopped
1 tablespoon seedless raisins,
  chopped
Freshly made bread crumbs
3 tablespoons olive oil
1 tablespoon vinegar
½ teaspoon orégano
3 tablespoons tomato paste
1 bay leaf
1 medium onion, coarsely
  chopped

Put the tongue into a large, heavy, covered casserole that will hold it comfortably. Cover with cold water, bring slowly to the boil, boil for 5 minutes, remove scum, reduce heat to a simmer, cover and cook for 2 hours. When cool enough to handle, remove from stock, skin, and trim the root end. Make a lengthwise incision down the front of the tongue, taking care not to sever the two halves. Reserve stock and rinse out casserole.

Meanwhile make a stuffing from the garlic, finely chopped onion, ham, carrot, salt, pepper, capers, tomato, raisins and enough bread crumbs to hold the mixture together. Stuff into the tongue and secure with toothpicks.

Heat the oil in the casserole and sauté the stuffed tongue on all sides. Turn right side up. Add enough of the reserved stock barely to cover, add the vinegar, orégano, tomato paste, bay leaf and onion. Simmer, partially covered, until the tongue is tender, about 1 hour.

If the sauce is very abundant and thin, remove tongue to a warmed serving platter and reduce the sauce over brisk heat until it is of medium thick consistency. Potatoes are often cooked with this dish. If liked, add 6 to 8 peeled potatoes during the last half hour of cooking. Serves 6 to 8.

lapin aux pruneaux   *martinique*

Rabbit with Prunes

1 rabbit, about 2½ lb.,
  ready-to-cook and cut into
  serving pieces
1 teaspoon thyme
½ pint dry red wine
4 oz. bacon, chopped
2 tablespoons olive oil
2 tablespoons plain flour

Salt, freshly ground pepper
  to taste
3 onions, coarsely chopped
1 bay leaf
2 sprigs parsley
Celery stalk with leaves
8 oz. pitted prunes, soaked
  in ½ pint dry red wine
2 tablespoons dark rum

Marinate the rabbit for 24 hours in red wine and thyme. Heat the oil in a heavy covered casserole and render the bacon. Season the flour with salt and pepper. Drain the rabbit, reserving the marinade. Pat the rabbit pieces dry with paper towels and dredge with the seasoned flour. Sauté the rabbit in the bacon fat and oil until lightly browned on both sides, a few pieces at a time. Set aside. In the fat remaining in the casserole, sauté the chopped onions until lightly browned.

Return the rabbit pieces to the casserole, add the bay leaf, parsley, celery, the reserved marinade and the prunes with the wine in which they have soaked. Bring to the boil, reduce the heat, cover and simmer until the rabbit is tender, about 2 hours. Adjust the seasoning, stir in the rum and cook for 2 or 3 minutes longer. Serves 4 to 6.

l'épaule de porc fourrée　　　　　*guadeloupe*

Stuffed Shoulder of Pork

4 lb. shoulder of pork
¼ pint dark rum
8 oz. dry bread crumbs
½ pint milk
½ teaspoon each sage and
　thyme
1 tablespoon chopped chives
½ small fresh hot pepper,
　seeded and chopped

1 bay leaf, crushed
1 tablespoon chopped parsley
2 large cloves garlic, chopped
Salt, freshly ground pepper
6 melegueta peppercorns (see
　Glossary) crushed
½ pint chicken stock

Have the butcher bone the shoulder of pork, or do it yourself.
Score the skin, which should be left on, at intervals of about
⅛ inch. Pour two thirds of the rum over the meat and let it
stand while the stuffing is prepared. Soak the bread crumbs in
the milk then squeeze dry. Mix with the sage, thyme, chives,
hot pepper, bay leaf, parsley, garlic, salt, and pepper to taste and
the melegueta peppercorns. Drain the rum from the meat and
pour it over the stuffing, mixing lightly. Stuff the shoulder and
sew it up. Roast on a rack in a roasting pan in a 325°F (gas 3)
oven for 2 hours and 45 minutes or until a meat thermometer
registers 180°F. Remove the meat to a serving platter and keep
warm.

Pour off the fat from the pan, add the remaining rum to
the pan, stir and scrape up all the brown bits. Pour in the chicken
stock and simmer until reduced to ½ pint. Serve in a sauceboat
separately. The skin of the shoulder should be crisp and crunchy.
Serves 6.

meat patties   *jamaica*

I used to buy these patties for a mid-morning snack during recess, when I attended Wolmer's School, in Kingston, Jamaica. The old woman who made them, and sold them to us from a big straw basket covered with a white cloth, had a generous hand with the hot peppers that give the patties their special flavour. She also used annatto which adds a subtle extra flavour. I have made the patties using other types of fresh hot peppers, but the result is not the same. However, hot crushed peppers, put up in vinegar and salt, from one or other of the Caribbean islands, are available in some West Indian and Indian shops and Pickapeppa hot pepper sauce will also give the authentic flavour to the patties. The amount used is a matter of taste.

2 tablespoons vegetable oil
1 lb. lean minced beef
1 medium onion, finely chopped
1 clove garlic, crushed
½ lb. tomatoes, peeled, seeded and chopped
Salt, freshly ground pepper

1 whole fresh red pepper, minced, or 1 teaspoon crushed peppers in vinegar
½ teaspoon thyme
2 eggs, slightly beaten
1 egg white, beaten until foamy
Flaky pastry

Heat the oil in a large frying pan and add the beef and cook it, breaking it up with a fork, until it begins to brown. Add the onion and garlic and cook until the onion is tender. Add the tomatoes, salt, pepper, hot pepper and thyme and cook, stirring, for 5 minutes longer. The mixture should be quite dry. Remove from the heat and stir in the 2 beaten eggs. Return to the heat and cook, stirring for 2 or 3 minutes longer. Cool to room temperature.

Roll out the pastry ⅛ inch thick and cut into 5-inch circles. Place 2 or 3 tablespoons of the meat mixture on one side of each circle, fold over into a crescent. Seal the edges by pinching with the fingers or crimping with a fork. Brush with beaten egg white and prick the tops to let the steam escape.

Bake on an ungreased cooking sheet in a 425°F (gas 7) oven for 20 to 30 minutes, or until lightly browned. Serve for lunch with a vegetable or a salad, or as a snack. Makes about 12 patties.

For cocktails put 1 teaspoon of the meat mixture on 2-inch pastry circles, bake 15 to 20 minutes.

A teaspoon of paprika may be used instead of the annatto seeds and 2 slices of bread, soaked in milk and squeezed dry, may be used instead of the 2 eggs.

FLAKY PASTRY

8 oz. plain flour
½ teaspoon salt
3 oz. unsalted butter

3 oz. lard
Cold water

Sift the flour and salt into a basin. Divide the butter and lard into 4 equal parts. Rub 1 part each of lard and butter into the flour, and add enough cold water to make an elastic dough.

Roll out the dough onto a floured board into a strip about 8-inches wide. Cut 1 part each of the remaining butter and lard into small pieces and dot two thirds of the pastry with it. Dredge lightly with flour.

Fold the section of pastry without fat over the middle one-third of the pastry strip. Then fold the first portion over to form a square. Press the open edges lightly together with a rolling pin to prevent the air escaping, and turn the pastry so that an open end faces you. Roll the pastry into a strip as before, and repeat the process until the remaining fat is used. Wrap the pastry in waxed paper and refrigerate for at least 1 hour before using.

mondongo
puerto rico
Tripe Stew

3 lb. tripe
6 tablespoons Seville orange
  juice, or orange and lemon
  juice mixed in the propor-
  tion of ⅔ orange to ⅓
  lemon
2 oz. salt pork, chopped
1 large onion finely chopped
4 oz. ham, coarsely chopped
2 large tomatoes, peeled and
  chopped
1 fresh hot green pepper,
  seeded and chopped

1 pimento, chopped
2 or 3 sprigs fresh coriander,
  coarsely chopped
2 or 3 sprigs parsley, coarsely
  chopped
8 oz. cooked chick peas
6 medium sized potatoes,
  peeled and halved
1 lb. pumpkin, peeled and
  cut into 1-inch cubes
Salt to taste

Put the tripe into a heavy, covered casserole. Pour the Seville orange juice over it and let it stand for 5 minutes or so. Cover with cold water, bring to the boil, reduce the heat, cover and simmer for 1½ hours. Drain, reserving stock, cool, cut into squares and return to the casserole.

In a heavy skillet render the salt pork, add the onion and sauté until it is tender. Add the ham, tomatoes, hot peppers, pimento, coriander and parsley and cook for a few minutes longer. Add to the tripe. Add the chick peas, potatoes and pumpkin and enough of the reserved stock to cover, a good pint. Season to taste with salt, cover and simmer until the tripe and potatoes are done, about half an hour. The pumpkin will disintegrate and thicken the sauce lightly. Serves 6.

mondongo de cerdo, estilo coloma

dominican republic

Pork Tripe, Coloma Style

3 lb. pork tripe, or use
  honeycomb tripe
1 tablespoon salad oil
1 onion, sliced
1 clove garlic, chopped
1 bell pepper, seeded and
  chopped
1 hot green pepper, chopped
1 medium tin Italian plum
  tomatoes
Salt, freshly ground pepper
  to taste

1 tablespoon capers and 1
  tablespoon vinegar from
  capers
1 tablespoon fresh coriander
  chopped
¼ teaspoon dried orégano
1 tablespoon Worcestershire
  sauce
1 tablespoon tomato paste
6 tablespoons dark, dry
  Bacardi rum
Grated Parmesan cheese

Cook the tripe in salted water until tender, about 2 hours. Drain and cut into squares. Transfer to a heavy casserole. Heat the oil in a skillet and sauté the onion, garlic, bell pepper, and hot pepper until the onion is transparent. Add the tomatoes, salt, pepper, capers, caper vinegar, coriander, orégano, and Worcestershire sauce. Pour over the tripe and simmer for 15 minutes. Add the tomato paste. Add the rum and simmer for a few minutes longer. Serve with grated cheese passed separately. Serves 6 to 8.

olive's seasoned-up pot roast

st kitts

3 lb. fresh brisket of beef
2 tablespoons malt vinegar
2 tablespoons soy sauce
1 teaspoon fresh thyme,
  coarsely chopped, or

½ teaspoon dried, crumbled
1 teaspoon fresh marjoram,
  coarsely chopped, or
  ½ teaspoon dried, crumbled

1 tablespoon coarsely chopped
  parsley, preferably flat
  Italian type
1 tablespoon coarsely
  chopped celery leaves
2 tablespoons chopped chives,
  or spring onions, using
  green and white parts
1 teaspoon salt
¼ teaspoon freshly ground
  pepper

2 teaspoons brown sugar
1 oz. unsalted butter
1 carrot, scraped and
  quartered
2 coarsely chopped shallots
1 whole fresh hot red or
  green pepper, stem left on
¾ pint beef stock, or water
2 teaspoons arrowroot
  (optional)

Sprinkle the meat with the vinegar and soy sauce. Mix the thyme, marjoram, parsley, celery leaves, chives, salt and pepper together and rub into the meat. Leave at room temperature, uncovered, for 2 or 3 hours.

Scrape off and reserve the herbs together with any liquid. Pat the meat dry with paper towels and rub in the brown sugar.

Heat the butter in a heavy, covered casserole and brown the meat on all sides, adding carrot and shallots to lightly brown at the same time. Add the whole pepper, the reserved herbs, marinade liquid, and the beef stock or water. Cover and simmer gently until the meat is tender, about 2½ hours, turning the meat once or twice during the cooking. Remove and discard the pepper before serving.

Potatoes, tannias, more carrots, or any other root vegetables may be added during the last half hour of cooking. If a thicker gravy is preferred, mix the arrowroot with 1 tablespoon of cold water, stir into the casserole and cook, stirring, until the gravy is lightly thickened. Serves 6 to 8.

patas de cerdo guisada   *puerto rico*

Stewed Pig's Feet

8 fresh pig's feet
2 cups sofrito
½ lb. chorizo sausage, sliced
½ lb. cooked chick peas
1 tablespoon fresh coriander,
  chopped

½ lb. potatoes, peeled and
  cut into 1-inch slices
½ lb. West Indian pumpkin,
  peeled and cut into 1-inch
  cubes
Salt

Put the pig's feet into a large casserole with enough cold water to cover by about 1 inch, bring to the boil, cover, reduce the heat and simmer until they are almost tender, about 3 hours. Drain, reserve liquid, and return the pig's feet to the casserole. Add the sofrito, sausage, chick peas, coriander, potatoes and pumpkin. Add as much of the reserved liquid as necessary to cook the potatoes and pumpkin, and simmer gently, covered, until the potatoes are done, about 30 minutes. Taste for seasoning, and add a little salt, if necessary. Serves 4.

For a meatier dish, use 4 fresh pork hocks instead of the pig's feet.

pastel de mondongo   *dominican republic*

Tripe Soufflé

1 lb. tripe
4 tablespoons freshly grated
  Parmesan cheese
2 oz. freshly made bread
  crumbs

Salt, white pepper
1 oz. unsalted butter,
  melted
4 eggs

Cut the tripe into squares and place in a heavy saucepan with water to cover by about 1 inch. Cook until tender, about 2½ hours, partially covered so that when the tripe is cooked there is very little liquid left. Be careful not to let the tripe burn. Transfer the tripe and liquid to a blender and reduce to a purée on high speed.

Pour the tripe into a mixing bowl. Add the cheese and bread crumbs. Season to taste with salt and pepper. Add the butter. Beat the eggs until light and fold into the mixture. Pour into a 2½-pint soufflé dish or baking dish and bake in a 400°F (gas 6) oven until set, about 20 minutes. Serves 3 to 4.

pepperpot   *trinidad, barbados, st kitts*

This meat stew is a very ancient Amerindian dish from Guyana that has spread throughout the English-speaking Caribbean islands. I have had it in Trinidad, and in St Kitts, and it is popular in Barbados.

The ingredient which gives the dish its distinctive character is cassareep, which the Guyanese pronounce cassarip. It is made by grating raw cassava and squeezing out the juice, which is then boiled down. When it begins to turn brown, it is flavoured with salt, brown sugar, cinnamon and cloves and the boiling continued until the cassareep has the consistency of a thick, dark brown syrup. Some cooks add a little gravy-browning to get the rich colour needed. Commercially bottled cassareep can be bought in some West Indian shops.

Cassareep keeps indefinitely, and the 'trash', the squeezed dry grated raw cassava can be used to make cassava bread, or biscuits. Cooked and drained, it can be adapted for the cassava in the Cuban dish, brazo gitano, a baked cassava roll with a corned beef filling.

All sorts of stories are told about cassareep. It is said to be a meat tenderizer, and/or a preservative and since meats can be added to the pot daily there are stories of pepperpots kept going from generation to generation.

It should not be confused with Jamaican pepperpot, which is a soup.

1 lb. oxtail, cut into joints
1 calf's foot, quartered
2 lb. lean pork or beef, cut
   into 2-inch cubes
1 stewing chicken, cut into
   serving pieces

½ lb. salt beef
6 tablespoons cassareep
2 or 3 hot peppers, tied in
   cheesecloth
Salt

Put all the ingredients into a large casserole or soup pot with enough cold water to cover, bring to the boil, lower the heat and simmer gently until the meats and the chicken are tender and the sauce quite thick. Remove the hot peppers before serving. Serves 8 to 10. Serve with boiled rice.

picadillo   *cuba*

Beef Hash

3 tablespoons oil
1 large onion, finely chopped
1 large green bell pepper,
   seeded and finely chopped
1 clove garlic, finely chopped
1 fresh hot red or green
   pepper, seeded and
   chopped
2 lb. minced steak

2 large tomatoes, peeled and
   chopped
½ teaspoon ground cumin
Salt
Freshly ground pepper
2 oz. seedless raisins
2 tablespoons pimento-stuffed
   green olives, chopped
1 tablespoon capers

Heat the oil in a large frying pan and cook the onion, bell pepper, garlic and hot pepper until the onion is tender but not browned. Add the meat and cook, stirring and breaking it up until it has lost its colour. Add the tomatoes, cumin, salt and pepper to taste. Add the raisins, mix thoroughly and simmer gently, uncovered, until cooked, about 20 minutes. Add the olives and capers, and cook for a few minutes longer. Serve with plain boiled white rice, black beans and fried ripe plantains. Serves 6.

If liked, this hash may be made with 1 ½ lb. minced beef and ½ lb. minced pork.

pernil al horno a la criolla *puerto rico*

Roast Leg of Lamb, Creole Style

4 lb. leg of lamb	1 teaspoon freshly ground
2 cloves garlic	black pepper
2 teaspoons orégano	1 tablespoon olive oil
1 teaspoon salt	1 tablespoon plain flour
	½ pint lamb or chicken stock

Remove the tough, fibre-like covering from the leg. Score the fat in a criss-cross pattern. Crush the garlic and mix it with the orégano, salt, pepper and olive oil. Rub into the meat, cover and refrigerate for 24 hours.

Before cooking let the meat come to room temperature. Drain off any liquid that has collected and pour it over the meat as a marinade. Put the lamb on a rack in a roasting pan and roast in an oven preheated to 350°F (gas 4) for 1 ¼ hours for underdone meat when the juices will run rosy if meat is pricked with a fork, to 1 ½ hours for well-done meat. Transfer the lamb to a platter.

Spoon off excess fat from the roast pan, leaving about 1 tablespoon. Over low heat stir in the flour, scraping up all the brown bits. Cook for a minute or two, add the stock, bring to the boil, lower heat and simmer for a few minutes. Adjust seasoning, add any juices that may have run out of the meat, and pour into a sauceboat. Serves 6 to 8.

picadillo de carne cocida   *cuba*

Beef Hash

This traditional dish is served with plain white rice, black beans, fried ripe plantains and Cuban-style fried eggs.

2–2½ lb. boiled beef, preferably brisket, coarsely chopped
2 tablespoons vegetable oil
1 oz. unsalted butter
2 green bell peppers, seeded and chopped
1 large onion, finely chopped
1 clove garlic, chopped
4 large tomatoes, peeled, seeded and chopped
1 bay leaf
¼ teaspoon ground cloves
Salt, freshly ground pepper to taste
1 tablespoon white distilled vinegar

Heat the butter and oil in a large frying pan and add the green peppers, onion and garlic and cook until the onion is lightly browned. Add the tomatoes, bay leaf, cloves, salt and pepper and cook gently for about 10 minutes. Add the vinegar and the boiled beef and cook until the meat is heated through. Serves 6.

HUEVOS ESTILO CUBANO

Deep-fried Eggs, Cuban Style

Vegetable oil for deep frying   6 eggs

Pour the oil to a depth of about 1½ inches into a heavy frying pan large enough to hold at least 3 eggs at a time. Heat the oil until the surface ripples gently (175°F on a frying thermometer).

Be careful not to overheat the oil as this will make the whites puff and brown. They should remain smooth, almost like an egg poached in water. Break the eggs into saucers and slide into the frying pan. Gently lift the whites over the yolk with a tablespoon. Deep fry the eggs for 2 or 3 minutes. The yolks should be soft. Lift out with a slotted spatula and drain on paper towels. Serve immediately as an accompaniment to the picadillo.

port royal lamb cutlets   *jamaica*

6 lamb cutlets, trimmed
Salt, freshly ground pepper
2 oz. unsalted butter
Bay leaf
1 tablespoon vinegar
Juice of 6 oranges

Grated peel of 2 oranges
½ teaspoon Angostura bitters
½ teaspoon Pickapeppa hot
   pepper sauce
Chicken stock, if necessary
2 egg yolks

Rub the cutlets with salt and plenty of pepper. Heat the butter in a heavy, covered casserole, add lamb and brown all over. Add the bay leaf, vinegar, orange juice and grated peel, bitters, hot pepper sauce, and a little stock if necessary to barely cover the lamb. Cover and cook over low heat until the lamb is tender, about 1½ hours.

Remove the cutlets to a serving dish and keep warm. Remove excess fat from the pan liquid and boil to reduce to about ¾ pint. Beat the egg yolks lightly and beat in 2 or 3 tablespoons of the hot liquid. Gradually add the egg mixture to the casserole, beating constantly. Do not allow the mixture to boil. When the sauce is thickened, pour over cutlets. Serves 6.

piononos   *puerto rico*

Stuffed Plantains

The name of this dish is an unsolved mystery. Pio means pious and nono means ninth in Spanish, so that the nearest translation would seem to be Pious the Ninth. Perhaps the idea behind the name is that only a Pope could equal the dish in goodness. I once saw it translated as pious nuns, a dreadful error as nuns in Spanish are monjas, not nonos.

3 ripe plantains, each cut
   into 4 lengthwise slices

Lard or oil for frying

FOR STUFFING

3 tablespoons oil or lard
1 lb. lean minced beef
1 medium onion, finely
  chopped
1 clove garlic, minced
½ green bell pepper, seeded
  and finely chopped
2 medium tomatoes, peeled,
  seeded and chopped

2 oz. boiled ham, finely
  chopped
½ teaspoon orégano
Salt, freshly ground pepper
  to taste
1 tablespoon capers, chopped
2 tablespoons pimento-
  stuffed green olives,
  chopped
3 eggs, well beaten
Oil for deep frying

Heat the lard or oil in a heavy frying pan and sauté the plantain pieces on both sides until they are golden. Remove carefully to a platter. As soon as they are cool enough to handle, shape each slice into a circle and secure with a tooth pick. Set aside.

To make the filling heat the oil in a heavy frying pan and sauté the beef until it is browned and all the particles separate. Add the onion, garlic and sweet peppers and sauté until tender. Add the tomatoes, ham, orégano, salt and pepper, and cook, stirring until the mixture is well blended and thick. Stir in the capers and olives. Remove from the heat. Fill each plantain ring with the meat stuffing, dip in the beaten egg, and deep fry in hot oil or lard on both sides. Serves 6.

Pork may be used instead of beef, if liked.

pulpeta   *cuba*

Meat Sausage

It is impossible to translate pulpeta literally since it means a small slice of stuffed meat. It might more accurately have been called pulpetón, a large slice of stuffed meat. Whatever its name, it is excellent hot for dinner, or cold for lunch or picnics.

1½ lb. lean minced beef
¼ lb. lean minced ham
¼ lb. lean pork, minced
1 medium onion, finely
    chopped
2 cloves garlic, chopped
3 tablespoons parsley, finely
    chopped
2 oz. soft bread crumbs

Milk
2 eggs
Salt, freshly ground pepper
¼ teaspoon hot pepper sauce
    (optional)
3 hard-boiled eggs, shelled
1 medium onion, sliced
1 bay leaf
3 tablespoons dry sherry

Combine the beef, ham, pork, onion, garlic and parsley in a large bowl. Soak the bread crumbs in a little milk and squeeze dry. Add to the meat. Add the eggs, unbeaten, salt and pepper to taste and the hot pepper sauce if liked. Mix thoroughly until the mixture is smooth and light. Shape half the meat into a rectangle about 12 inches long and 4 inches wide. Lay the hard-boiled eggs lengthwise down the centre. Cover with the remaining meat mixture to form a cylinder. Wrap in a cloth, or in a double thickness of cheesecloth, keeping the sausage shape and tie the ends firmly with string.

Fill a heavy casserole, large enough to hold the sausage comfortably, about halfway with water, bring to the boil, add the onion, bay leaf and sherry and the sausage. Cover, and simmer for 1½ to 2 hours, or until the sausage feels firm to the touch. Unwrap and arrange on a warm serving platter, and cut into 1-inch slices. If liked, the sausage may be served with a fresh tomato sauce poured over it, or with tomato sauce served separately. If served cold, garnish the platter with sliced tomatoes, lettuce, parsley sprigs, green olives and radishes. Serves 6 to 8.

pudding and souse   *barbados*

This is popular in Barbados as an informal Saturday night meal.
It also makes a good lunch, or appetizer. The pudding is black
pudding or blood pudding, a large sausage made from pig's
blood encased in an intestine. It can be bought ready-made and
can be heated in the oven, grilled, or fried in lard or butter.

SOUSE

Young pig's head   4 pig's feet

FOR THE PICKLE

½ pint lime juice   1 tablespoon salt
2 or 3 fresh hot red peppers,   Water
  sliced

FOR THE GARNISH

1 medium cucumber, peeled   1 green bell pepper, seeded
  and thinly sliced   and sliced
1 medium onion, chopped   Watercress, if liked
1 red bell pepper, seeded and
  sliced

FOR THE SAUCE

4 tablespoons lime juice   1 fresh hot green pepper,
1 teaspoon salt   seeded and chopped
1 medium cucumber, peeled   ½ pint stock reserved from
  and thinly sliced, or   cooking pig's head
  coarsely chopped

Wash the pig's head and feet. Place in a large saucepan with
cold, salted water to cover. Bring to the boil, lower the heat,

cover and simmer until the meat is tender, 2 hours or longer, depending on the age of the pig. Drain, reserving ½ pint of stock for the sauce, and plunge into cold water. Cut the pig's feet in half. Cut the meat from the head. Skin and slice the tongue. Put all the meats into a large bowl with a pickle made from the lime juice, hot peppers, salt, and enough water to cover. Allow to steep overnight in refrigerator. Drain, and arrange on a platter with the garnish.

If preferred, make a sauce by mixing the lime juice, salt, cucumber, hot pepper and stock. Omit the garnish and serve the meats with the sauce in a separate bowl.

Many islands, among them St Kitts, serve souse without the blood sausage. In the Spanish-speaking islands the sausage is called morcilla.

rabbit and groundnut stew *leeward islands*

2½ lb. rabbit, ready-to-cook and cut into serving pieces
2 oz. salt pork, cut into cubes
1 onion, chopped
1 clove garlic, chopped
¾ pint chicken stock, or water
1 bay leaf
¼ teaspoon thyme

¼ teaspoon marjoram
Sprig parsley
Salt, freshly ground pepper to taste
3 oz. chopped peanuts
2 fresh hot peppers, preferably red, seeded, or Tabasco to taste
¼ teaspoon nutmeg

In a heavy, covered casserole render the salt pork. Sauté the rabbit pieces until browned all over. Add the onion and garlic and sauté lightly. Add the stock or water, bay leaf, thyme, marjoram, parsley, salt and pepper to taste. Cover and simmer until the rabbit is almost tender, about 1 hour, depending on the age of the rabbit.

Place the peanuts, the hot peppers and the nutmeg in an electric blender with ½ pint of the rabbit stock and blend until smooth. Pour into a saucepan with ¼ pint more of the stock, and simmer gently for 15 minutes. Taste for seasoning. Add the rabbit pieces and simmer on very low heat just long enough to heat the meat through. Serve with plain rice, or any root vegetable, and a hot pepper sauce on the side. Serves 4 to 6.

riñones con jerez   *puerto rico*

Kidneys with Sherry

8 lamb's kidneys	¼ teaspoon freshly ground
2 oz. clarified butter	pepper
1 large onion, finely chopped	4 tablespoons plain flour
1 teaspoon salt	6 tablespoons dry sherry

Remove skin and excess fat from kidneys. Cut lengthwise in halves. Soak in salted water for 15 minutes. Remove from water and pat dry with paper towels. Set aside.

Heat the butter in a frying pan and sauté the onion until tender and lightly browned. Remove with a slotted spoon and keep it warm. Mix the salt, pepper and flour. Toss the kidneys in this mixture.

If necessary add a little more butter to the frying pan, and sauté the kidneys, over a medium to high heat, turning frequently until they are done, about 5 minutes. Do not overcook as kidneys toughen very quickly. Return the onion to the pan, add the sherry, stir, cook for a minute or so and serve on buttered toast. Serves 4.

This makes an excellent breakfast, luncheon or late supper dish.

riñones guisados   *dominican republic*

Kidney Stew

8 lamb's kidneys
4 tablespoons peanut oil
1 large onion, coarsely
  chopped
1 green bell pepper, seeded
  and chopped
3 medium tomatoes, peeled,
  seeded and chopped

1 tablespoon fresh green
  coriander, chopped, or flat
  leaved parsley
1 teaspoon orégano
1 tablespoon tomato paste
6 tablespoons Seville orange
  juice
6 tablespoons chicken stock
Salt, freshly ground pepper
  to taste

Remove skin and excess fat from the kidneys. Cut lengthwise
into halves. Soak in salted water for 15 minutes. Remove from
water and pat dry with paper towels.

Meanwhile prepare the sauce. Heat 2 tablespoons of the oil in
a frying pan and sauté the onion and bell pepper until both are
tender, but not browned. Add the tomatoes, coriander or parsley,
orégano, tomato paste, orange juice, chicken stock, salt and
pepper. Stir to mix thoroughly, pour into a small saucepan, bring
to a simmer, cover and cook until the kidneys are ready. Rinse
out and dry the frying pan.

Heat the remaining 2 tablespoons of oil in the frying pan and
over medium to high heat sauté the kidneys, turning often, until
they are done, about 5 minutes. Do not overcook as kidneys
toughen very quickly. Turn the kidneys into the sauce and serve
immediately. Serves 4.

The kidneys may be served on toast for breakfast or lunch, or
with plain boiled white rice, or a starchy root vegetable and a
green vegetable or salad, for a main meal.

If Seville orange juice is not available use 2 parts orange juice
mixed with 1 part lemon juice and a drop or so of oil squeezed
from the orange peel.

VARIATION: The Puerto Ricans serve the kidneys in a sauce of onion, garlic, tomatoes, hot pepper and a tablespoon of wine vinegar seasoned with salt, pepper and a pinch of sugar.

roast pork calypso   *jamaica*

5–6 lb. loin of pork	2 bay leaves, crumbled
½ teaspoon freshly ground black pepper	8 fl. oz. dark, dry Jamaican rum
1 teaspoon salt	1 pint chicken stock
1 teaspoon ground ginger	4 oz. brown sugar
½ teaspoon ground cloves	4 tablespoons lime juice
2 cloves garlic, crushed	2 teaspoons arrowroot

Have the butcher saw through the chine bone (the backbone or spine) of the pork loin. Score fatty side in a diamond pattern. Mix the pepper, salt, ginger, cloves and garlic and rub well into the scored surface. Lay crumbled bay leaves on top.

Put roast on a rack in a roasting pan with half the rum and ¼ pint of the stock. Roast in a preheated 325°F (gas 3) oven, allowing 30 minutes to the pound. Halfway through cooking baste with a sauce made by combining the brown sugar, lime juice and remaining rum. Spoon it over the pork 3 or 4 times. Add more stock to the pan during cooking if necessary.

When roast is done, remove bay leaves, set meat on a platter, and keep warm. Spoon off excess fat, measure liquid, add any remaining basting sauce, and bring the quantity up to ¾ pint by adding remaining stock. Bring to the boil. Mix the arrowroot with a little water, add to the pan, stirring constantly until the gravy has thickened. Adjust seasoning, pour into a sauceboat and serve with the roast. Serves 8 to 10.

roast suckling pig   *all islands*

This is a great favourite in all the islands, especially at Christmas time. In the past the pigs were roasted on a spit over a wood fire, a method that is still popular and nowadays is made easier by modern barbecueing equipment. However, many suckling pigs today are cooked in the oven. The method of roasting the pig does not vary materially from island to island, but stuffings do, and so do accompanying sauces, a selection of which are given here.

10–12 lb. oven-ready suckling pig	3 tablespoons vegetable oil, or melted butter
Salt	Stuffing

Wash the cleaned and prepared pig in cold water and wipe dry. Sprinkle inside and outside with salt. Fill the cavity loosely with the stuffing and close the opening with skewers and kitchen string or sew together. Draw the legs back and tie with string. Stuff the mouth with a piece of crumpled aluminium foil to keep it open during cooking.

Brush pig with oil or butter, place on a rack in a large, shallow roasting pan. Cover pig loosely with foil and roast in a 325°F (gas 3) oven for 2½ hours, basting 2 or 3 times. Remove the foil, and cook for 30 minutes longer basting frequently.

To test for doneness, prick the thigh with a fork, or the tip of a small knife. The juices will run clear if the pig is done. Cook for a little, longer if necessary.

Transfer the pig to a heated platter. Remove the foil from the mouth and replace it with an orange, an apple, or a baked potato. Allow the pig to rest for 10 to 15 minutes at room temperature before carving. Serves 10 to 12.

In Barbados and Trinidad, the pig is rubbed inside before stuffing, with Seasoning Mixture (see Index), a typical Bajan seasoning, also used for fish.

In the Spanish-speaking islands, the pig is seasoned inside and out, with an adobo that is left on all night. While cooking, the pig is basted with the adobo and its own juice and fat. It is more often than not left unstuffed. Though stuffings, when used, tend to be elaborate. (For Adobo see Index.)

In Martinique, Guadeloupe, and Haiti the pig may be rinsed out with a cupful of good, dark rum, which is saved and added to the stuffing. Lemon juice is used to baste the pig until the last half hour of cooking when it is basted with olive oil mixed with a little vinegar.

STUFFING (JAMAICA NO. 1)

¾ lb. bread crumbs
Milk
2 cloves garlic, minced
3 oz. chopped pitted green olives
6 oz. cooked green peas, slightly crushed

2 tablespoons coarsely chopped capers
½ teaspoon allspice
1 teaspoon thyme
Salt, freshly ground pepper

Moisten the bread crumbs with a little milk and add all the remaining ingredients. Season to taste with salt and pepper.

This stuffing is very similar to one used in Barbados. For the Bajan version sauté 2 medium onions, finely chopped, and the garlic cloves as above, in 1½ oz. of unsalted butter, and add to the stuffing.

For a stuffing more typical of Trinidad, add 2 medium onions finely chopped, 2 oz. unsalted butter, 3 oz. seedless raisins, 2 medium tomatoes, peeled and chopped, and 1 teaspoon of finely chopped fresh hot red pepper. Omit the allspice and green peas. Mix all the ingredients together as in the Jamaican stuffing.

STUFFING (JAMAICA NO. 2)

2 oz. unsalted butter
1 large onion, finely chopped
1 clove garlic, chopped

¾ lb. bread crumbs
6 oz. seedless raisins, coarsely chopped

1 tablespoon fresh hot red
  peppers, chopped
1 tablespoon ground ginger

½ teaspoon grated lime rind
3 tablespoons Pickapeppa sauce
Salt

Heat the butter in a frying pan and sauté the onion and garlic until the onion is tender, but not browned. Transfer to a large bowl. Add all the rest of the ingredients, except the Pickapeppa sauce and the salt, and toss lightly to mix well. Add the Pickapeppa sauce and toss again. Taste for seasoning and add salt if necessary.

STUFFING (DOMINICAN REPUBLIC)

1½ oz. unsalted butter
½ lb. pork sausages
2 medium onions, finely
  chopped
1 clove garlic, chopped
Liver of suckling pig

¾ lb. bread crumbs
2 tablespoons chopped parsley
1 egg, well beaten
3 tablespoons milk
Salt, freshly ground pepper
6 tablespoons brandy

Heat the butter in a frying pan and sauté the sausages until lightly browned all over. Remove from the pan, cool, slice and place in a large bowl.

In the fat remaining in the pan, sauté the onions and garlic until the onions are tender but not browned. Lift out with a slotted spoon and add to the sausages. Sauté the liver over fairly brisk heat until it is browned on both sides, but still pink inside. Cool, chop coarsely and add to the bowl with the bread crumbs, parsley, egg, milk, and salt and pepper to taste. Toss lightly with a fork to mix, add the brandy and toss again.

STUFFING (GUADELOUPE)

8 fl. oz. dark rum
Pig's heart, liver, kidneys,
  lungs, etc. washed and
  cleaned

½ lb. bread crumbs
3 tablespoons milk
1 teaspoon fresh, hot, red
  pepper, chopped

1 head garlic, peeled and
chopped
1 teaspoon sage
1 bay leaf, crumbled

½ teaspoon melegueta
peppercorns (see Glossary)
ground
1 teaspoon thyme
3 tablespoons chopped chives
Salt, freshly ground pepper

Rinse out the suckling pig with the rum. Reserve the rum that runs out of the animal's body. Chop the heart and other organs, using whatever you wish, and place in a large bowl. Add the bread crumbs mixed with the milk, hot pepper, garlic, sage, bay leaf, melegueta pepper, thyme, chives and salt and pepper to taste. Pour the rum over the contents of the bowl and toss lightly with a fork to mix well.

STUFFING (MARTINIQUE)

1 lb. chopped spring onions
2 fresh hot green peppers,
chopped
1 bunch parsley, chopped
3 cloves garlic, chopped
3 tablespoons *rhum vieux*, or
use a dark rum

3 tablespoons vegetable oil
2 large onions, chopped
Pig's heart, liver, kidneys,
lungs, etc. washed, cleaned
and chopped
White wine
Oil and lime juice

Combine the spring onions, peppers, parsley and garlic in a large bowl. Add the rum. Heat the oil in a large frying pan and lightly sauté the onions and the pig's heart, liver, kidneys, lungs, etc. Add to the mixture in the bowl. Moisten with a little white wine. Toss lightly to mix and stuff into the suckling pig.

Rub the skin of the pig with oil and lime juice and place on a rack in a large baking pan. Roast for 3 hours in a 400°F (gas 6) oven. Serves 10 to 12.

This very interesting stuffing is from the kitchen of the De Leyritz Plantain Inn at Basse Pointe in Martinique and was given me by Mme. Yveline de Lucy de Fossaríeu after I had eaten and admired a portion of the dish.

In the English-speaking islands the sauces popularly served with suckling pig are Mango, Papaya 'Applesauce', and Créole Sauce.

The French-speaking islands have their own version of sauce créole, and in the Spanish-speaking islands Mojo and Ajilimójili are perhaps the most popular sauces.

They can all be found in the chapter on sauces.

salpicón estilo camagüey   *cuba*

Meat Salad, Camagüey Style

1½ lb. cold boiled beef, chopped
½ lb. fresh pineapple, diced

3 oranges, peeled, sectioned and membrane removed
Lettuce leaves or watercress for garnish

DRESSING

12 tablespoons olive oil
4 tablespoons white wine vinegar
1 teaspoon Dijon mustard

Pinch of sugar
Salt, freshly ground pepper to taste

In a salad bowl combine the beef, pineapple and orange sections. Mix together the oil, vinegar, mustard, sugar, salt and pepper, whisking to blend well. Pour over the beef and fruit and toss lightly. Garnish with lettuce or watercress. Serves 6.

Roast beef may also be used for this dish. Soup meat is also traditionally used.

salpicón   *cuba*

Meat Salad

¾ lb. cold roast beef,
  chopped
¾ lb. cold roast chicken,
  chopped
1 lb. boiled potatoes, cubed
1 large green bell pepper,
  peeled,* seeded and
  chopped

a small lettuce, chopped
2 tablespoons finely chopped
  onion
1 tablespoon capers
3 oz. sliced pimento-stuffed
  green olives
2 pimentos, chopped

DRESSING

12 tablespoons olive oil
4 tablespoons white vinegar
Salt, freshly ground pepper
  to taste

Lettuce leaves or watercress
  for garnish

In a salad bowl combine all the ingredients. Mix together the
oil, vinegar, salt and pepper whisking to blend well. Pour over
the salad, and toss lightly.

Garnish with lettuce leaves or watercress. Serves 6.

Roast veal or pork may be used, if liked in place of beef and
chicken.

*To peel the bell pepper, impale on a kitchen fork and hold over a
gas flame or electric heat turning constantly. The thin, tough skin
covering the pepper will blister and blacken. Wrap the pepper in a
damp kitchen towel, and leave for about 15 minutes, when the skin
will peel off easily.

ropa vieja   *cuba*

Old Clothes

This is a traditional Spanish dish that migrated early to the Caribbean, and remains popular in the Spanish-speaking islands, as indeed it does throughout Latin America. This Cuban version is a very good one.

2½ lb. flank steak
1 carrot, scraped and sliced
1 turnip, peeled and cubed
1 leek, chopped
2 tablespoons olive oil
1 large onion, finely chopped
1 clove garlic, chopped
1 green bell pepper, seeded and chopped
1 fresh hot red or green pepper, seeded and chopped

2 large tomatoes, peeled and chopped
1 bay leaf
⅛ teaspoon ground cinnamon
⅛ teaspoon ground cloves
Salt, freshly ground pepper
2 tinned pimentos, chopped
1 tablespoon capers (optional)

Put the beef with the carrot, turnip and leek on to cook in sufficient water to cover, and simmer gently until it is tender, about 1½ hours, in a covered pot. Allow it to cool sufficiently to handle then shred it until it resembles its name, old clothes which are in rags. Reserve the stock.

Heat the oil in a large, heavy frying pan and sauté the onion, garlic, bell pepper and hot pepper until the onion is tender but not browned. Add, the tomatoes, bay leaf, spices, salt and pepper and cook until the sauce is thick and well blended. Add ¾ pint of the stock in which the steak was cooked, the shredded steak and the pimentos and simmer for about 5 minutes longer. Add the capers if liked. The sauce, which should be abundant, may be thickened with bread crumbs if liked. Serve garnished with triangles of fried bread. Serves 6.

sancoche   *trinidad*

This Trinidadian plantation meal certainly started life as Sancocho, like its South American and Caribbean relations, but time
has altered its spelling.

4 oz. salt pork, diced
½ lb. corned beef, cut into
    ½-inch cubes
2 lb. lean, boneless beef, cut
    into 2-inch cubes
2 large onions, coarsely
    chopped
5 pints beef stock
½ lb. dried yellow split peas
½ lb. each yam, dasheen
    (taro root), and cassava
    root, peeled and cut into
    slices 1-inch thick

1 lb. sweet potatoes, peeled
    and cut into 1-inch slices
1 lb. potatoes, peeled and cut
    into 1-inch slices
1 whole fresh very hot red or
    green pepper, intact with
    stem on
8 fl. oz. coconut cream
Salt, freshly ground pepper
    to taste
Corn Meal Dumplings
2 green plantains

In a heavy, covered casserole render the salt pork. Lightly sauté
the corned beef and fresh beef, and the onions in the fat from
the salt pork. They should not be heavily browned. Add the stock
and the split peas, cover and simmer gently for 1 hour. Add the
yam, dasheen, cassava, sweet potatoes and potatoes with the whole
pepper and the coconut cream. Cover and continue to simmer
gently for 15 minutes. Season to taste with salt and pepper. Add
the dumplings and cook partially covered for 20 minutes longer.
In the meantime cook the green plantains, with their skins on,
for half an hour in water to cover. As soon as they are cool enough
to handle, peel, and cut into 1-inch slices. Add to the casserole
just long enough to heat through. Serves 6 to 8.

CORN MEAL DUMPLINGS

2 oz. yellow corn meal
2 oz. plain flour
1 teaspoon baking powder

1 teaspoon salt
Pinch of nutmeg
1 ½ oz. unsalted butter

Sift the corn meal, flour, baking powder, salt and nutmeg into a large bowl. Rub in the butter with the fingertips and add just enough cold water, about 3 tablespoons, to make a soft dough. Divide the dough into 12 equal portions, form gently into balls and drop 1 at a time into the sancoche. Continue cooking as described.

wilma's pork and spinach *st lucia*

1 ½ lb. lean pork, cut into
1-inch cubes
1 onion, halved
Salt, freshly ground pepper

1 teaspoon ground ginger
¾ pint chicken stock, or
water
1 ½ lb. spinach

Put the pork, onion, salt and pepper to taste, the ginger and enough stock or water to cover the pork, into a heavy saucepan or casserole. Cover, and simmer until the pork is tender, about 1 ½ hours. Lift out the pork and reserve. Strain the stock, return it to the saucepan and reduce it over brisk heat to ¼ pint. Adjust the seasoning and add a little more ginger if necessary. Wash the spinach, drain thoroughly and chop coarsely. Add to the saucepan with the pork. Cover, and simmer until the spinach is done, about 5 minutes. Serve with rice. Serves 4.

sancocho de carne de cerdo

dominican republic

Pork Stew

3 lb. pork loin, cut in 2-inch chunks
Salt, freshly ground pepper to taste
2 onions, chopped fine
1 leek, chopped
4 cloves garlic, chopped
1 tablespoon each chopped parsley and fresh coriander
Bay leaf
1 hot pepper, chopped
1 tablespoon vinegar
3 tablespoons Seville orange juice, or 2 tablespoons

orange and 1 tablespoon lime juice
2 green plantains, peeled and sliced
3 tablespoons lime, or lemon, juice
1 lb. longaniza sausage, or Polish boiling ring
1 tablespoon salad oil
1 lb. each yuca, yautía, pumpkin, sweet potatoes, and yam, peeled and sliced
3 ears sweet corn, each cut into 3 pieces

Season the pork with salt and pepper. Put into a heavy, covered 6 pint casserole with the onions, leek, garlic, parsley, coriander, bay leaf, hot pepper, vinegar, and bitter orange juice. Add enough water to barely cover. Simmer over low heat.

Meanwhile soak the plantains in the lime or lemon juice for 10 minutes. Drain, and add to the casserole.

Fry the sausage lightly in the salad oil, drain, cool, cut in slices and add to the casserole with the yuca, yautía, pumpkin, sweet potatoes, yam, and sweet corn. Bring to the boil, cover, and simmer very gently until all the ingredients are tender. The pumpkin will disintegrate and thicken the sauce. Serves 6 to 8.

sancocho de rabo de vaca   *dominican republic*

Oxtail Stew

3 lb. oxtail, cut up
4 cloves garlic, mashed
2 medium onions
1 green bell pepper, seeded and chopped
1 teaspoon each parsley and coriander, chopped
3 grains melegueta pepper
1 teaspoon orégano
2 tablespoons cider vinegar
2 tablespoons Seville orange juice
5 pints beef stock, or half stock, half water

1 lb. each white and yellow yautía, peeled and cut into 1-inch slices
1 lb. cush-cush yams, peeled and cut into 1-inch slices
1 lb. West Indian pumpkin, (calabaza) peeled and cubed
1 lb. cassava root, peeled and cut into ½-inch slices
3 ripe plantains, peeled and cut into 1-inch slices
Salt to taste
Tabasco sauce to taste

Put the oxtail into a soup pan or heavy casserole big enough to hold all the ingredients. Add the garlic, onions, bell pepper, parsley, coriander, melegueta pepper, orégano, vinegar, Seville orange juice and stock. Cover, and simmer gently for 2 hours. Add the yautía, yams, pumpkin, cassava, plantains, salt and Tabasco to taste, cover and simmer for 1 hour longer, or until the oxtail and the vegetables are done. Serves 6 to 8.

seasoned-up pork stew   *st kitts*

3 lb. boneless pork, cut into 2-inch cubes
2 tablespoons distilled white vinegar

1 tablespoon Worcestershire sauce
2 sprigs coarsely chopped parsley, preferably flat Italian type

1 teaspoon fresh sage,
coarsely chopped, or ½
teaspoon dried, crumbled
1 tablespoon celery leaves
coarsely chopped
2 tablespoons chopped chives,
or spring onions, using
green and white parts
2 cloves garlic crushed,
1 onion, grated

¼ teaspoon fresh ground
pepper
Salt to taste
1 tablespoon golden rum
2 teaspoons brown sugar
1 oz. unsalted butter
¾ pint chicken, or pork,
stock
1 tablespoon tomato ketchup
2 teaspoons arrowroot

Mix together the vinegar, Worcestershire sauce, parsley, sage, celery leaves, chives, garlic, onion, pepper, salt, and rum in a large bowl. Add the meat and mix thoroughly. Leave, loosely covered, at room temperature for 3 to 4 hours, turning from time to time so that all the pieces of meat are able to absorb the flavours of the marinade.

Scrape off the marinade and if liked, purée it in an electric blender with some of the stock, or strain, discarding the solids. Sprinkle the pork pieces with the brown sugar. In a heavy, covered casserole heat the butter and sauté the pork lightly. Add the marinade and enough stock to cover. Stir in the tomato ketchup. Cover and simmer until the pork is tender, 1½ to 2 hours. Taste for seasoning. Mix the arrowroot with a little cold water and stir into the stew. Cook, stirring until the gravy is lightly thickened. Serve with any root vegetable or with rice. Serves 6.

stobá di concomber   *curaçao*

Kid and Cucumber Stew

The cucumbers used in Curaçao are the small round tropical variety sometimes called apple, or lemon, cucumbers. If they are not available, use ordinary cucumbers, peeling them if they have been waxed. Do not peel the apple cucumbers.

1 lb. corned beef
2 tablespoons vegetable oil
2 oz. unsalted butter
3 lb. lean, boneless kid, or
lamb, cut in 3-inch pieces
3 medium onions, finely
chopped
3 cloves garlic, chopped
2 shallots, chopped
2 stalks celery, finely chopped
1 medium green bell pepper,
seeded and chopped
1 or 2 fresh hot red or green
peppers, seeded and
chopped

2 medium tomatoes, peeled
and chopped
2 tablespoons lime juice
1 tablespoon white vinegar
Salt, freshly ground pepper
1 teaspoon ground cumin
1 teaspoon ground nutmeg
2 lb. cucumbers, coarsely
chopped
8 small potatoes, peeled and
cubed
1 tablespoon capers
10 pitted green olives

Put the corned beef into a heavy saucepan, cover with cold water, bring to the boil, reduce heat and simmer, covered for 45 minutes. Set aside.

Heat the oil and butter in a heavy casserole and lightly brown the kid (or lamb). Add the onions, garlic, shallots, celery, peppers, and tomatoes and cook until the onion is tender. Drain the corned beef, cut it into 1-inch cubes and add to the casserole with the lime juice, vinegar, salt and pepper to taste, cumin, nutmeg and ½ pint of water. Cover, and simmer until the kid is tender, about 1½ hours. Check from time to time to see if there is enough liquid, adding hot water if necessary. Add the cucumbers, potatoes, capers, and olives and cook for about 15 minutes longer, or until the potatoes are done. Serves 6.

vaca frita
cuba

Fried Cow

2½ lb. flank steak
1 carrot, scraped and sliced
1 turnip, peeled and cubed

1 onion, chopped
Bay leaf
3 tablespoons olive oil

Put the steak on to cook in water to cover with the carrot, turnip and onion. Cover and simmer gently until it is tender, about 1½ hours. Remove the meat from the stock when it is cool enough to handle. Pound it thoroughly. Heat the oil in a large frying pan and fry the meat on both sides. Drain the oil from the pan and serve the meat masked by the Tomato Sauce. Serves 6.
Refrigerate the stock for use in other dishes.

TOMATO SAUCE

Salsa de Tomate

3 tablespoons olive oil
2 large tomatoes, peeled and
  chopped
2 cloves garlic, peeled and
  chopped
1 fresh hot red pepper,
  seeded and chopped, or
  ½ teaspoon cayenne

4 whole tinned pimentos and
  the liquid from the tin
6 tablespoons tomato purée
½ teaspoon orégano
¼ teaspoon freshly ground
  pepper
½ teaspoon sugar
Salt to taste

To make the sauce, heat the olive oil in a large frying pan. Add the tomatoes, garlic, and fresh hot pepper and cook, stirring over medium heat until the mixture is well blended. Add all the rest of the ingredients, lower the heat and cook gently, stirring from time to time, until the sauce is thick. Makes about 1 pint.

almond chicken   *trinidad*

This dish has a very strong Asian influence, not uncommon in Trinidad. The technique of stir-frying is not difficult. Food is fried quickly at a high temperature while being stirred constantly. A little liquid is added and the cooking quickly finished.

3 boned chicken breasts, thinly sliced
3 tablespoons peanut oil
1 small onion, chopped
3 spring onions, chopped, using green and white parts
½ cucumber, peeled and coarsely chopped
2 medium carrots, scraped and coarsely chopped
8 oz. tin water chestnuts, drained and sliced
4 oz. mushrooms, sliced
8 oz. tin bamboo shoots, drained and chopped
2 teaspoons salt
3 tablespoons soy sauce
4 oz. whole blanched almonds
Butter or oil

Heat the oil in a heavy frying pan or wok and stir-fry the chicken over brisk heat for 3 minutes. Add the onion, spring onions, cucumber, carrots, water chestnuts, mushrooms, bamboo shoots and salt and cook stirring constantly over brisk heat, for about 5 minutes longer. Pour soy sauce over the mixture and cook without stirring for 1 minute more. Meanwhile, sauté the almonds in a little butter or oil until golden brown. Pile the chicken–vegetable mixture into a warmed serving dish and top with the almonds. Serve with rice. Serves 4 to 6.

asopao de pollo   *puerto rico*
Chicken and Rice Stew

½ teaspoon orégano
2 cloves garlic, crushed
1 teaspoon salt
2½–3 lb. chicken, cut into
  6 to 8 pieces
3 tablespoons lard, or
  vegetable oil
1 medium onion, finely
  chopped
1 green bell pepper, seeded
  and chopped
2 oz. ham, coarsely chopped
2 medium tomatoes, peeled
  and chopped

¾ lb. long-grain rice
Freshly ground pepper
2½ pints chicken stock
6 oz. cooked green peas
1 tablespoon capers,
  preferably Spanish
2 oz. small pimento-stuffed
  green olives
4 oz. freshly grated Parmesan
  cheese
2 pimentos, cut into strips
Asparagus tips for garnish

Mix the orégano, garlic and salt together and rub into the chicken pieces. Heat the lard or oil in a heavy casserole, and sauté the chicken, a few pieces at a time, until lightly golden. Set chicken aside. Add the onion and green pepper to the casserole and cook, stirring, until the onion is tender but not browned. Add the ham, then the tomatoes and cook for a few minutes longer, until the mixture is well blended. Return the chicken pieces to the casserole, cover and cook over low heat for 30 minutes, or until the chicken is tender. Remove the chicken pieces to a plate and when they are cool enough to handle, remove the bones and cut the meat into 2-inch squares. Set aside. Add the rice, freshly ground pepper and chicken stock to the casserole, cover, and cook over low heat until the rice is tender, about 20 minutes. Add the peas, capers, olives, cheese and chicken. Garnish with the pimento strips, cover and simmer just long enough to heat the chicken through. The rice should not be dry but soupy, which is what asopao means. Garnish with asparagus tips. Serves 6.

arroz con pollo

*cuba, puerto rico,
dominican republic*

Chicken with Rice

This traditional Spanish dish is popular not only in the Spanish-speaking islands of the Caribbean, but throughout Latin America. The Caribbean version is slightly different from the parent recipe, but differs little from island to island. Sometimes French-cut green beans replace the traditional green peas.

3–3 ½ lb. chicken, cut into
  serving pieces
2 cloves garlic
½ teaspoon orégano
2 teaspoons salt
¼ teaspoon freshly ground
  pepper
2 tablespoons red wine
  vinegar
4 tablespoons olive oil
1 onion, chopped
1 green bell pepper, seeded
  and chopped

2 medium tomatoes, peeled,
  seeded and chopped
1 bay leaf
4 oz. ham, chopped coarsely
1 tablespoon fresh coriander,
  or parsley, chopped
1½ pints chicken stock, about
¾ lb. rice
1 tablespoon capers
2 oz. pitted green olives,
  sliced
3 tablespoons dry sherry
6 oz. cooked green peas
2 pimentos, sliced

Mix together the garlic, orégano, salt, pepper and vinegar and rub into the chicken pieces. Let them stand for about an hour. Heat the oil in a frying pan and sauté the drained chicken pieces until golden. Transfer to an earthenware* casserole. Add any remaining marinade. In the oil remaining in the pan sauté the onion and bell pepper until the onion is lightly browned. Add the contents of the pan to the casserole with the tomatoes, bay leaf, ham, coriander, and ¾ pint of the chicken stock. Cover and

*When using earthenware make sure it is heavy enough not to crack over direct heat. Use one or more asbestos mats if necessary.

simmer for 30 minutes. At the end of this time, lift out the chicken pieces and other solids and set aside. Measure the liquid and add enough chicken stock to make the quantity up to 1½ pints. Pour into a saucepan and bring to the boil.

Wash the rice thoroughly, drain and pour into the casserole. Pour in the boiling stock and stir. Add the capers and olives and chicken pieces, and other solids. Cover and cook over low heat until the liquid has been absorbed and the rice is tender. Remove the bay leaf. Sprinkle the rice with the sherry and garnish with the peas and pimento strips and cook just long enough to heat through. Serve directly from the casserole. Serves 6.

annie's tropical chicken   *jamaica*

3 tablespoons peanut oil
3½–4 lb. chicken, cut into
  serving pieces
1 onion, finely chopped
2 cloves garlic, chopped
1 lb. fresh pineapple,
  chopped or
1 lb. unsweetened pineapple
  chunks tinned in own juice
6 oz. water chestnuts, sliced
1 fresh hot red pepper,
  seeded and chopped

3 medium tomatoes, peeled
  and chopped, or 1 medium
  tin Italian plum tomatoes,
  drained
Salt, freshly ground pepper
  to taste
Chicken stock, if necessary
½ lb. mange-tout peas
1 tablespoon chopped chives
  or spring onion tops

Heat the oil in a heavy frying pan and sauté the chicken pieces until golden on both sides. Transfer chicken to a heavy covered casserole. In the oil remaining in the frying pan sauté the onion and garlic until the onion is tender but not browned. Add to the chicken, together with the pineapple and any juice, or the tinned pineapple and juice, the water chestnuts, hot pepper, tomatoes, salt and pepper, cover and simmer gently until the chicken is tender, about 45 minutes. Add a little chicken stock if necessary. During the last ten minutes add the mange-tout peas and the chives. Serves 6.

chicken calypso   *dominica*

5 tablespoons olive oil
3 ½ –4 lb. chicken, cut into
   serving pieces
2 cups rice
1 medium onion, finely
   chopped
1 clove garlic, chopped
1 green bell pepper, seeded
   and chopped

1 small hot green pepper,
   seeded and chopped
½ lb. mushrooms, sliced
½ teaspoon saffron
2- to 3-inch piece of lime peel
1 tablespoon lime juice
¼ teaspoon Angostura bitters
4 cups chicken stock
Salt, freshly ground pepper
3 tablespoons light rum

Heat 3 tablespoons of the olive oil in a skillet and sauté the chicken pieces until brown all over. Remove to a heavy casserole. Add the rice, onion, garlic, bell pepper, and hot pepper to the oil remaining in the skillet, and sauté, stirring, until the oil is absorbed, being careful not to let the rice scorch. Add to the chicken in the casserole. Add the remaining 2 tablespoons of oil to the skillet and sauté the mushrooms over fairly high heat for 5 minutes. Add to the casserole with the saffron, lime peel, lime juice, bitters, chicken stock, and salt and pepper to taste. Cover and simmer gently until rice and chicken are tender and the liquid is absorbed, about ½ hour. Add the rum and cook, uncovered, for 5 minutes longer. Serves 6.

chicken in orange sauce   *trinidad*

2 oz. plain flour
2 teaspoons salt
½ teaspoon freshly ground
  pepper
3½–4 lb. chicken, cut into
  serving pieces
3 tablespoons peanut oil
¾ pint orange juice
2 tablespoons dark brown
  sugar

2 tablespoons white vinegar
1 teaspoon freshly ground
  nutmeg
1 teaspoon fresh basil,
  chopped, or ½ teaspoon
  dried
2 cloves garlic, finely
  chopped
3 oranges peeled, sectioned
  and membrane removed

Combine the flour, salt and pepper and dredge the chicken pieces heavily with the mixture. Heat the oil in a frying pan and sauté the chicken pieces until golden on both sides. As they are done, transfer them to a heavy, covered casserole. Pour off and discard any oil remaining in the frying pan, but scrape the brown bits into the casserole, deglazing the pan with a little of the orange juice if necessary.

Add all the ingredients, except the orange sections, to the casserole, cover and simmer gently until the chicken is almost done, about 45 minutes. Add the orange sections and cook for 5 minutes longer. The flour in which the chicken was dredged will have thickened the sauce lightly. Serves 6. Serve with plain boiled white rice, or a starchy root vegetable and either a green vegetable or a salad.

chicken pilau   *st vincent*

3½–4 lb. chicken, cut into
  serving pieces
Salt, freshly ground pepper
  to taste

2 tablespoons Worcestershire
  sauce
3 tablespoons cooking oil
Stock or water

4 oz. butter
1 onion, finely chopped
1 clove garlic, chopped
¾ lb. rice

½ teaspoon cinnamon
2 oz. seedless raisins
2 oz. roasted peanuts

Season chicken pieces with salt, pepper, and Worcestershire sauce. Heat the oil in a large, heavy, covered frying pan, and sauté the chicken pieces until golden. Add stock or water to cover and simmer, covered, until half-done, about 15 minutes. Remove from heat, drain stock from pan and reserve it. Heat the butter in another skillet and sauté the onion and garlic until golden brown. Add the rice and sauté until all the butter is absorbed. Add the cinnamon and the raisins. Transfer to the skillet with the chicken and add the reserved stock. Add enough extra stock or water to make the quantity up to 1 ½ pints. Cover, and cook until the rice is tender and all the liquid is absorbed. Sprinkle with roasted peanuts. Serves 6.

chicken pelau   *trinidad*

3½–4 lb. chicken, cut into
   serving pieces
1 lb. pork, cut into 1-inch
   cubes
Salt, freshly ground black
   pepper
1 fresh hot green pepper,
   seeded and minced
1 onion, peeled and finely
   chopped
3 or 4 blades of chive,
   chopped

1 sprig thyme, crumbled
1 medium tomato, peeled
   and chopped
2 teaspoons brown sugar
3 tablespoons oil
¾ lb. long-grain rice, well
   washed
½ oz. butter
12 almonds, blanched and
   chopped
12 small pimento-stuffed
   green olives, halved

Season the chicken pieces and the pork with salt, pepper, fresh hot pepper, onion, chives, thyme, tomato and sugar, and allow to stand for several hours or overnight in the refrigerator. Scrape off and reserve seasonings. Heat the oil in a large, covered frying pan and sauté the chicken and pork until golden brown. Add the reserved seasonings, pour in enough water to barely cover the meat, cover the pan and simmer gently until half done, about 30 minutes. Remove the meat from the frying pan, strain the stock, measure it and bring the quantity up with extra stock or water to make 1½ pints. Return the meat to the frying pan, add the stock and stir in the rice, cover, and simmer, until the rice is tender and all the liquid absorbed, about 20 minutes. Add the butter, nuts and olives. Serves 6 to 8.

chicken fricassée   *jamaica*

3½–4 lb. chicken, cut into serving pieces
4 cloves garlic, crushed
1 teaspoon paprika
1 teaspoon ground ginger
1 teaspoon salt
½ teaspoon freshly ground pepper

2 oz. chicken fat, about
2 large onions, coarsely chopped
3 medium tomatoes, peeled and coarsely chopped
1 hot fresh pepper, red if possible
Chicken stock if necessary

Rub the chicken pieces with the garlic, paprika, ginger, salt and pepper mixed together. Refrigerate in a covered container overnight. Scrape off and reserve the seasonings. Pat the chicken pieces dry with paper towels. Heat the chicken fat in a heavy frying pan and sauté the chicken pieces until golden on both sides. Transfer to a heavy covered casserole. In the chicken fat remaining in the frying pan, adding a little more if necessary, sauté the onions until golden. Add the onions to the casserole with the tomatoes, the reserved seasonings, and the hot pepper, left whole and with the stem still on. Cover, and simmer gently until the chicken is tender, adding a little chicken stock if there is not sufficient liquid. The sauce should not be watery. Before serving, remove and discard the hot pepper. Serves 6.

chicken pie with sweet potato crust   *barbados*

The boniato sweet potato, which has a brown or pink skin and white flesh, should be used in this dish. The yellow-fleshed sweet potato, often called a Louisiana yam, is far too sweet and its texture too moist for this pie crust.

1 lb. cubed cooked chicken
6 small white boiled onions
6 oz. cooked diced carrots
6 oz. cooked green peas
1 tablespoon chopped parsley
Salt, freshly ground pepper
3 tablespoons plain flour

1 ½ oz. butter
8 fl. oz. chicken stock
8 fl. oz. milk
2 tablespoons sherry
   (optional)
Sweet Potato Crust

Combine the chicken, onions, carrots, peas, parsley, and salt and pepper to taste and place in a soufflé or baking dish. Mix the flour and butter together. Heat the chicken stock and milk in a small saucepan and add the flour mixture. Cook, stirring, until thickened. Add sherry if liked, and pour over the chicken. Top with the crust. Bake in a 350°F (gas 4) oven until golden brown, about 45 minutes. Serves 4 to 6.

SWEET POTATO CRUST

4 oz. plain flour
1 teaspoon salt
1 teaspoon baking powder

8 oz. cold, mashed white
   sweet potato
4 oz. unsalted butter

Sift the flour, salt and baking powder together into a bowl. Add the sweet potato and mix well. Rub in the butter to make a smooth mixture. Add a little water if necessary. Gather the dough into a ball and transfer to a floured board. Roll out lightly to fit the top of the soufflé or baking dish. Place on top of the chicken mixture inside the dish.

empanada de pollo   *cuba*

Chicken Pie

This is an old Cuban dish from Oriente province. The recipe was given me by my friend Nieves Rendueles who was given it by her mother-in-law. It has been handed down through the generations, and goes back to early colonial times when the family received land grants from the Spanish crown. The pastry is particularly interesting.

PARA EL RELLENO

For the Filling

2 2½ lb. frying chickens, cut into serving pieces	1 pound tomatoes,* peeled and chopped
Lemon juice	1 teaspoon Spanish (hot) paprika
Salt, freshly ground pepper	Bay leaf
3 tablespoons olive oil	2 tablespoons chopped, pitted green olives
3 medium onions, finely chopped	2 teaspoons capers
2 green bell peppers, seeded and chopped	2 tinned pimentos, chopped
	2 hard-boiled eggs, sliced

Pat the chicken pieces dry, rub with lemon juice and season to taste with salt and pepper. Heat the oil in a large, heavy frying pan and sauté the chicken pieces until golden. Lift out and set

*It is important to use very ripe, flavourful tomatoes. If good fresh ones are not available, use the best available tinned ones.

aside. Add the onions and green peppers to the frying pan and sauté until the onion is tender but not browned. Add the tomatoes, paprika, and bay leaf. Season to taste with salt and pepper, stir to mix well, cover and simmer gently for 15 minutes. Return the chicken pieces to the pan, cover and simmer for about 30 minutes, or until the chicken can be boned easily. Do not overcook the chicken. Allow to cool, bone the chicken, and cut the meat into bite-sized pieces. At this point check if the sauce is at all watery and if necessary reduce it over brisk heat for a few minutes. It should be quite thick. Remove and discard the bay leaf. Add the olives, capers, pimentos and chicken and mix gently. Set aside.

Remove the pastry from the refrigerator and roll out the larger ball to fit a 2- to 2½- inch deep by 12- inch rectangular pyrex, or other baking dish. Line the pie dish allowing the pastry to overlap the edges. Fill with the chicken and sauce mixture. Arrange the egg slices on top. Roll out the smaller ball of pastry to cover the dish. Trim, then moisten the edges of the lower crust with water, cover with the top crust, and seal well. Pinch with the fingers to make a decorative border, or mark with a fork. Cut three or four slits in the top to allow the steam to escape during cooking. Bake in a 350°F (gas 4) oven for 45 minutes, or until the crust is golden. Serve hot or cold. Serves 8 to 10.

PASTEL PARA LA EMPANADA

Pastry for the Pie Crust

1 lb. plain flour
1 teaspoon baking powder
1 tablespoon sugar
4 oz. lard, chilled and cut into ¼-inch pieces

2 oz. unsalted butter, chilled and cut into ½-inch pieces
2 egg yolks and 1 whole egg
4 tablespoons dry white wine

Sift the flour, baking powder and sugar into a large bowl. Rub the fat into the flour with the tips of the fingers until the mixture resembles coarse meal. Beat the egg yolks and the egg lightly with 2 tablespoons of the wine and blend into the fat–flour mixture. Knead quickly into a ball. If the dough crumbles, sprinkle up to 2 tablespoons more wine over it until it holds together. Shape into 2 balls, one slightly larger than the other, wrap in wax paper and refrigerate until ready to use.

VARIATION: Puerto Rico has a chicken pie, Pastelón de Pollo, that bears a strong family resemblance to the Cuban version. It is baked with a double crust in a straight-sided 9-inch pie dish using the same pastry as Deep Dish Meat Pie, St Thomas (see Index), and serves 4 to 6. The filling is made with a 2 lb. chicken seasoned with salt, freshly ground pepper, 2 cloves of crushed garlic and ½ teaspoon of orégano, then marinated in ¼ pint each Seville orange juice and olive oil for 2 hours. It is simmered in a heavy saucepan with a bay leaf, and ⅜ pint each of sofrito (see Index) and chicken stock. Olives and capers are added as in the Cuban version (3 oz. chopped olives, 1 tablespoon capers), but the pimentos and eggs are omitted. Instead 1 medium potato cut into ½-inch cubes, 3 oz. fresh or frozen green peas, and 1½ oz. raisins are added 15 minutes before the chicken is done. The chicken is boned and the pie assembled in the same way as for Empanada de Pollo. It is baked for 10 minutes in a 450°F (gas 8) oven, then at 350°F (gas 4) for 45 minutes longer, or until the crust is golden brown. It is served hot, directly from the pie dish.

gallina en pepitoria   *puerto rico*

Chicken in Almond Sauce

3½ lb. chicken, cut into
  serving pieces
Flour
3 tablespoons olive oil

1 medium onion, finely
  chopped
1 clove garlic, chopped
1 large tomato, peeled,
  seeded and chopped

1 or 2 sprigs parsley	Salt
2-inch piece stick cinnamon	¼ teaspoon white pepper
4 whole cloves	2 teaspoons lime, or lemon,
¾ pint chicken stock	juice
2 oz. blanched almonds	2 eggs

Dredge the chicken pieces with flour, shaking to remove the excess. Heat the oil in a frying pan and sauté the chicken until golden. Transfer to a heavy casserole. Sauté the onion and garlic in the frying pan and add to the chicken together with the tomato, parsley, cinnamon, cloves and chicken stock. Pulverize the almonds in an electric blender at high speed and add to the casserole. Season with salt, if necessary, and white pepper. Cover and simmer gently until the chicken is tender, about 45 minutes.

Remove the chicken pieces to a serving platter and keep warm. Skim off any grease from the sauce and reduce the sauce to ¾ pint over brisk heat. Ajdust seasoning, and strain the sauce through a fine sieve. Place over low heat. Beat the eggs with the lime juice. Pour a few tablespoons of the sauce on to the eggs, beating it in with a wire whisk. Then pour the egg mixture into the sauce, beating constantly over low heat until the sauce has thickened. Do not let the sauce boil as it will curdle. Pour over the chicken. Serve with plain white rice. Serves 6.

fowl down-in-rice   *barbados*

This is an Arroz con Pollo (Chicken with Rice) that has wandered into English-speaking territory and changed its character somewhat en route. It is quite astonishingly good.

3½–4 lb. chicken, cut into serving pieces	1 teaspoon salt
	¾ pint chicken stock
4 tablespoons lime, or lemon, juice	¾ lb. rice
	Bay leaf

2 or 3 sprigs parsley
½ teaspoon thyme
Salt, freshly ground pepper
   to taste

2 medium onions, thinly
   sliced
2 medium tomatoes, sliced
1½ oz. butter
1 teaspoon dry mustard

Season the chicken pieces with the salt and 2 tablespoons of the lime or lemon juice and allow to stand at room temperature for 1 hour. Transfer to a heavy casserole, earthenware* if possible. Drain and discard the marinade. Add the chicken stock, bring to a simmer and cook, covered, for 40 minutes. Lift out the chicken from the casserole and set aside. Measure the liquid and add enough water to bring it up to 1½ pints. Wash the rice, drain and add to the casserole with the bay leaf, parsley, thyme and salt and pepper to taste. Bring to the boil, add the chicken pieces, reduce the heat, cover, and simmer until the chicken and rice are tender and all the liquid is absorbed, about 20 minutes.

Meanwhile make the sauce. Combine the onions, tomatoes, butter, mustard, and salt and pepper to taste in a small saucepan. Bring to the boil, cover and simmer for 5 minutes. If serving directly from the casserole, pour the sauce over the chicken or make a bed of the rice on a warmed platter, arrange the chicken pieces on top, and cover with the sauce. Serves 6 to 8.

fricassée de poulet au coco   *martinique*

Chicken in Coconut Milk

3 tablespoons vegetable oil
3 lb. chicken, quartered
1 large onion, finely chopped
1 clove garlic, chopped

¼ lb. mushrooms, sliced
Salt, freshly ground pepper
Sprig parsley
Sprig thyme

*If using earthenware make sure it is heavy enough not to crack over direct heat. Use one or more asbestos mats if necessary.

| 1 fresh hot red pepper | ¾ pint coconut milk |
| (optional) | |

Heat the oil in a heavy, flameproof casserole and add the chicken pieces. Cook over medium heat until they have stiffened and are very lightly golden on both sides, about 5 minutes. They should not brown. Remove and set aside. Add the onion, garlic and mushrooms and sauté until the onion is tender, but not browned. Return the chicken pieces to the casserole. Season to taste with salt and pepper. Tie the parsley, thyme and pepper in a square of cheesecloth and add. Pour in the coconut milk. Simmer gently, covered, until the chicken is tender, about 1 hour. Remove the *bouquet garni*. Serve with Riz Créole. Serves 4.

VARIATION: This is sometimes served as a sauté (Sauté de Poulet au Coco, Sautéed Chicken with Coconut Milk Sauce). For this, heat 3 tablespoons each of oil and unsalted butter in a heavy casserole and sauté the chicken pieces over medium heat until they are golden on both sides, about 8 minutes. Season with salt and pepper, cover and cook over low heat until the chicken is tender, about half an hour. Remove the chicken pieces to a serving platter and keep warm. Add the onion, mushrooms and garlic to the casserole and sauté over fairly brisk heat until the onion is tender. Add ⅜ pint of rich coconut milk, 1 tablespoon finely chopped parsley, ¾ teaspoon of thyme and, if liked, ½ a fresh hot pepper seeded and chopped. Cook, stirring from time to time, over low heat, until the sauce is well blended and heated through. Pour over the chicken. Serves 4.

keshy yena coe galinja   *curaçao*

Cheese with Chicken Stuffing

4 lb. Edam cheese
2 tablespoons vegetable oil
1 oz. butter
3½–4 lb. chicken, cut into pieces
¾ pint chicken stock, about
2 medium onions, finely chopped
2 green bell peppers, seeded and coarsely chopped

1 fresh hot green pepper, seeded and chopped
1 large tomato, peeled, seeded and chopped
1 tablespoon seedless raisins
Salt, freshly ground pepper
2 or 3 chopped gherkins
¼ pint tomato purée
1 oz. freshly made bread crumbs

Peel the red wax covering from the cheese, cut a 1-inch slice from the top, hollow out the slice and reserve. Scoop out the cheese leaving a shell about ½ inch thick. Cover the shell and top slice with cold water and soak for an hour. Store the scooped out cheese for another use.

Heat the oil and butter in a frying pan and sauté the chicken pieces lightly. Transfer the chicken to a saucepan, add enough stock to cover and cook gently, covered, until the chicken is done, about 45 minutes. Cool, take out of the stock, remove the skin and bones and cut the meat into bite-size pieces. Set aside.

Meanwhile, in the fat remaining in the frying pan, sauté the onions and peppers until the onions are tender. Add the tomato and raisins and cook for about 5 minutes. Season to taste with salt and pepper, add the gherkins, tomato purée and bread crumbs, cook for a minute or two, mixing well. Add the chicken.

Remove the cheese from the water and pat dry. Stuff with the chicken mixture. Replace top of cheese. Put stuffed cheese into a greased 5-pint oven-proof casserole. Bake uncovered in a pre-heated 350°F (gas 4) oven for 30 minutes. Do not overcook as the cheese becomes tough, instead of soft and bubbly. Slide the cheese out of the casserole onto a warmed serving dish. Cut into wedges and serve immediately. Serves 6 to 8.

A popular way of cooking this dish is to peel off the outer wax covering of the cheese, then cut it into ¼-inch slices. Line a greased 5-pint oven-proof casserole on bottom and sides with the cheese slices overlapping. Pour in the chicken mixture and cover with the remaining slices of cheese. Bake for 30 minutes in a 350°F (gas 4) oven. Small individual casseroles may also be used, in which case, reduce the baking time to 15 to 20 minutes.

curri de pollo con salsa de ciruelas pasas   *cuba*

Chicken Curry with Prune Sauce

3½–4 lb. chicken, cut into serving pieces	1 tablespoon mild curry powder
3 cloves garlic, crushed	4 oz. unsalted butter
½ teaspoon orégano	½ lb. mushrooms
¼ teaspoon cumin	¾ pint unsweetened prune juice
1 teaspoon salt	Chicken stock, if necessary
¼ teaspoon freshly ground pepper	2 teaspoons arrowroot (optional)

Mix the garlic, orégano, cumin, salt, pepper and curry powder together and rub into the chicken pieces. Refrigerate overnight. Heat half the butter in a heavy frying pan and lightly sauté the chicken pieces. Transfer the contents of the pan to a heavy, covered casserole. Rinse out the pan and heat the rest of the butter. Sauté the mushrooms (whole if small, sliced if large) over fairly high heat until they are lightly browned, 4 or 5 minutes. Add to the casserole. Pour the prune juice over the chicken pieces and add chicken stock, if necessary, to cover. Cover the casserole and simmer until tender, about 45 minutes to 1 hour. Cook partially covered for the last 15 minutes to reduce the sauce. If the sauce is too thin, mix the arrowroot with a tablespoon of cold water, stir into the sauce and cook until lightly thickened. The sauce should not be very thick. Serve with Arroz con Ajo (Garlic Rice). Serves 6.

le colombo   *martinique–guadeloupe*

The Colombo, which is a type of curry, was introduced into Martinique and Guadeloupe around the middle of the last century by migrant Hindu workers, mostly from Bengal. They brought with them the ingredients for a sort of curry powder which is made from mustard seeds, toasted rice, garlic, hot peppers, coriander, saffron, and black pepper. The spices and herbs are ground, then fried in oil. Tamarind pulp is always added to the curries, which may be made from chicken, pork, kid, lamb, fish or shellfish. Tropical vegetables, onions and garlic complete the dish, which has become a great favourite for holidays. Pork is traditionally used for the Christmas *Colombo* in Martinique. The cooking liquid more often than not is white wine, perhaps combined with stock, and a little *rhum vieux* or dry Madeira. Coconut milk is sometimes used, though not for fish or shellfish curries. Curry powder is often used nowadays instead of the original poudre de colombo though many islanders still make their curry powder from old recipes. I have included here a curry powder recipe from St Kitts, as well as the poudre de colombo. Recipes for the Colombos tend to be flexible, depending on the talents and inclinations of the cook.

In Martinique the curries are considered Northern dishes, as the Hindus settled mainly in Basse Pointe and Macouba in the north of the island. If two different kitchens seems an extravagance in an island only fifty miles by nineteen miles it must be remembered that distance is relative, and Martinique is mountainous, so that before the invention of the internal combustion engine, a trip from south to north was indeed a journey.

In Trinidad, Indians, again mostly from Bengal, make up about a third of the population. There is a whole world of Indian cooking on this island, differing subtly from the original, and embracing both Moslem and Hindu.

curry powder *st kitts*

1 oz. coriander seeds
2 oz. cumin seeds
1 tablespoon poppy seeds
1 tablespoon cloves
1 tablespoon mustard seeds,
   preferably brown

1 oz. peppercorns
2 oz. ground turmeric
1 oz. ground ginger,
   preferably Jamaican

Toast the coriander, cumin, cloves, peppercorns, poppy and mustard seeds in a heavy iron frying pan until the mustard seeds begin to jump about. Grind in a mortar or in an electric blender, and mix with the turmeric and ginger. Put through a fine sieve and store in a glass jar. Makes about 8 oz. As a general rule use 1 tablespoon of curry powder for each 2 lb. of meat or poultry, rather less for fish and shellfish.

poudre de colombo

⅛ teaspoon turmeric
1 teaspoon ground coriander
1 teaspoon ground mustard
   seeds

3 cloves garlic, crushed
2 fresh hot red peppers,
   seeded and mashed

Combine all the ingredients and mix to a paste. Use as directed for Colombo de Poulet (Chicken Curry). This amount is enough for a curry made from chicken, pork, kid, lamb, fish or shellfish to serve 6 to 8.

colombo de poulet *martinique–guadeloupe*

Chicken Curry

3½ lb. chicken, cut into
  serving pieces
4 tablespoons peanut or
  coconut oil
2 medium onions, finely
  chopped
2 cloves garlic, crushed
1 or 2 tablespoons curry
  powder, or 1 recipe Poudre
  de Colombo
1 tablespoon tamarind pulp
  (see Glossary)
1 green mango, peeled and
  coarsely chopped
½ lb. West Indian pumpkin,
  peeled and sliced
½ lb. green papaya, peeled
  and sliced (optional)

½ lb. aubergine, peeled and
  sliced
1 christophene (chayote),
  peeled and sliced
1 lb. dasheen (taro), peeled
  and sliced, or use white
  tropical yam
⅜ pint dry white wine, or
  coconut milk, if liked
⅜ pint chicken stock
1 or more fresh, hot peppers,
  seeded and chopped
1 teaspoon lime juice
Salt
2 tablespoons dry Madeira,
  or *rhum vieux*

Heat the oil in a heavy frying pan and sauté the chicken pieces
lightly on both sides. Transfer to a heavy casserole, earthenware* if possible. In the oil remaining in the pan, sauté the
onions until golden. Add the garlic and curry powder or Poudre
de Colombo and cook, stirring from time to time, for 3 or 4
minutes. Transfer to the casserole. Add all the remaining ingredients, except the lime juice. Cover and simmer gently until
the chicken is tender and the vegetables done. Add salt to taste,
and stir in the lime juice. Just before serving stir in the Madeira
or *rhum vieux*. Serve with Riz Créole. Serves 6 to 8.

As a rule the Colombo is extremely spicy and hot. For non-

*If using earthenware make sure it is heavy enough not to crack
over direct heat. Use one or more asbestos mats if necessary.

Caribbean people, or those not accustomed to this sort of dish, the amount of fresh hot pepper could be reduced.

le caneton aux ananas   *guadeloupe*

Duckling with Pineapple

4½ lb. ready-to-cook duckling
Salt, freshly ground pepper
1 oz. unsalted butter
¼ pint dark rum
¼ pint unsweetened pineapple
    juice, fresh if possible

½ pint stock made from neck,
    giblets and liver of
    duckling
¾ lb. chopped fresh, or
    unsweetened tinned,
    pineapple
2 teaspoons arrowroot

Pull any loose fat from the cavity of the duckling, and prick all over the fatty parts with a fork. Season with salt and pepper. Heat the butter in a heavy casserole large enough to hold the duckling comfortably. Brown the bird all over, lift out, and discard all the fat. Return the duckling to the casserole with 6 tablespoons of the rum and 6 tablespoons of pineapple juice. Cover and cook in a 325°F (gas 3) oven for 1 to 1½ hours.* Remove the duckling to a serving platter and keep it warm. Discard all the fat that has accumulated in the casserole. Add the remaining rum, stir and scrape up all the brown bits. Pour into a saucepan. Add the rest of the pineapple juice and the giblet stock, cook over brisk heat until reduced to ¾ pint. Adjust the seasoning, add the chopped pineapple and cook for 5 minutes longer, over very low heat. Mix the arrowroot with 3 tablespoons cold water and stir into the sauce. Cook just long enough to thicken lightly. Serve separately to accompany the duckling. Serves 4.

*The duckling is cooked when its juices run pale pink for medium rare, clear yellow for well done. One hour cooks the duckling to the medium rare stage.

le caneton au rhum   *guadeloupe*

Duckling with Rum

5–6 lb. ready-to-cook duckling
1 oz. unsalted butter
Salt, freshly ground pepper
1 medium onion, finely
    chopped
½ pint stock made from neck,
    giblets, liver of duckling
1 clove garlic, chopped
1 sprig parsley

¼ teaspoon each sage,
    thyme, marjoram
1 bay leaf
1 leaf bois d'inde (see Glossary,
    under Bay rum) or
3 grains melegueta pepper
    (see Glossary)
6 tablespoons dark rum

Pull any loose fat from the cavity of the duck and prick all over the fatty parts with a fork. Heat the butter in a heavy casserole large enough to hold the duck comfortably and lightly brown the bird all over. Discard all but 2 tablespoons of the fat. Season the bird with salt and pepper. Add the onion and garlic to the casserole and sauté until the onion is tender. Return the bird to the casserole with the herbs tied in a square of cheesecloth. Add the giblet stock, cover and simmer gently until the duckling is tender, about 1½ hours. Discard the *bouquet garni* and remove any fat that has accumulated. Warm the rum, pour it over the duck and flame it. Serve on a bed of Riz Créole, with the sauce separately. Serves 6.

To make the stock put the neck, giblets, liver and lower wing tips to cook with 1 pint of water. Simmer, partially covered, for 1½ hours or until the liquid is reduced to ½ pint. Season to taste with salt and pepper.

pato con piña   *dominican republic*

Duck with Pineapple

5 ½ lb. ready-to-cook duck

STUFFING

2 oz. white bread in ½-inch
  cubes
4 oz. unsalted butter
4 tablespoons finely chopped
  blanched almonds
2 finely chopped onions
2 teaspoons finely chopped
  garlic
Liver of duckling
½ lb. lean, boneless ham
  chopped into ¼-inch dice

1 tomato, peeled, seeded and
  chopped
2 tablespoons finely chopped
  parsley
2 oz. pimento-stuffed green
  olives, chopped
2 oz. seedless raisins
1 tablespoon capers
Salt, freshly ground pepper
  to taste

PINEAPPLE GARNISH

1 oz. butter
¾ lb. coarsely chopped fresh
  pineapple, or unsweetened
  tinned pineapple in its own
  juice

6 tablespoons dry white wine
3 tablespoons pineapple juice
6 tablespoons chicken stock
1 teaspoon arrowroot, mixed
  with 2 tablespoons water

TO MAKE THE STUFFING

Heat 2 oz. of the butter in a heavy frying pan and sauté the
bread cubes until crisp and golden brown. Remove with a
slotted spoon. Add the rest of the butter and sauté the almonds
for 2 or 3 minutes until golden, then add onions and garlic and
sauté stirring until the onions are tender but not brown. Add the
duck liver and cook until it is lightly browned but still pink

inside. Remove the liver, chop finely and reserve. Add the ham and tomatoes to the frying pan and cook until most of the liquid has evaporated, stirring from time to time. Remove from the heat, add the liver, parsley, olives, raisins, capers, bread cubes, salt and pepper to taste, and toss to mix.

Stuff the duck with this mixture. Truss and prick all over with a fork to release the fat. Place on a rack in a baking pan and roast in an oven preheated to 450°F (gas 8) for 20 minutes. At the end of this time remove any fat that has accumulated. Reduce oven to 250°F (gas ½) and roast for 2½ hours, removing fat as it accumulates. When the duck is cooked remove it to a warmed platter and allow it to rest. Meanwhile make the pineapple garnish. Pat the pineapple pieces dry. Pour off all the fat from the baking pan, add the butter and sauté the pineapple until lightly brown. Lift out and arrange around the duck on the platter. Pour wine, pineapple juice and stock into the pan, scraping up all the brown bits. Add the arrowroot and cook, stirring, until the sauce is lightly thickened. Pour over the pineapple or serve separately if preferred. Serves 4 to 6.

pollo a la pepitoria   *cuba*

Chicken Fricassée with Onions

This is another recipe given me by my friend Nieves Rendueles. It comes from Cuba's Oriente province, and like the recipe for Empanada de Pollo (Chicken Pie) has been handed down from early colonial times in the Rendueles family. It reminds me of Poulet Antiboise in Elizabeth David's *A Book of Mediterranean Food*, which I have cooked many times with great pleasure. The two dishes, which may have a common origin, come to table very different. The name cannot be translated literally since pepitoria means a medley of things and 'Chicken with a Medley of Things' sounds odd, and is not very enlightening.

1 3½–4 lb. chicken, cut into
   serving pieces
3 tablespoons plain flour
Salt, freshly ground pepper
4 tablespoons olive, or
   vegetable oil

2 lb. Spanish onions, very
   finely sliced
Bay leaf
6 tablespoons dry white wine
2 eggs, well beaten

Pat the chicken pieces dry. Season the flour with salt and pepper
and place in a plastic or paper bag. Shake the chicken pieces, one
at a time, in the bag, take out and shake again to remove any
excess flour. Heat 2 tablespoons of the oil in a large, heavy,
frying pan and sauté the chicken pieces until they are golden on
both sides. Transfer to a heavy casserole. If the oil in the pan is
discoloured, discard it, and wash and dry the pan. Heat the
remaining 2 tablespoons of oil in the pan, or if the oil is not
discoloured, add enough oil to bring the amount to 2 tablespoons.
Add the onions and mix well. Add a teaspoon of salt which helps
release the juice in the onions, and stir. Add the bay leaf and the
wine, and cook for 2 or 3 minutes. Pour over the chicken in the
casserole and mix gently, using a rubber spatula. Cover and
simmer for about 45 minutes, or until the chicken is tender.
Shake the pot two or three times during the first 20 minutes of
cooking to make sure the chicken does not scorch on the bottom.
The onions will release their juice, creating a sauce, as they cook
down.

Lift out the chicken pieces on to a serving dish and keep warm.
The onions should have melted into a purée. If necessary cook
them for a few minutes longer. Take out and discard the bay
leaf. Beat a cupful of the hot sauce into the eggs, a tablespoon at
a time, then pour the mixture into the casserole and cook,
stirring constantly over very low heat, until the sauce has
thickened. Do not let the sauce come to the boil as it will curdle.
Pour a little of the sauce over the chicken pieces and serve the
rest separately in a sauceboat. Serve with plain white rice. Serves
6 to 8.

pollo con lentejas y piña   *dominican republic*

Chicken with Lentils and Pineapple

2 tablespoons vegetable oil
2½ lb. frying chicken, cut
  into serving pieces
1 onion, finely chopped
1 clove garlic, chopped
1 medium-sized fresh
  pineapple, or a 20 oz. tin
  of pineapple chunks,
  unsweetened in own juice

½ teaspoon orégano
1 fresh hot pepper, seeded
  and chopped
Salt, freshly ground pepper
1 lb. brown lentils
¾ pint pineapple juice
¾ pint chicken stock

Heat the oil in a frying pan and sauté the chicken pieces lightly on both sides. Transfer to a heavy casserole. In the oil remaining in the frying pan, adding a little more if necessary, sauté the onion and garlic until the onion is tender but not browned. Transfer to the casserole together with the pineapple, peeled and cut into 1-inch cubes if fresh; if tinned, drained, but with the juice reserved. Add the orégano, the hot pepper, and salt and pepper to taste.

If using unprocessed lentils these should be picked over and soaked in cold water for several hours before cooking. They should then be cooked half an hour in plain water, drained and added to the casserole with the pineapple juice and chicken stock. Simmer, covered for 45 minutes. If using the quick cooking type, add the juice and stock to the casserole, cover and simmer for 20 minutes, then add the lentils and cook for 25 minutes longer as they tend to get mushy if overcooked. By the time the lentils and chicken are both tender, the liquid should be absorbed. Serve from the casserole. Serves 4.

pollo con uvas   *dominican republic*

Chicken with Grapes

2½ lb. chicken, quartered
3 large cloves garlic, crushed
Salt, freshly ground pepper
1½ oz. unsalted butter
1 large onion, finely
  chopped
1 bay leaf
5 tablespoons dry white wine

5 tablespoons dry red wine
½ pint chicken stock
4 oz. pitted prunes, halved
3 oz. pimento-stuffed green
  olives
1 lb. seedless white grapes
2 teaspoons arrowroot, or
  potato flour

Season the chicken pieces with the garlic, and salt and pepper to taste. Allow to stand for about half an hour. Heat the butter in a heavy casserole and sauté the chicken pieces, 2 at a time, until lightly golden on both sides, and set aside. Add the onion to the butter remaining in the casserole and sauté until tender but not browned. Return the chicken pieces to the casserole. Add the bay leaf, both wines, the chicken stock and the prunes. Cover and simmer gently for half an hour. Cut the olives in halves cross-wise and add to the casserole with the grapes. Cover and cook for 15 minutes longer, or until the chicken is tender. Lift out the chicken onto a serving platter and keep it warm. Dissolve the arrowroot in cold water and stir into the casserole. Cook, stirring, until the sauce is lightly thickened. Pour the sauce over the chicken pieces and serve with rice or a starchy vegetable. Serves 4.

pollo con piña a la antigua   *cuba*

Chicken with Pineapple in the Old Style

Juice and grated rind 1 large
lime
3½–4 lb. chicken, cut into
serving pieces
Salt, freshly ground pepper
to taste
3 tablespoons olive oil
1 medium onion, chopped
1 clove garlic, chopped
2 very ripe tomatoes, peeled
and coarsely chopped

3 tablespoons seedless raisins
1 fresh hot pepper,
preferably red, seeded and
chopped
¼ teaspoon orégano
1 bay leaf
½ pint rich chicken stock,
about
¾ lb. coarsely chopped fresh
pineapple and juice
4 tablespoons golden rum

Rub the lime juice and rind into the chicken pieces, season with
salt and pepper, and let stand for half an hour. Heat the oil in a
frying pan and sauté the chicken pieces until just coloured.
Transfer them to a heavy casserole large enough to hold them
comfortably, in layers. In the oil remaining in the pan sauté the
onion and garlic until the onion is tender but not browned, add
the tomatoes, raisins, hot pepper, orégano and bay leaf and cook,
stirring occasionally for 5 minutes or so to blend the flavours.
Pour over the chicken in the casserole and add enough chicken
stock barely to cover. Partially cover the casserole and cook over
low heat until the chicken is tender, about 45 minutes.

Put the pineapple and any juice in a small saucepan and cook
until reduced to half. Add the rum, mix thoroughly and cook for
a minute or two. Pour over the chicken and cook 5 minutes
longer. Serves 6.

pollo en escabeche
dominican republic and spanish-speaking islands

Pickled Chicken

3 ½ lb. chicken, cut into
   serving pieces
Salt, freshly ground pepper
3 medium onions, thinly
   sliced
6 large cloves garlic

1 fresh hot green pepper,
   left whole
Bay leaf
1 teaspoon orégano
½ pint olive oil
¼ pint white wine vinegar

Season the chicken pieces with salt and pepper, and place in a heavy casserole with the onions and garlic. Tie the hot pepper, bay leaf and orégano in a small square of cheesecloth and add to the casserole. Pour the oil and vinegar over the chicken, cover and simmer gently for 30 minutes. If the onions are very watery, continue cooking, with the casserole partially covered, to reduce the sauce, for 15 minutes longer, or until the chicken is tender. Otherwise continue cooking with the casserole covered as before. Remove and discard the cheesecloth bag before serving. Serve with plain white rice, or any plainly cooked starchy vegetable. This is equally good served cold. Refrigerate and serve with the jellied sauce, lettuce, sliced tomato, radishes, avocado, and olives. Serves 6.

pollo en salsa
de almendras y avellanas
dominican republic

Chicken in Almond and Hazelnut Sauce

3 ½ lb. chicken, cut into
   serving pieces
Flour

Salt, freshly ground pepper
3 tablespoons olive oil

1 medium onion, finely
  chopped
1 whole head garlic,
  blanched and peeled
2 large tomatoes, peeled,
  seeded and chopped
Grated rind ½ lime, or
  lemon

3 oz. blanched almonds
3 oz. hazelnuts
2 slices white bread toasted
¾ pint chicken stock
1 whole fresh or tinned hot
  pepper
Liver of the chicken
2 tablespoons dry sherry

Dip the chicken pieces into flour seasoned with salt and pepper.
Shake to remove the excess. Heat the oil in a frying pan and
sauté the chicken pieces until golden on both sides. Transfer to a
heavy casserole. In the oil remaining in the pan sauté the onion
and garlic cloves until the onion is tender but not browned,
taking care not to let the garlic burn. Add to the casserole with
the tomatoes and grated lime peel.

Pulverize the almonds in an electric blender at high speed.
Spread the hazelnuts on a baking sheet and toast in a 350°F
(gas 4) oven for 15 minutes. Then drop them into a bowl of boiling water, drain immediately and rub off the skins in a kitchen
towel. Break the toast into small pieces and pulverize in the
blender. Pulverize the hazelnuts in the blender at high speed.
Add the nuts and toast crumbs to the casserole with the chicken
stock and the hot pepper, stir to mix, cover and simmer gently
until the chicken is tender, about 45 minutes. Shake or stir the
casserole mixture from time to time during the cooking to
prevent the sauce catching.

Transfer the chicken pieces to a serving platter and keep it
warm. Remove the hot pepper. Skim off any grease from the
sauce and strain the sauce through a fine sieve. Return it to the
casserole. Push the raw chicken liver through a sieve and stir
into the sauce. Add the sherry and cook for a minute or two
longer. Pour over the chicken pieces and serve with plain white
rice, or any plainly boiled root vegetable. Serves 6.

poulet à la créole   *haiti*

Chicken Creole Style

Though this very simple, very good chicken dish is labelled Créole, its influences are clearly Asian, perhaps brought by the French from India, or perhaps it is Burmese influence making its way into the Caribbean via what was French Indo-China.

3½–4 lb. chicken, cut into
   serving pieces
6 tablespoons peanut oil
4 large onions, finely chopped
2 teaspoons curry powder
¼ teaspoon powdered saffron

2 very hot fresh peppers,
   preferably red, seeded and
   finely chopped
Salt, freshly ground pepper
   to taste
¾ pint coconut milk

Heat the oil in a heavy frying pan and sauté the chicken pieces until golden on both sides. Transfer to a heavy, covered casserole. In the oil remaining in the pan sauté the onions until tender but not browned, add the curry powder, saffron, and hot peppers and cook for 3 or 4 minutes longer. Add to the chicken. Season to taste with salt and pepper, add the coconut milk, cover and simmer until the chicken is tender, about 45 minutes. Serve with rice. Serves 6.

poulet farci   *haiti*

Stuffed Chicken

3 tablespoons vegetable
   shortening
3 oz. freshly made coarse
   bread crumbs
Salt, freshly ground pepper
   to taste

¼ teaspoon cayenne pepper
Juice and grated rind of 1
   large lime
1 teaspoon brown sugar
¼ teaspoon grated nutmeg
6 tablespoons dark dry rum

3½–4 lb. chicken
3 or 4 bananas peeled and
  chopped

2 oz. butter
⅜ pint chicken stock

Heat the shortening and fry the bread crumbs until golden. Drain. Season the breadcrumbs with salt, pepper and cayenne. Add the lime juice (reserve a few drops) and rind, sugar, nutmeg and 2 tablespoons of rum, mixing to a stiff paste. Stuff this paste into the chicken breast cavity, lifting skin over breast to do so. Season the bananas with salt, pepper, a few drops of lime and a sprinkle of rum. Stuff the cavity of the bird with the bananas and insert a crumpled piece of aluminium foil into the tail end to prevent the banana oozing out during the cooking. Truss the bird, set it on a rack in a roasting pan. Roast in a preheated 350°F (gas 4) oven for 1 hour and 20 minutes, basting with butter every 15 minutes.

Remove trussing strings and set bird on a serving platter. Keep it warm. Add the stock to the juices in the pan together with 1 tablespoon of rum. Set over high heat, stirring and scraping up all the brown bits. Cook until the gravy is slightly reduced. Adjust seasoning, and pour gravy into a sauceboat. Just before serving heat the remaining rum, pour over the bird, and set aflame. Serves 6.

pavo relleno   *puerto rico*

Stuffed Turkey

3 tablespoons salt
3 cloves garlic, crushed
¼ teaspoon freshly ground
  pepper

3 tablespoons olive oil
1 tablespoon cider vinegar
8–9 lb. ready-to-cook turkey

Mix salt, garlic, pepper, oil and vinegar together and rub the bird thoroughly, inside and out. Cover loosely with foil and refrigerate for at least 8 hours, or overnight.

STUFFING

½ lb. firm white bread
½ pint chicken stock
2 oz. butter
4 tablespoons blanched
almonds, coarsely chopped
2 tablespoons vegetable oil
1 medium onion, finely
chopped
1 lb. lean boneless pork,
minced

¾ lb. lean, boneless ham,
coarsely chopped
6 tablespoons dry sherry
1 teaspoon finely crumbled
bay leaf
Salt, freshly ground pepper
to taste
4 oz. unsalted butter, melted

Cut the crusts off the bread and tear it into ½-inch pieces. Place bread in a large bowl and pour the chicken stock over it. Mix well and set aside.

Heat the 2 oz. of butter in a heavy frying pan and sauté the almonds, stirring constantly, until they are golden. Lift out with a slotted spoon and add to the bread.

Add the vegetable oil to the butter remaining in the frying pan, and sauté the onion until it is tender but not browned. Add the minced pork, mashing with a fork to break up any lumps. Cook until the meat has lost all trace of pink. Add the contents of the frying pan to the bread mixture together with the ham, sherry, bay leaf, salt and pepper, and mix gently but thoroughly.

Stuff the turkey with the mixture, close the vent with foil or with metal skewers, then truss the bird. Brush all over with about 2 tablespoons of the melted butter then place on a rack in a roasting pan and roast in a preheated 350°F (gas 4) oven, un-covered, basting frequently, and allowing 25 minutes to the pound. To test for doneness, pierce the thigh joint with a fork. If the juice runs clear the bird is done. If it runs red roast for 5 minutes longer and test again. Do not overcook turkey as this makes the meat dry and flavourless. Serves 8 to 10.

pelau

Chicken and Rice Stew

All the pilaus and pelaus in the Caribbean have a common origin, having been introduced by Moslems from India. This one is simple, but very pleasant.

1½ oz. unsalted butter
3½–4 lb. chicken, cut into
  serving pieces
2 medium onions, finely
  chopped
1 clove garlic, chopped
Sprig thyme, or ½ teaspoon
  dried thyme
2 or 3 sprigs parsley
Bay leaf
1 sprig celery with leaves

1 small fresh hot red pepper,
  or 1 hot dried pepper
1 lb. tomatoes peeled and
  chopped, or use 1 medium
  tin tomatoes
Salt, freshly ground pepper
  to taste
Chicken stock
¾ lb. rice
10 oz. package frozen green
  peas, thawed

Heat the butter in a heavy, covered frying pan large enough to hold the chicken pieces comfortably. Sauté the chicken pieces until golden brown. Remove from the pan and set aside.

In the same pan sauté the onions and garlic until tender but not browned. Return the chicken pieces to the pan. Tie the thyme, parsley, bay leaf, celery and hot pepper in a small square of cheesecloth, and add to the pan with the tomatoes, and salt and pepper to taste. Add enough chicken stock barely to cover. Simmer gently, covered, for 30 minutes. Remove the chicken pieces from the pan. Strain the stock and discard the cheesecloth bag. Bring the quantity of stock up to 1½ pints. Return the chicken pieces to the pan, add the stock, stir in the rice, cover and cook for 15 minutes. Add the peas, cover and continue cooking for about 10 minutes longer, or until the rice is tender and all the liquid is absorbed. Serves 6 to 8.

pavo guisado   *dominican republic*

Turkey Stew

8–8½ lb. turkey, cut into
  serving pieces
4 cloves garlic, crushed
Salt, freshly ground pepper
2 tablespoons red wine
  vinegar
6 tablespoons vegetable oil
5 tablespoons tomato purée
¾ pint chicken or turkey
  stock

½ pint dry red wine
1 green bell pepper, seeded
  and chopped
24 pitted green olives
4 tablespoons capers
1 lb. potatoes, peeled and
  sliced
10 oz. package frozen peas,
  thawed

Season the turkey pieces with a mixture of the garlic, salt and
pepper to taste, and the vinegar. Leave for 1 hour. Heat the oil
in a heavy casserole large enough to hold the turkey and sauté
the pieces 2 or 3 at a time until lightly browned. Add any of the
marinade that remains. Add the tomato purée, stock, wine and
pepper, cover and cook for 1 hour. Add the olives, capers and
potatoes and cook for half an hour longer, or until both the
potatoes and turkey are tender. Add the peas and cook 5 to 7
minutes longer. Serves 8 to 10.

sancocho de pollo   *dominican republic*

Chicken and Vegetable Stew

5 lb. chicken, cut into serving
  pieces
3 tablespoons Seville orange
  juice
1 lb. cassava root, peeled and
  cut into 1-inch slices

6 pints chicken stock, or
  half stock, half water
3 green plantains
3 tablespoons lime juice
1½ lb. West Indian pumpkin
  (calabaza) peeled and cubed

4 cloves garlic, crushed
1 large onion, finely chopped
1 teaspoon orégano
2 fresh hot red or green
   peppers, seeded and
   chopped, or Tabasco to
   taste
3 grains melegueta pepper
   (see Glossary)
2 or 3 sprigs each of parsley
   and fresh coriander
1 lb. potatoes, peeled,
   and cut into 1-inch slices
1 lb. yam, peeled and cut
   into 1-inch slices

1 lb. sweet potatoes,
   preferably white, peeled
   and cut into 1-inch slices
1 lb. each of white and
   yellow yautía, peeled and
   cut into 1-inch slices
3 ears sweet corn, cut into
   1-inch slices
Salt, freshly ground pepper
   to taste
1 small cabbage, cut into 6
   wedges
2 tablespoons cider vinegar

Wash the chicken in the orange juice and put into a heavy casserole big enough to hold all the ingredients. Add the cassava root and the chicken stock, bring to the boil, reduce the heat to a bare simmer and cook, covered, for 1 hour.

Peel the plantains using a paring-knife as the skin will not come off readily, and cut into 1-inch slices. Pour the lime juice over the plantain pieces and set aside.

Add all the other ingredients, except the vinegar and the cabbage to the pan. The pumpkin will disintegrate, thickening the sauce lightly. Drain the plantains, and add. Simmer for half an hour. Add the cabbage and cook 5 to 10 minutes longer, or until the cabbage is done. Add the vinegar and cook for a minute or two more.

Taste for seasoning and check that all the ingredients are done. When serving cut the cabbage wedges crosswise in halves. Serve in large, rimmed soup plates with a hot pepper sauce on the side. Serves 10 to 12.

poulet aux pruneaux   *martinique*

Chicken with Prunes

4 lb. roasting chicken
10 oz. pitted prunes, halved
10 oz. seedless raisins
½ pint Martinique *rhum
vieux,* or use a dark rum
4 oz. sausage meat

2 large apples, peeled, cored
and chopped
1 medium onion, finely
chopped
Salt, freshly ground pepper
1 oz. butter, melted

Allow the chicken to come to room temperature. Combine the
prunes and raisins in a bowl, add the rum and allow to stand for
2 hours. Then add the sausage meat, apples, onion, and salt and
pepper to taste, mixing well. Stuff the chicken with the prune
mixture and truss. Place in a baking pan with any remaining
stuffing wrapped in aluminium foil. Roast in a 350°F (gas 4)
oven, basting with the butter every 15 minutes. Roast 1½ hours,
or until the juices run clear when the chicken is pierced with a
fork in the thickest part of the leg. Remove the trussing string,
transfer chicken to a hot platter. Serve with the extra stuffing,
and Riz Créole. Serves 4 to 6.

vegetables and salads

alu talkari

trinidad

Potato Curry

4 tablespoons coconut, or
  vegetable, oil
1 tablespoon fenugreek
  (optional)
2 cloves garlic, finely
  chopped
2 tablespoons massala (curry
  powder or paste)

2 lb. potatoes, peeled and
  sliced
1 small green mango, peeled
  and sliced (optional)
Salt
½ pint water

Heat the oil in a heavy frying pan or saucepan and add the
fenugreek, if liked, and the garlic cloves. Cook over medium heat
stirring with a wooden spoon, until the garlic is dark brown.
Lift out, and discard the fenugreek and garlic. Add the massala
to the pan and cook, stirring, for 3 or 4 minutes. Add the potatoes,
the green mango slices, if liked, salt to taste and the water.
Cover and simmer until the potatoes are tender. If necessary,
add a little water during the cooking, but the finished dish
should be quite dry. This is very good as a stuffing for Roti (see
Index), one of which makes a light lunch, supper or snack.
Serves 4.

ackee soufflé   *jamaica*

1½ oz. unsalted butter
3 tablespoons plain flour
⅜ pint milk
½ teaspoon salt
¼ teaspoon white pepper

1 teaspoon Worcestershire
  sauce
4 egg yolks
1 cup tinned ackees, mashed
  to a purée
5 egg whites, stiffly beaten

Melt the butter in a heavy saucepan and stir in the flour. Cook
stirring constantly with a wooden spoon for a minute or two,
without letting the flour brown. Heat the milk and add all at
once to the flour mixture. Cook, stirring until thick and smooth.
Add the salt, pepper, and Worcestershire sauce. Remove from
the heat and allow to cool a little.

Stir in the egg yolks one by one. Stir in the ackee purée. Stir
in about a quarter of the egg whites, then fold in the rest,
gently but thoroughly. Pour into a buttered 2½-pint soufflé dish
mould. Bake in a 375°F (gas 5) oven for about 30 minutes or until
the soufflé is firm. Serves 4.

acrats d'aubergine   *martinique–guadeloupe*

Aubergine Fritters

1½ lb. aubergines
1 egg, well beaten
2 tablespoons milk
Salt, freshly ground pepper

⅛ teaspoon cayenne
4 oz. plain flour
1 teaspoon baking powder
Oil for deep frying

Peel the aubergines and cut into 1-inch cubes. Cook in boiling
salted water until tender, about 15 minutes. Drain thoroughly
and mash into a smooth purée. Add the egg, milk, salt, pepper
and cayenne, mixing well. Sift baking powder with the flour
and beat in the flour tablespoon by tablespoon into the aubergine

mixture until it is smooth and light. Deep fry by tablespoons in oil heated to 375°F on a frying thermometer until golden brown. Serve hot as an accompaniment to drinks, or as a vegetable with meat, fish or poultry. Makes about 18 fritters.

acrats de chou palmiste *martinique–guadeloupe*

Palm Heart Fritters

14 oz. tin palm hearts, drained and coarsely chopped
4 oz. plain flour
1 teaspoon baking powder
1 teaspoon salt
2 eggs, lightly beaten
1 medium onion, finely chopped
1 clove garlic, minced

2 fresh hot red or green peppers, seeded and chopped
1 tablespoon parsley, chopped
½ teaspoon thyme, crumbled
Salt, freshly ground pepper to taste
3 tablespoons milk, if necessary
Oil for deep frying

Sift together, into a large bowl, the flour, baking powder and salt. Stir in the eggs, onion, garlic, peppers, parsley, thyme, salt, pepper and the palm hearts, folding the ingredients lightly together to form a stiffish dough. Add the milk, if necessary. Allow the batter to stand for about 1 hour, then deep fry by tablespoons in oil heated to 350°F to 375°F on a frying thermometer until golden brown. Drain on paper towels, keep warm and serve as a first course, or as an accompaniment to drinks. Makes about 24 fritters. Serves 6.

arroz blanco   *dominican republic*

White Rice

2 cups long-grain rice
Juice 1 large lime
3 cups water

1 teaspoon salt
3 tablespoons peanut oil

Wash the rice thoroughly. Drain, cover with cold water, add the lime juice and allow to stand for 2 or 3 minutes. Drain. Pour the water into a heavy saucepan with a tight-fitting lid, add the salt, bring to the boil and pour in the rice. Stir, bring back to the boil, cover, lower the heat and cook for 10 minutes. Stir the oil into the rice, cover and cook on the lowest possible heat until the rice is tender. Serves 6.

arroz con ajo   *cuba*

Garlic Rice

2 oz. unsalted butter
2 cloves garlic, crushed
2 cups long-grain rice

4 cups chicken stock
Salt, white pepper to taste

Heat the butter in a heavy saucepan, add the garlic, stir, add the rice, and cook, stirring constantly, until the butter has been absorbed. Take care not to let the rice brown. Add the stock, season to taste, cover, bring to the boil then reduce the heat as low as possible and cook until the rice is tender and all the liquid absorbed, 20 to 30 minutes. Serves 6.

arroz con frijoles   *dominican republic*

Rice with Beans

1⅜ pints coconut milk (see Index)

2 oz. boiled ham, coarsely chopped

1 fresh hot pepper, seeded and chopped

3 cloves garlic, minced

2 medium tomatoes, peeled, seeded and chopped

1 tablespoon fresh coriander, chopped

Salt to taste

¾ lb. long-grain rice

4 oz. cooked red kidney beans

Put 6 tablespoons of coconut milk into a heavy saucepan with a tight-fitting lid. Add the ham, hot pepper, garlic, tomatoes, coriander and salt to taste. Cook, stirring, over low heat for 3 or 4 minutes or until the mixture is well blended. Stir in the rice, the beans and the remaining coconut milk. Stir gently, then cover and cook over low heat until the rice is tender and the liquid absorbed. Serves 6 to 8 as a side dish, or 4 if served with a salad, as a main course.

asparagus pudding   *u.s. virgin islands*

This recipe is of Danish origin and is a good example of the pluralist nature of Caribbean cooking. Both foods and cooking methods illustrate the history of the islands.

4 oz. unsalted butter, plus butter for mould

2 oz. plain flour

Salt, white pepper

6 tablespoons liquid from tinned asparagus

6 tablespoons milk

1 teaspoon onion juice

8 eggs

19 oz. tin asparagus, cut into ½-inch pieces

Thickly butter a covered 1½-pint mould. In a heavy saucepan melt the butter over low heat, stir in the flour and cook, stirring for 2 minutes without letting the flour colour. Add salt, pepper, asparagus liquid, milk, and onion juice. Stir over low heat to make a smooth, thick sauce. Off the heat beat in the eggs, one by one. Carefully fold in the asparagus. Pour in the mould. Cover the mould and set it in a large pan with hot water coming about halfway up the mould. Cover the pan and steam on top of the stove for about 30 minutes, or until firm. Add a little boiling water to the pan during cooking, if necessary. Serve with Lemon Butter Sauce, or Curry Sauce (see Index). Serves 6.

Fresh or frozen asparagus may be used for this dish. If using frozen asparagus thoroughly defrost 2 10 oz. packages, and cut into ½-inch pieces. If using fresh asparagus, cut the tough ends off 1½ lb. asparagus, peel and cook in boiling salted water for 12 to 15 minutes. Drain thoroughly and cut into ½-inch pieces. Use ½ pint milk to make up the liquid.

berehein na forno   *st maarten*

Aubergine in Coconut Cream

1 large aubergine, weighing
   about 1 lb.
½ oz. butter, softened
3 large onions, finely
   chopped
1 teaspoon dried hot red
   peppers, crumbled, or

1 fresh hot red pepper,
   seeded and chopped
Salt, freshly ground pepper
¾ pint coconut cream (see
   Index)

Peel the aubergine and slice thinly. Butter an oven-proof dish and arrange the aubergine slices in it. Cover with the onions, sprinkle with the peppers, season to taste with salt and pepper and pour the coconut cream over it. Cover the dish with a lid, or with foil, and bake in a 350°F (gas 4) oven for 45 minutes. Uncover and bake for 10 minutes longer. Serves 4 to 6.

baked pawpaw   *jamaica*

Papaya is known as pawpaw in Jamaica. When ripe it is eaten as a fruit, when unripe as a vegetable.

1 green (unripe) papaya,
  weighing about 5 lb.
2 oz. unsalted butter
1 large onion, finely chopped

2 medium tomatoes, peeled
  and chopped
Salt, freshly ground pepper
3 oz. bread crumbs
2 oz. grated Parmesan cheese

Cut the unpeeled papaya in half, lengthwise. Scoop out and discard the seeds. Drop the fruit into boiling salted water and cook until tender, 15 to 20 minutes. Lift out and drain. Carefully scoop out the flesh, reserving the shells. Heat 1 oz. butter in a frying pan and sauté the onion until tender but not browned. Add the tomatoes, salt and pepper to taste and the papaya mashed. Mix thoroughly. Stuff the shells with the mixture, sprinkle with the bread crumbs and cheese, and dot with the remaining butter. Bake in a 400°F (gas 6) oven on a baking sheet until the tops are browned. Serves 6.

VARIATION: Boiled papaya is also popular as a vegetable. Choose a green (unripe) papaya weighing 2–3 lb. Wash, peel and slice it crosswise. Remove and discard the seeds. Put it into a saucepan with enough salted water to cover. Cover and simmer 15 minutes or until tender. Serve with melted butter and freshly ground pepper. Serves 4 to 6.

banane jaune avec sauce blanche   *martinique*

Green Bananas with White Sauce

3 large green plantains, or 6
    fairly small green bananas
1 ½ oz. unsalted butter
3 tablespoons plain flour
⅝ pint milk

Salt, white pepper to taste
⅛ teaspoon grated nutmeg
2 oz. grated gruyère cheese
    (optional)

Peel the plantains or bananas by cutting through the skin
lengthwise with a sharp knife in 3 places, then peeling off the
skin. Cut the plantains in half cross-wise. The bananas should
be left whole. Put into a saucepan with salted water to cover and
cook until tender, about 30 minutes for the plantains, 15
minutes for bananas.

Heat the butter in a small saucepan and stir in the flour. Cook
stirring constantly with a wooden spoon for a minute or two.
Heat the milk and pour all at once into the butter–flour mixture.
Cook, stirring until the sauce is smooth and thick. Season to taste
with salt and pepper; add the nutmeg. Arrange the bananas or
plantains in a serving dish and pour the sauce over them. Serves 6.

2 oz. grated gruyère cheese may be added to the white sauce,
stirred in with the seasonings.

breadfruit stuffed
with salt fish and ackee   *jamaica*

1 recipe Salt Fish and Ackee
1 breadfruit, peeled, or

1 lb. 10 oz. tin breadfruit,
    drained and mashed
Butter

If using fresh breadfruit, rub the breadfruit with butter and
wrap in aluminium foil. While preparing the salt fish and ackee,
bake the breadfruit in a 350°F (gas 4) oven until tender, about
45 minutes. Allow to cool a little. Remove the core and, if

necessary a little of the flesh from the stem end. Stuff with the fish mixture. Rub more butter on the outside and return to the oven for about 15 minutes, or until heated through. If using tinned breadfruit, line a buttered casserole with the mashed breadfruit, fill with the fish mixture, and top with more breadfruit. Dot with butter and bake in a 350°F (gas 4) oven for 30 minutes, or until heated through. Serves 6.

Breadfruit may also be stuffed with the filling used for Deep Dish Meat Pie, St Thomas, either of the Cuban Picadillos, or the beef filling for Keshy Yena, Curaçao. Run Down, Jamaica, can also be used. (See recipes in Index.)

chou palmiste en sauce blanche   *martinique–guadeloupe*

Palm Hearts in White Sauce

2 14 oz. tins palm hearts
1 ½ oz. sweet butter
3 tablespoons plain flour
½ pint milk

3 tablespoons double cream
Salt, white pepper to taste
2 oz. freshly grated
· Parmesan or gruyère cheese

Heat the palm hearts in their own liquid. Drain thoroughly and chop coarsely. Place in a buttered oven-proof dish.

Meanwhile melt the butter in a small saucepan, stir in the flour and cook over low heat, stirring constantly for about a minute. Heat the milk and cream together and pour on to the butter–flour mixture, stirring constantly until smooth. Season to taste with salt and pepper and pour over the palm hearts. Top with the grated cheese and run under the grill until the cheese is lightly browned. Serves 6.

VARIATION: Heat the palm hearts, cut into lengthwise pieces and serve with a freshly made tomato sauce and freshly grated Parmesan or gruyère cheese.

concombre en daube   *martinique*
Stewed Cucumbers

3 medium-sized cucumbers
3 tablespoons olive, or
   vegetable, oil
1 medium onion, finely
   chopped

1 lb. tomatoes, peeled and
   chopped
Salt, freshly ground pepper
Pinch sugar

Peel the cucumbers and cut into halves, lengthwise. Scrape out
the seeds and cut the cucumbers into 1-inch crosswise slices. Set
aside. Heat the oil in a saucepan and sauté the onion until tender,
but not browned. Add the tomatoes, salt and pepper to taste, and
sugar. Add the cucumbers, stir to mix, cover and simmer very
gently for 45 minutes. Serves 6.

concombres en salade   *martinique*
Cucumber Salad

2 medium-sized cucumbers
1 teaspoon salt
1 large clove garlic, crushed
1 tablespoon lime, or lemon
   juice

1 or 2 teaspoons fresh hot
   pepper, seeded and finely
   chopped

Peel the cucumbers and cut into halves lengthwise. Scrape out
the seeds. Chop the cucumbers coarsely and mix with the salt.
Allow to stand for 10   minutes, then drain thoroughly. Toss
with the garlic, lime juice and hot pepper. Serves 4.

COO-COO

Though Coo-Coo is traditionally credited to Barbados, it turns up in a great many islands including Jamaica, Trinidad, and Tobago. In the Netherlands Antilles and the Virgin Islands it is called Funchi or Fungi, and is cooked without the okras, sometimes even without butter, though this produces a rather dull dish. There is also a sweet Fungi, popular in the Virgin Islands (see Breads, Puddings and Desserts).

Coo-Coo in Barbados is served with the island speciality, steamed flying fish, but is also served in other islands as a starchy vegetable with any meat or fish, and sometimes with tomato sauce. The word coo-coo means a cooked side dish, and in addition to corn meal coo-coo there are Breadfruit Coo-Coo, an interesting corn meal and coconut version from Grenada, and one from Trinidad made with fresh sweet corn.

Cold Coo-Coo can be cut into slices and fried in butter or vegetable oil.

breadfruit coo-coo   *barbados*

1 breadfruit about 2 lb., or a
    26 oz. tin
½ lb. salt beef, coarsely
    chopped
1 onion, finely chopped
½ teaspoon thyme
1 bay leaf

1 sprig parsley
2 or 3 stalks of chives
3 oz. unsalted butter
Salt, freshly ground pepper
    to taste
A little chicken stock

Peel the breadfruit, cut out the core, and cut up roughly. If using tinned breadfruit, drain and chop coarsely. Put on to cook with the salt beef and onion, with the thyme, bay leaf, parsley and chives tied up in a piece of cheesecloth, in enough water to cover. Cook until breadfruit is tender. Drain, remove and discard *bouquet garni* and mash in 2 oz. of the butter, over very low heat, adding a little chicken stock if necessary to achieve a smooth mixture with the consistency of rather stiff mashed potatoes. Season to taste with salt and pepper. Turn into a buttered basin to mould, then turn out onto a warmed serving platter. Garnish with the remaining butter. Serves 6 as a vegetable dish.

COO-COO   *barbados*

12 small, young okras
2½ pints water
Salt to taste

8 oz. yellow corn meal
1½ oz. unsalted butter

Wash the okras, cut off stems and slice crosswise, about ¼-inch thick. Bring the water to the boil, add salt and okras and cook, covered, for 10 minutes. Pour the corn meal into the water and okras in a slow steady stream, stirring with a wooden spoon. Cook, stirring constantly, over medium heat until the mixture is thick and smooth, about five minutes. Turn into a greased basin to mould, then turn out onto a warmed serving platter and spread the butter on top, or turn out directly onto a warmed platter without moulding. Serve hot. Serves 6 as a vegetable dish.

COO-COO   *tobago*

12 small, young okras
2½ pints chicken, or beef, stock
Salt to taste
8 oz. yellow corn meal
1 oz. unsalted butter

1 lb. sweet potatoes, peeled, cooked and sliced
2 medium tomatoes, peeled and sliced
2 pimentos, sliced
Lettuce for garnish

Wash the okras, cut off stems and slice crosswise, about ¼-inch thick. Bring the stock to the boil, add salt to taste, and add okras, and cook, covered, for 10 minutes. Pour the corn meal into the water and okras in a slow, steady stream, stirring with a wooden spoon. Cook, stirring constantly, over medium heat until the mixture is thick and smooth, about five minutes. Put the butter into a warmed basin, add the coo-coo and shake until it forms a ball and absorbs the butter. Turn onto a warmed serving platter and decorate with the sweet potatoes, tomatoes, pimentos and lettuce. Serves 6.

corn and coconut coo-coo   *grenada*

1½ pints freshly made   Salt to taste
  coconut milk (see Index)   8 oz. yellow corn meal

Put the coconut milk on to boil with salt to taste in a heavy saucepan. When boiling pour in the corn meal in a slow, steady stream, stirring constantly with a wooden spoon. Cook until the mixture is thick and smooth. Serves 6 as a vegetable dish.

lavina's codfish coo-coo   *jamaica*

1 oz. lard or butter   1 fresh hot red or green
2 oz. ham or bacon, chopped   pepper, seeded and
1½ pints water   chopped
8 oz. yellow corn meal   Salt to taste
1 lb. cooked, shredded salt
  codfish

Heat the lard in a large saucepan. Fry the ham or bacon in it, add the water and bring to a rolling boil. Pour in the corn meal in a slow steady stream and cook, stirring constantly with a wooden spoon over medium heat until the mixture is smooth and thick. Add the codfish and hot pepper and cook until the fish is heated through. Season to taste with salt if necessary. Serves 4 as a luncheon dish.

sweet corn coo-coo   *trinidad*

12 small young okras
¾ pint water
Salt to taste

¾ lb. fresh sweet corn, grated
1 oz. butter

Wash the okras, cut off stems and slice crosswise, about ¼ inch thick. Bring the water to the boil, add salt and okras and cook, covered, for 10 minutes. Add the corn and cook, stirring, until the mixture is thick and creamy. Stir in the butter and serve hot. Serves 6.

colombo de giraumon   *martinique–guadeloupe*

Pumpkin Curry

2 tablespoons vegetable oil
1 oz. unsalted butter
¼ lb. bacon, chopped
1 medium onion, chopped
1 bell pepper, seeded and
  chopped
1 teaspoon curry powder
¼ teaspoon ground cloves

2 medium tomatoes, peeled
  and chopped
1 lb. West Indian pumpkin
  (calabaza), peeled and cut
  into 1-inch cubes
Salt, freshly ground pepper,
  to taste
1 large clove garlic, crushed

Heat the oil and butter in a heavy saucepan, add the bacon, onion and pepper and cook, stirring from time to time, until the onion is tender but not browned. Add the curry powder and cook, stirring for a minute or two. Add the cloves, tomatoes, pumpkin, salt and pepper, stir to mix, cover and cook on the lowest possible heat, stirring occasionally to prevent the mixture from burning. When the pumpkin is very tender and almost reduced to a purée, stir in the garlic and cook, uncovered for a minute or so longer.

Serve by itself or as an accompaniment to any plainly cooked meat or poultry. Serves 6.

congris   *cuba*

Red Beans and Rice

This is the popular rice and bean dish of the eastern part of the island, a speciality of Santiago de Cuba.

1 oz. lard (see Index)
1 medium onion, finely chopped
1 clove garlic, minced
1 green bell pepper, seeded and chopped

2 medium tomatoes, peeled, seeded and chopped
Salt, freshly ground pepper to taste
8 oz. cooked red kidney beans
6 oz. raw rice
¾ pint cold water

Heat the lard in a heavy, covered casserole or saucepan, add the onion and garlic, and sauté until the onion is tender but not browned. Add the pepper and tomatoes and cook, stirring, until the mixture is thick and well blended. Season to taste with salt and pepper. Stir in the beans, mixing well. Add the rice and water, mixing lightly. Cover and cook over very low heat until the rice is tender and all the water absorbed, about 20 minutes. The rice should be fluffy and dry. Serves 4 to 6.

christophene au gratin   *martinique*

Chayote with Cheese and Onion Stuffing

3 large chayotes (see
   Glossary), each weighing
   about ¾ lb.
2½ oz. unsalted butter

1 large onion, finely chopped
Salt, freshly ground pepper
5 oz. grated Parmesan cheese

Boil the whole chayotes in salted water until tender, about 30 minutes. Remove from the saucepan, and when cool enough to handle, cut into halves lengthwise. Scoop out the pulp, including the edible seed, mash and set aside. Reserve the shells.

    Heat 1½ oz. of the butter in a frying pan and sauté the onion until tender but not browned. Add the mashed chayote pulp, salt and pepper to taste and cook, stirring, for a few minutes to dry the mixture out a little. Off the heat, add 4 oz. of cheese, stirring to mix well. Stuff the shells with the mixture, dot with the remaining butter and sprinkle with the extra cheese. Place on a baking sheet and bake in a 350°F (gas 4) oven for 15 minutes, or until the tops are lightly browned. Serve as a luncheon or supper dish. Serves 6.

VARIATION: This vegetable is also popular as a salad in Martinique. For Christophene en Salade (Chayote Salad), peel 2 large chayotes and cut lengthwise into 4 pieces. Do not remove edible seed. Boil in salted water for 20 minutes, or until tender. Drain thoroughly and when cool cut into ½-inch crosswise slices and toss gently with Sauce Vinaigrette (see Index), and 2 chopped shallots. Serve on lettuce leaves. Serves 6.

foo-foo   *trinidad–barbados*

Pounded Green Plantain Balls

3 green plantains, unpeeled   Salt

Cook the plantains in unsalted water until tender, about half an hour. When soft, peel, chop coarsely, and pound in a mortar until smooth, moistening the pestle with water from time to time as it gets sticky. Season with salt to taste, and form into small balls. Keep warm. Serve with Callaloo (see Index) or any creole soup. Serves 6.

dal   *trinidad*

Split Pea or Lentil Purée

Dal is the Hindi name for all the legumes. The spelling varies, but dal is the closest. In Trinidad, where split peas, or less popularly, brown lentils, are the favourite dal, it is also spelled dhal or dholl.

1 lb. split peas, or lentils   2 tablespoons coconut oil,
1 ½ pints water   ghee, or vegetable oil
1 teaspoon ground turmeric   2 cloves garlic, chopped
Salt   1 teaspoon cumin seeds
1 medium onion, finely
   chopped

Soak the peas or lentils overnight, unless they are the quick-cooking variety, in which case omit this step. Add the turmeric to the peas and cook, covered, at a simmer until they are tender. Season to taste with salt and stir in the onion. Remove from the heat. Heat the oil in a small pan and add the garlic and cumin. Sauté until the garlic is dark brown. Strain the oil into the peas. Stir, cover and let stand for a minute or two. Serve with boiled rice. Serves 6 to 8. The dal should have about the consistency of mashed potatoes. If it seems too watery, simmer, uncovered, for part of the cooking time.

frijoles negros   *cuba*

Black Beans

Black beans and white rice are a great favourite in Havana, either served separately, or together as Moros y Cristianos (Moors and Christians).

1 lb. black beans	1 clove garlic, minced
1½ pints cold water	1 green bell pepper, seeded
3 tablespoons olive oil	and chopped
2 oz. salt pork, chopped	1 bay leaf
1 medium onion, finely	Salt, freshly ground pepper
chopped	to taste

Wash the beans thoroughly, but do not soak them. Put them into a large saucepan with the cold water, cover and simmer gently until they are tender, about 1½ to 2 hours. Add a little hot water from time to time as necessary.

Heat the oil in a frying pan and render the salt pork. Add the onion, garlic, and pepper and sauté until the onion is tender but not browned. Add to the beans with the bay leaf and salt and pepper to taste. At this point the beans should still have quite a lot of liquid. Simmer, partially covered, for half an hour longer, stirring once or twice. Crush a spoonful or so of the beans to thicken the sauce, remove the bay leaf and serve. The beans should not be dry, but neither should the sauce be abundant. Serves 6 to 8.

VARIATION: Frijoles Colorados (Red Beans) are popular in the eastern part of Cuba. The beans most popularly used are California pink beans, or red kidney beans. They are cooked in the same way as Frijoles Negros (Black Beans) except that lard is used instead of olive oil.

daube de giraumon   *martinique–guadeloupe*

Seasoned West Indian Pumpkin

1 ½ lb. West Indian pumpkin (calabaza)
2 tablespoons plain flour
3 tablespoons vegetable oil
4 oz. salt pork, cut into ¼-inch cubes
2 cloves garlic, minced
1 tablespoon parsley, finely chopped
½ teaspoon marjoram
½ teaspoon thyme
1 bay leaf
Salt, freshly ground pepper
1 tablespoon white wine vinegar

Peel the pumpkin and cut into 1-inch cubes. Toss the pumpkin pieces in the flour, using up all the flour. Heat the oil in a heavy saucepan and add the pumpkin pieces and the salt pork. Sauté for about 10 minutes stirring from time to time. Add the garlic, parsley, marjoram, thyme, bay leaf, salt and pepper, and sauté for a minute or two longer. Add ½ pint of hot water, a little at a time, stirring occasionally, and cook with the saucepan partially covered, until the pumpkin is tender and there is a fairly thick sauce. Just before serving stir in the vinegar. Serve as a starchy vegetable with meats or poultry. Serves 6.

fried ripe plantains   *all islands*

When plantains are ripe their skins are quite black, but they must still be cooked before they can be eaten. They are served, fried, with almost any meat or fish dish in the islands, though with some dishes, such as Picadillo in Cuba, they are traditional. In Guadeloupe they are often served as a dessert, in which case they are sprinkled with sugar after they are fried, then flamed with *rhum vieux*. In French they are Bananes frites, in the Spanish-speaking islands, Plátano Frito.

| 3 large, ripe plantains | Butter, or vegetable oil |

Cut off both ends of the plantains, peel and halve lengthwise. Ripe plantains can usually be peeled as easily as ripe bananas. If there is any difficulty, cut through the skins lengthwise on the ridges, with a small, sharp knife, and peel the segments. Slice the plantains in halves crosswise, giving 12 slices in all. Heat the butter or oil in a large, heavy frying pan and sauté the pieces until browned on both sides. Drain on paper towels and serve immediately. Serves 6.

If bananas are used as a substitute, use them when they are ripe, but still firm and the skins yellow, not black.

funchi   *netherlands antilles*

Corn Meal Pudding

| 1½ pints water | 8 oz. yellow corn meal |
| 1 tablespoon salt | 2 oz. unsalted butter |

Bring the water and salt to a rolling boil, pour in the corn meal in a slow, steady stream and cook, stirring, over medium heat until the corn meal is thick and smooth, about 5 minutes. Beat in the butter, and turn out on to a warmed serving dish. Serves 6.

jug-jug   *barbados*

It is said that Jug-Jug is derived from haggis, and was created by
Scots who were exiled to Barbados after the Monmouth Rebellion
of 1685. Millet, called guinea corn in Barbados, is used for what
has become a Christmas, rather than a New Year dish, as haggis
is. If Jug-Jug is haggis transported, then like all dishes arriving
in the Caribbean it has changed a great deal from the original.

4 oz. lean corned beef, cut
   into ½-inch cubes
4 oz. lean pork, cut into
   ½-inch cubes
1 lb. fresh green pigeon peas,
   or use tinned, drained peas
   (see Glossary)
2 medium onions, finely
   chopped
1 tablespoon finely chopped
   parsley

3 stalks celery, with leaves,
   very finely chopped
½ teaspoon dried thyme,
   crumbled
2 spring onions, finely
   chopped, using green and
   white parts
2 oz. ground millet
Salt, freshly ground pepper
1½ oz. unsalted butter

Put the meats on to cook in a heavy saucepan with water to
cover and simmer, covered, for 1 hour. Add the pigeon peas, if
they are fresh, and cook until both meats and peas are tender,
about 20 minutes. If using tinned peas, add when meats are
tender and cook only long enough to heat through.

Strain the meat and pea mixture and set aside. Return the
stock to the saucepan with the onions, parsley, celery, thyme,
spring onions, millet and salt and pepper to taste. Cook for about
15 minutes over low heat, stirring constantly. Mince the meat
and pea mixture and add to the millet and cook, stirring, for 20
to 30 minutes, until the mixture is fairly stiff. Stir in 1 tablespoon of the butter. Turn the mixture out onto a warmed serving
dish and mould into a smooth shape. Spread with the rest of the
butter. Traditionally this is served as an accompaniment to ham
or roast chicken. Serves 4 to 6 according to appetite.

If fresh pigeon peas are not available, dried ones may be used. In which case use 2 cups (¾ lb.) and put them on to cook with the meats adding a little hot water during the cooking if the peas absorb the liquid too fast.

frijoles negros pascuales   *cuba*

Holiday Black Beans

1 lb. black beans
⅜ pint peanut oil
1 medium onion, finely chopped
4 cloves garlic, minced
1 fresh hot green pepper, seeded and chopped
½ teaspoon dried orégano, crumbled

½ teaspoon ground cumin
1 bay leaf
Salt to taste
3 tablespoons cider or distilled white vinegar
4 oz. jar of pimentos chopped, and juice from jar
1 tablespoon sugar, or to taste
1 tablespoon cornflour

Wash the beans thoroughly, drain, and place in a heavy, covered casserole or saucepan with 1½ pints cold water. Cover and simmer gently until the beans are tender, 1½ to 2 hours, adding a little hot water from time to time as necessary. Heat the oil in a heavy frying pan and sauté the onion, garlic and pepper until the onion is tender, but not browned. Add the orégano, cumin and bay leaf, season to taste with salt and stir into the beans, which should have quite a lot of liquid. Cook, stirring from time to time, for half an hour longer then add the vinegar, the pimentos with their juice, and the sugar. Mix the cornflour with a tablespoon of cold water and stir into the beans. Cook, stirring from time to time for 5 minutes longer. Serves 6 to 8.

These beans are particularly good served with Salsa Roja para Frijoles Negros (Red Sauce for Black Beans).

la salade de leyritz   *northern martinique*

Salad Leyritz

4 green (unripe) bananas
Salt
Vinaigrette dressing (see
  below)
1 large tomato, peeled, seeded
  and coarsely chopped

1 medium cucumber, peeled
  and coarsely chopped
6 stalks sliced celery
2 medium carrots, scraped
  and shredded
1 medium avocado, sliced
Lettuce

Peel the green bananas by cutting through the skin, lengthwise, in 2 or 3 places, then peeling the skin off in sections. Put the bananas into a saucepan with enough cold, salted water to cover, and cook, covered until they are tender, 10 to 15 minutes. Drain, cool and cut crosswise into ½-inch slices. Mix all the ingredients, except the lettuce, lightly together, with the vinaigrette dressing. Line a salad bowl with lettuce and fill with the banana mixture. Serves 6 to 8.

VINAIGRETTE

6 tablespoons olive, or
  vegetable oil
2 tablespoons white wine
  vinegar

2 teaspoons prepared
  mustard, preferably Dijon
1 clove garlic, crushed
  (optional)
Salt, freshly ground pepper

Beat all the ingredients together with a fork.

matété de fruit à pain   *guadeloupe*

1 breadfruit, weighing about
  1 lb., peeled and cut into
  1-inch cubes, or use canned
  breadfruit

2 oz. salt pork, or corned
  beef, cut into ¼-inch
  cubes, or a pig's tail,
  chopped

1 tablespoon chives, finely
   chopped
2 cloves garlic, crushed
1 teaspoon parsley, chopped
¼ teaspoon thyme

1 fresh hot red or green
   pepper, seeded and
   chopped
Salt, freshly ground pepper
1 tablespoon vegetable oil,
   or lard
1 tablespoon lime juice

Put the breadfruit into a heavy saucepan with the meat, and enough water to cover. Cook, covered, at a gentle simmer until the breadfruit is half done, about 15 minutes. Add the chives, garlic, parsley, thyme, hot pepper, salt, and freshly ground pepper and continue cooking, partially covered until the breadfruit is tender. Add the oil and lime juice, and continue cooking for 5 minutes or so longer, stirring constantly with a wooden spoon. The breadfruit will partly disintegrate forming a thick, creamy sauce for the pieces of it that remain whole. Serve as a starchy vegetable with meat or poultry, or by itself. Serves 6.

moros y cristianos   *cuba*

Moors and Christians

Leftover Frijoles Negros (Black Beans) may be used for this recipe.

2 tablespoons olive oil
1 medium onion, finely
   chopped
1 clove garlic, minced
1 small green bell pepper,
   seeded and finely chopped

2 medium tomatoes, peeled,
   seeded and chopped
Salt, freshly ground pepper
8 oz. cooked black beans
6 oz. raw rice
¾ pint cold water

Heat the oil in a heavy, covered casserole or saucepan, add the onion, garlic and pepper and sauté until the onion is tender. Add the tomatoes and cook, stirring, until the mixture is well blended and quite thick. Season to taste with salt and pepper. Stir in the beans, mixing well. Add the rice and water, mixing lightly. Cover and cook over very low heat until the rice is tender and all the water absorbed. Serves 4 to 6.

This is often served with fried egg and fried, ripe plantains.

otro arroz blanco   *dominican republic*

Another White Rice

5/4 lb. long-grain rice
3 tablespoons lard or
  vegetable oil

Salt to taste
1 1/4 pints boiling water

Wash the rice thoroughly in several waters, drain and allow to dry. In a heavy saucepan with a tight-fitting lid, melt the lard or oil. Add the rice and cook, stirring until the rice has absorbed the fat, taking care not to let the rice brown. Add the salt and boiling water, cover, and cook on the lowest possible heat until the rice is tender and all the liquid absorbed, 20 to 30 minutes. Serves 6.

mrs bessie byam's rice and peas   *trinidad*

This recipe given me by a friend, Mrs Byam of Trinidad, is particularly good, and because of the amount of meat, is a meal in itself.

1/2 lb. smoked ham hocks
1 lb. lean beef, chuck or
  shin, cut into 1-inch cubes
1 teaspoon salt
1 teaspoon crushed garlic
1 teaspoon ground cloves

2 tablespoons vegetable oil
2 tomatoes, peeled, seeded
  and chopped
1 medium green bell pepper,
  chopped

1 fresh hot green pepper,
  seeded and chopped
2 onions, coarsely chopped
½ lb. fresh or tinned
  pigeon peas

2 cups (¾ lb.) long-grain rice,
  washed
3 cups (1¼ pints) chicken or
  beef stock, about

Soak ham hocks overnight in water to cover. Drain. Cut meat off the bones in 1-inch pieces. Mix with the beef and season with salt, garlic and cloves. Heat the oil in a heavy, covered casserole and sauté the meat until browned. Add ½ pint of water and simmer, covered, until the meats are tender, about 1½ hours, adding a little water from time to time if necessary.

Measure the liquid. Add the tomatoes, sweet and hot peppers, onions, pigeon peas and rice. Make up the quantity of liquid to 1½ pints with stock, or water, bring to the boil, cover and cook over very low heat until the rice is tender and all the liquid absorbed. Serves 6. Serve with Mrs Bessie Byam's Mango Relish (see Index).

Fresh pigeon peas can sometimes be bought, but the season is quite short. Tinned fresh pigeon peas can be bought in tropical food shops often labelled in Spanish, gandules verdes. Dried peas can also be used, in which case reduce the amount to 1 cup (6 oz.), soak overnight, and cook together with the meats.

palmito guisado   *dominican republic*

Stewed Palm Hearts

2 tablespoons vegetable oil
4 oz. lean boiled ham, cut
  into ½-inch cubes
2 cloves garlic, minced
1 fresh hot red or green
  pepper, seeded and
  chopped

2 tablespoons chopped chives
2 tablespoons tomato purée
3 medium tomatoes, peeled
  and coarsely chopped
1 tablespoon chopped parsley
1 tablespoon distilled white
  vinegar

Salt, freshly ground pepper
to taste

2 14 oz. tins palm hearts,
drained and coarsely
chopped

1 tablespoon chopped
pimento-stuffed green olives

1 tablespoon chopped capers,
preferably Spanish

Freshly grated Parmesan
cheese

Heat the oil in a heavy 12-inch frying pan and sauté the ham, garlic and hot pepper for a few minutes. Add the chives, tomato purée and tomatoes, parsley, vinegar, salt and pepper and cook until the mixture is thick and well blended. Add the palm hearts and cook just long enough to heat them through. Add the olives and capers and cook for a minute or two longer. Serve accompanied by a bowl of grated Parmesan cheese. Serves 6.

palmito revuelto
con huevos   *dominican republic*

Hearts of Palm Scrambled with Eggs

Cook the hearts of palm as in the recipe for Palmito Guisado.

Lightly beat 6 eggs and scramble them into the palm hearts mixture. Cook just long enough for the eggs to set, stirring with a wooden spoon to reach the entire surface of the pan, about 3 or 4 minutes. Serves 6.

VARIATION: Heat the palm hearts in their own liquid. Drain thoroughly, and chop coarsely. Heat 1 oz. of butter in a heavy frying pan, add the palm hearts, and season to taste with salt and white pepper. Pour in 6 lightly beaten eggs and cook, stirring with a wooden spoon to reach the entire surface of the pan until the eggs are set, about 3 or 4 minutes. Serves 6.

pepinos en salsa de naranja　　　　*puerto rico*

Stewed Cucumbers in Orange Sauce

3 cucumbers, about 8 inches
　long
1½ oz. butter
1 tablespoon flour

½ pint fresh orange juice,
　strained
Salt, freshly ground white
　pepper
1 teaspoon grated orange rind

Peel the cucumbers, cut in half lengthwise, scrape out the seeds
with a spoon and cut into ½-inch crosswise slices. Drop into
boiling salted water and cook for 5 minutes. Drain. Place in a
warmed vegetable dish. Melt the butter in a small saucepan.
Stir in the flour and cook without letting the flour take on any
colour, for a minute or two. Add the orange juice, stir and cook
until smooth and thickened. Season to taste with salt and pepper,
add rind, mix thoroughly and pour over the cucumbers. Serves 4.

pois et riz　　　　*guadeloupe*

Rice and Beans

This is the recipe for rice and red beans as they are cooked by
Mme Jean-Noël Villahaut Ces François at her restaurant Aux
Raisins Clairs in Guadeloupe. The large red kidney beans may
be used, but the smaller type, sometimes called California pink
is to be preferred. This very simple form of rice and beans is
delicious with either meat or fish.

8 oz. red beans
1 small onion, finely chopped
1 clove garlic, crushed
1 bay leaf

Sprig of thyme
1 fresh, hot red or green
　pepper (optional)
9 oz. long-grain rice

Wash the beans thoroughly, drain and put into a heavy saucepan, large enough to hold both beans and rice. Add the onion, garlic, bay leaf, thyme and hot pepper, left whole. Add enough cold water to cover the beans by about 2 inches. Bring to the boil, lower the heat and cook, covered, at a gentle simmer until the beans are almost tender. If necessary add a little hot water from time to time. Drain the beans. Reserve the liquid. Remove the bay leaf and pepper and discard. Measure the liquid and add enough water to bring the quantity up to 1¼ pints. Return the beans and liquid to the saucepan. Wash the rice several times in cold water, drain, then add to the beans. Stir once, then bring to the boil, lower the heat and cook, covered, for 20 minutes, or until the rice is just tender and all the liquid absorbed. Serves 6 to 8.

VARIATION: In Haiti a slightly different recipe is followed. Cook the beans in water for 1½ to 2 hours, drain and reserve the liquid. Then heat 2 tablespoons of oil and fry 2 chopped up rashers of bacon until crisp. Add a finely chopped onion, 2 chopped shallots and a hot green pepper, seeded and chopped. Sauté until the onion is soft. Add the beans, season with salt and cook for a minute or two. Pour in 1½ pints of bean water, bring to the boil and add ¾ lb. rice. Lower the heat, cover and simmer until the rice is cooked and the water has evaporated, about 20 minutes. Stir in 2 oz. butter before serving.

pois rouges en sauce   *haiti*

Red Beans in their Own Sauce

1 lb. red kidney beans	3 tablespoons chopped parsley,
1 oz. unsalted butter	preferably flat Italian type
1 clove garlic, finely chopped	Salt, freshly ground pepper
	to taste

Put the beans into a large, covered casserole with 2½ pints of cold water. Bring to the boil, cover, lower the heat and simmer until the beans are tender, 1½ to 2 hours. Drain the beans and measure the liquid; there should be 1¼ pints. If there is too much liquid, reduce it quickly over brisk heat. If insufficient, make up the quantity with water. Measure 6 oz. of the cooked beans and reduce to a purée in an electric blender with ½ pint of the bean liquid. Stir the purée into the remaining liquid, together with the whole beans. Set aside.

Heat 1 tablespoon of the butter in a small frying pan and sauté the garlic and parsley, being careful not to let the garlic burn. Stir into the beans and season to taste with salt and pepper. Cook very gently, stirring from time to time, until the sauce is thick and creamy. Stir in the remaining tablespoon of butter. Serves 6 to 8.

okra in tomato sauce   *st croix*

1 lb. young okra pods, or
2 10 oz. packages frozen
okra
3 tablespoons olive oil
1 medium onion, finely
chopped
1 clove garlic, chopped
1 green bell pepper, seeded
and chopped

1 fresh hot green pepper,
seeded and chopped
3 medium tomatoes, peeled
and chopped or, 1 cup
tinned Italian plum
tomatoes, drained
Salt
Pinch sugar

Wash the okras, pat dry with paper towels, and cut off the stem ends. If using frozen okra, thaw completely and pat dry. Heat the oil in a heavy frying pan, and sauté the okra until lightly browned all over. Lift out with a slotted spoon and transfer to a saucepan. In the oil remaining in the pan, sauté the onion, garlic and peppers until the onion is tender and very lightly browned. Add the tomatoes, salt, and sugar, and cook until the mixture is well blended, 2 or 3 minutes. Pour the tomato mixture over the okra, stir to mix, cover and cook until the okra is tender, about 5 minutes. Serves 6.

VARIATION: In Puerto Rico okra is cooked in sofrito. If the okras are small and young, leave whole, otherwise cut in ½-inch slices. Simmer them in the sofrito for 15 to 20 minutes until tender. Quantities are 1½ lb. okra and 1 recipe Sofrito (see Index).

pois rouges maçonne   *guadeloupe*

Mashed Red Beans

It is impossible to translate this literally. It means red beans in the style of a mason's plaster, not a flattering description. It really does *not* have the consistency of plaster or wet concrete, but is a bit gloopy when contrasted with the very light texture of, say, Pois et Riz Collés. Whatever its name, it is a very good dish and an interesting example of the many forms rice and beans can take from island to island.

1 tablespoon peanut oil
2 slices bacon, coarsely chopped
1 medium onion, finely chopped
3 chopped shallots
1 clove garlic, minced
¾ lb. red kidney beans

1 fresh hot red or green pepper, seeded and chopped
9 oz. long-grain rice
Salt, freshly ground pepper to taste
1 teaspoon cassava meal, about

Heat the oil and sauté the bacon, onion, shallots and garlic until the onion is tender but not browned. Wash the beans, drain, and put into a heavy saucepan with the onion mixture. Add the hot pepper, pour in enough water to cover the beans by about 2 inches, bring to the boil, cover and simmer until the beans are just tender, about 1½ hours. Drain and measure the liquid. Make up the quantity to 1½ pints.

Add the rice and liquid to the beans, season to taste with salt and pepper, bring to the boil, lower the heat and cook, stirring frequently, until the rice is tender and the liquid almost evaporated. Test a grain of rice from time to time and if the liquid is nearly gone and the rice still uncooked, add a little more water.

When the rice is tender, stir in the cassava meal and cook, stirring, until the cassava has thickened any remaining liquid. Serves 6.

ratatouille créole   *guadeloupe*

The special feature of this dish is the gros concombre, the enormous, light green cucumber of Guadeloupe and Martinique and some other islands. The cucumbers weigh a pound or more each but, apart from size, differ very little from our cucumbers, which can be used instead. Simply choose the biggest ones available.

6 tablespoons olive oil
1 aubergine, weighing about
  1 lb.
1 or 2 large cucumbers,
  weighing about 1 lb.
1 lb. courgettes
1 lb. tomatoes, peeled and
  sliced

½ lb. green bell peppers,
  seeded and sliced
½ lb. ripe red bell peppers,
  seeded and sliced, or sliced
  tinned pimentos
1 teaspoon sugar
Salt, freshly ground pepper

Heat the oil preferably in an earthenware* casserole, or use any heavy saucepan or casserole large enough to hold all the in-

*If using earthenware make sure it is heavy enough not to crack over direct heat. Use one or more asbestos mats if necessary.

gredients comfortably. Peel the aubergine and cut into cross-wise slices about $\frac{1}{2}$ inch thick. Cut the widest of these in half. Arrange the slices in the casserole.

If the cucumbers are waxed, peel them and cut into $\frac{1}{2}$-inch crosswise slices; otherwise leave unpeeled. Add to the casserole with the courgettes, washed, with the ends cut off, and sliced into $\frac{1}{2}$-inch pieces. Add the tomatoes and the peppers. Season with the sugar, salt and pepper, cover and cook for 15 minutes. Uncover and cook for 15 minutes longer, or until most of the liquid has evaporated. Serves 6 to 8.

stuffed pawpaw   *jamaica*

Papaya is known as pawpaw in Jamaica.

1 green (unripe) papaya,
  weighing about 5 lb.
2 tablespoons vegetable oil
1 large onion, finely chopped
1 clove garlic, chopped
1 lb. lean minced beef
3 medium tomatoes, peeled
  and chopped

1 fresh hot red or green
  pepper, seeded and
  chopped
Salt, freshly ground pepper
$\frac{1}{2}$ oz. unsalted butter
4 tablespoons grated
  Parmesan cheese
Tomato sauce or brown
  sauce

Wash the papaya, peel, cut in half lengthwise, and remove and discard the seeds. Drop the papaya halves into boiling, salted water and parboil for 10 minutes. Drain thoroughly and pat dry with paper towels. Heat the vegetable oil in a frying pan and add the onion, garlic and minced beef. Sauté for 15 minutes, stirring from time to time to break up the meat. Add the tomatoes, hot pepper and salt and pepper to taste and cook, stirring until the mixture is well blended and thick. Arrange the papaya halves in a greased baking pan and fill them with the meat mixture. Sprinkle with grated cheese and dot with butter. Bake in a 350°F (gas 4) oven for 30 to 40 minutes. Serve with a tomato sauce or brown sauce served separately. Serves 6.

riz au djon-djon   *haiti*

Rice with Black Mushrooms

Rice is an immense favourite throughout the Caribbean and much ingenuity is shown in dishes that vary from island to island, or, as is the case with Riz au Djon-Djon, within themselves. In its simplest form it can accompany a main dish of fish or meat. A more elaborate version, accompanied by a green salad, can be served for lunch.

The mushrooms used are Haitian black mushrooms, tiny, with inch-long inedible stalks. European dried mushrooms, such as German pfifferlinge, give almost the same taste to the dish, though it will lack the fine black colour of the original.

1 oz. dried mushrooms	2 cloves garlic, finely
2 oz. unsalted butter	chopped
2 cups long-grain rice	½ teaspoon thyme
	Salt, freshly ground pepper

If using Haitian black mushrooms, remove the stems and soak them in 1 cup hot water. Soak the mushroom caps separately in another cup of hot water. If using European dried mushrooms, break them up coarsely and soak them in 2 cups hot water for half an hour. Discard the black mushroom stems, reserving the water which will be richly coloured as much of the colour is in the stems. Drain the caps, reserving the water. Drain the European mushrooms, reserving the water.

Heat the butter in a saucepan and sauté the rice with the garlic until the butter is absorbed. Add the reserved 2 cups of mushroom liquor plus 2 cups more water to the rice with the mushrooms, thyme, and salt and pepper to taste. Bring to the boil, cover, and turn the heat as low as possible. Cook for 20 to 30 minutes, or until all the liquid is absorbed and the rice is tender. Serves 6.

VARIATION:

1 oz. dried mushrooms
2 tablespoons vegetable oil
1 oz. unsalted butter
1 oz. salt pork, cut into ¼-inch dice
3 cloves garlic, finely chopped
1 medium green bell pepper, seeded and chopped
1 tablespoon chopped chives
½ teaspoon thyme
1 teaspoon parsley, chopped

A generous pinch of ground cloves
Salt, freshly ground pepper
4 oz. cooked, coarsely chopped corned pork, or 4 oz. coarsely chopped boiled ham
4 oz. cooked salt codfish shredded, or 4 oz. cooked shrimp, coarsely chopped
2 cups long-grain rice

Soak the mushrooms as in the recipe for Riz au Djon-Djon. Heat the oil and butter in a heavy saucepan and sauté the pieces of salt pork until they are crisp and brown. Add the garlic, bell pepper, chives, parsley, thyme, cloves, salt and pepper to taste, corned pork and codfish, and sauté lightly for a minute or two.

Add the rice, and stir for 2 or 3 minutes, or until the rice has absorbed the oil and butter, being careful not to let the rice brown. Add the mushrooms, 2 cups of mushroom liquid and 2 cups of water. Bring to the boil, cover and turn the heat as low as possible. Cook for 20 to 30 minutes, or until all the liquid is absorbed and the rice is tender. Serves 4.

rice and peas *jamaica*

Fresh gungo peas (pigeon peas) are used when they are in season, but dried red beans are more usually the 'peas' of Jamaican Rice and Peas.

8 oz. red kidney beans
2 tablespoons vegetable oil
1 medium onion, finely
    chopped
1 fresh hot red pepper,
    seeded and chopped

2 cups coconut milk (see
    Index)
½ teaspoon thyme
Salt, freshly ground pepper
    to taste
2 cups long-grain rice

Put the beans on to cook in a heavy, covered casserole or saucepan with enough cold water to cover by about 2 inches. Bring to the boil, cover, reduce the heat and cook at a gentle simmer until the beans are tender, adding hot water during the cooking if necessary. Drain the beans, measure the liquid and return both to the casserole.

Heat the oil in a frying pan and sauté the onion until it is golden. Add to the casserole with the hot pepper, coconut milk, thyme, salt and pepper to taste and the rice. Make up the quantity of liquid to 4 cups with cold water, if necessary. Cover and cook over very low heat for 20 to 30 minutes, or until the rice is tender and all the liquid absorbed. Serves 6.

If using fresh or tinned gunga (pigeon peas) simply add with the rice. Do not cook them beforehand. If using dried pigeon peas, cook exactly as the beans, using 8 oz.

riz créole   *martinique–guadeloupe*

Rice Creole Style

2 cups long-grain rice
6 cups water

1 tablespoon salt

Wash the rice thoroughly in several waters. Drain. Put the 6 cups of water on to boil with the salt and when it comes to a rolling boil pour in the rice. Cook, uncovered, at a vigorous simmer for 15 minutes. Drain, rinse quickly under cold running water and return to the saucepan. Do not add any water. Cook, covered, over very low heat until the rice is tender and dry, about 20 minutes. Stir with a two-pronged fork and serve. An asbestos mat or two is helpful in preventing the rice from catching. Serves 6 to 8.

Some cooks add 2½ times the volume of water to rice (5 cups water to 2 cups rice), and cook the well washed rice, covered, at a brisk simmer until the water has evaporated. The rice is then rinsed quickly in cold water, returned to the saucepan and put over very low heat, uncovered, to dry the grains.

stuffed cho-cho   *jamaica*

Chayote with Meat Stuffing

3 large chayotes (see
  Glossary), each weighing
  about ¾ lb.
2 tablespoons vegetable oil
1 large onion, finely chopped
1 clove garlic, chopped
1 lb. lean minced beef
1 tablespoon curry powder,
  or 1 fresh hot red pepper,

  seeded and chopped
3 medium tomatoes, peeled
  and chopped
Salt, freshly ground pepper
6 tablespoons grated
  Parmesan cheese
5 tablespoons bread crumbs
1½ oz. unsalted butter

Boil the whole chayotes in salted water until tender, about 30 minutes. Remove from the saucepan, and when cool enough to handle, cut into halves lengthwise. Scoop out the pulp, including the edible seed, mash and set aside. Reserve the shells. Heat the oil in a frying pan and sauté the onion, garlic and beef for 15 minutes, stirring from time to time. Add the curry powder or hot pepper, and cook for a few minutes longer. Add the tomatoes and the chayote pulp. Cook, stirring, until the ingredients are well blended, and the mixture is fairly dry. Season well with salt and pepper, pack into the chayote shells, sprinkle with cheese and bread crumbs, dot with butter and bake in a 350°F (gas 4) oven for 15 minutes, or until lightly browned. Serve as a luncheon or supper dish. Serves 6.

riz à l'aubergine   *haiti*

Rice with Aubergine

2 oz. sweet butter
3 tablespoons vegetable oil
2 lb. aubergine, peeled and
   cut into ½-inch cubes
4 oz. bacon, coarsely chopped

1 medium onion, finely
   chopped
2 cups long-grain rice
Salt to taste
⅜ pint tomato purée
4 oz. grated Parmesan cheese

Heat the butter and oil in a large, heavy frying pan and sauté the aubergine cubes over high heat until they are golden brown, about 3 minutes. Set aside.

In a heavy, covered casserole render the bacon. Add the onion and sauté until it is tender but not browned. Add 4 cups of water, bring to the boil, pour in the rice, add salt to taste and stir. Cover and cook over very low heat until the rice is tender and all the liquid absorbed, 20 to 30 minutes.

Make a bed of the rice in an ovenproof platter, cover with the aubergine, pour the tomato purée over the aubergine, then sprinkle with the cheese. Put under a grill until the cheese melts and browns. Serves 6.

creole sauce   *trinidad*

This sauce, or one very like it, turns up in a number of the English-speaking islands.

3 tablespoons vegetable oil
1 medium onion, finely
  chopped
1 green bell pepper, seeded
  and chopped
3 tablespoons plain flour
2 medium tomatoes, peeled
  and chopped

½ pint chicken stock, or dry
  white wine
Salt, freshly ground pepper
1 teaspoon lime juice
1 teaspoon vinegar
Hot pepper sauce to taste

Heat the oil in a saucepan, add the onion and pepper, and sauté until the onion is tender, but not browned. Stir in the flour and cook, stirring constantly with a wooden spoon, for a minute or two until the flour is lightly browned. Add the tomatoes and stir to mix well. Gradually stir in the stock or wine, season to taste with salt and pepper and cook, stirring until the sauce has thickened. Add the lime juice and vinegar, and hot pepper sauce to taste. Adjust the seasoning.

Serve with suckling pig, any meats or poultry or fish. If serving with fish use dry white wine or fish stock instead of chicken stock.

adobo   *spanish-speaking islands*

Marinade for Roasted Pig

1 medium onion, very finely
   chopped
1 head garlic, peeled and
   crushed
2 tablespoons orégano
2 tablespoons salt

1 tablespoon freshly ground
   pepper
6 tablespoons Seville orange
   juice
6 tablespoons peanut oil
   (optional)

Mix all the ingredients together and season the pig inside and outside with the adobo which should be left on overnight.

During roasting, baste the pig with the adobo and the meat's own juices and fat. If the peanut oil is omitted, increase the orange juice to 9 tablespoons. Makes enough for a 10 to 12 lb. suckling pig.

ajilimójili   *puerto rico*

Garlic and Pepper Sauce

3 fresh hot red peppers,
   seeded
3 ripe red bell peppers,
   seeded, or use 4 pimentos
4 peppercorns
4 large cloves garlic, peeled

2 teaspoons salt
6 tablespoons lime juice, or
   3 tablespoons each lime
   juice and vinegar
6 tablespoons olive oil

Pound the hot and sweet peppers with the peppercorns, garlic, and salt in a mortar. Transfer to a bowl and beat in the lime juice and oil, or combine the ingredients in an electric blender and reduce to a purée. Serve with suckling pig.

curry sauce

1 oz. unsalted butter
1 onion, finely chopped
1 small carrot, scraped and
   finely chopped
1 small stalk celery, chopped
2 tablespoons curry powder
½ teaspoon ground ginger
1 tablespoon plain flour

Bay leaf
½ pint beef stock
Salt, freshly ground pepper
¼ pint coconut milk, or
   single cream
1 teaspoon lime, or lemon,
   juice

In a heavy saucepan heat the butter and sauté the onion, carrot
and celery until the onion is tender and lightly browned. Add
the curry powder, ginger and flour and cook, stirring, for 3 or
4 minutes longer. Add the bay leaf and stock, season with salt
and pepper, mix, cover and simmer gently for 30 minutes. Add
the coconut milk and cook until heated through. Remove from
the heat and stir in the lime juice.

dr alex d. hawkes' pawpaw applesauce

Many islands make a mock applesauce from papaya, known in
Jamaica as pawpaw, or from chayote (christophene). This is one
of my favourite versions.

10 oz. green (unripe) papaya,
   peeled, seeded and
   chopped
¾ pint water

4 cloves
2 tablespoons sugar
4 tablespoons lime juice

Put the papaya into a heavy saucepan with the water, cloves,
sugar, and lime juice, cover and cook at a simmer until the

papaya is very soft and most of the liquid absorbed, about 1 hour. Remove from heat. Discard the cloves. Rub sauce through a sieve and serve hot or cold.

This is excellent with suckling pig, or any meat, or poultry.

green pawpaw chutney   *jamaica*

2 lb. green (unripe) papaya, cut into 1-inch cubes

¾ lb. finely chopped onions

6 oz. seedless raisins

4 cloves garlic, chopped

6 fresh hot red peppers, seeded and chopped

4 red or green bell peppers, seeded and chopped

2 tablespoons finely chopped fresh ginger root

½ teaspoon allspice

1 lb. tomatoes, peeled and chopped

1 tablespoon salt

¾ pint vinegar

1¼ lb. sugar

Put all the ingredients, except the sugar, into a large saucepan. Bring to the boil, lower the heat, cover and simmer gently for 30 minutes. Add the sugar and cook, uncovered, stirring from time to time until the mixture is thick, about 45 minutes.

Serve with cold meats, or with steak, lamb chops, roast chicken. Makes 4 pint jars. Seal and store for later use while still hot.

hot pepper sauces

Every island has its hot pepper sauce. Indeed there are hot pepper sauces, all slightly different, from Mexico, where peppers were first cultivated as far back as 7000 B.C., all the way south to Argentina and Chile. The hot peppers of the Caribbean are very hot, and very flavourful. It is wise to remove the seeds which harbour a great deal of the heat, and wise to wash the hands after handling the peppers.

hot pepper sauce   *dominica*

½ lb. yellow or red fresh hot peppers, seeded

1 medium onion, finely chopped

2 large cloves garlic, finely chopped

3 tablespoons green papaya, grated raw

½ teaspoon ground turmeric

1 teaspoon salt

3 tablespoons malt vinegar

Combine all the ingredients in an electric blender and reduce to purée. Pour into a saucepan and bring to the boil. Simmer for a minute or two. Pour into sterilized jars. Serve with any meat or fish.

hot pepper sauce   *st kitts*

½ cup seeded and finely chopped fresh hot peppers, preferably red

½ cup finely chopped onions

Salt

Combine the peppers and onions in a small, heavy saucepan and simmer over low heat. Do not add any water, the vegetables will give off enough liquid. When the mixture is thick, season with salt, cool and use as a sauce with any meat or fish.

hot pepper sauce   *trinidad*

1 small green papaya
12 fresh hot red peppers,
    seeded and chopped
2 medium onions, finely
    chopped
2 cloves garlic, finely chopped

1 tablespoon salt
½ teaspoon ground turmeric
1 teaspoon curry powder
4 tablespoons dry mustard
¾ pint malt vinegar

Put the papaya into a saucepan with enough cold water to cover, bring to the boil, cover and simmer until tender, about 15 minutes. Cool, peel and chop coarsely. Return to the saucepan with the hot peppers, onions, garlic, salt, tumeric, curry powder and the mustard mixed with the vinegar. Stir and simmer gently, uncovered, for 15 minutes. Cool and seal in sterilized jars.
    If liked the turmeric and curry powder may be omitted.

hot pepper sauce   *st lucia*

2 tablespoons vegetable oil
1 large onion, finely chopped
2 cloves garlic, chopped
3 spring onions, chopped,
    using the green and white
    parts

1 christophene (see Glossary),
    weighing about ½ lb.
12 fresh hot peppers, preferably
    red, seeded and chopped
Salt
½ pint malt vinegar

Heat the oil in a frying pan and sauté the onion, garlic and spring onions until very lightly browned. Put the christophene into a saucepan with cold water to cover, and simmer, covered until tender, about 20 minutes. Drain, cool, peel and chop coarsely, using the edible seed. Combine all the ingredients in an electric blender, or put the solids through the fine blade of a food mill then mix with the vinegar. Season to taste with salt. Serve with any meat or fish.

sauce piquante   *martinique*

Hot Sauce

6 tablespoons hot water
4 or 5 shallots, finely chopped
3 tablespoons chopped chives
2 cloves garlic, minced

1 or more fresh hot green
  peppers, finely chopped
3 tablespoons lime juice
Salt, freshly ground pepper

Pour the hot water over the shallots, chives, garlic, and hot
pepper and mix well. Stir in the lime juice, season to taste with
salt and pepper and allow to stand for 1 hour before using.

sauce ti-malice   *haiti*

Hot Pepper Sauce

2 large onions, finely chopped
2 shallots, finely chopped
6 tablespoons lime juice
2 cloves garlic, finely chopped

2 teaspoons finely chopped
  fresh hot peppers, red or
  yellow preferably
Salt, freshly ground pepper
  to taste
3 tablespoons olive oil

Mix the onions and shallots with the lime juice and allow to stand
for about 1 hour. Pour into a small saucepan, add all the other
ingredients and bring to the boil. Stir, remove from the heat and
allow to cool. Serve cold with Griots de Porc (see Index).

saus di promente pica   *saba*

Hot Pepper Sauce

Ideally for this sauce a mixture of hot peppers, green, yellow and red, is used. If this is not possible, use whatever hot peppers are available. There is a subtle difference in flavour between the pepper in its green, midway, and ripe stages, but not enough to outlaw the making of a one-colour sauce.

1 tablespoon each of green, yellow, and red fresh, hot peppers, seeded and finely chopped
1 large onion, finely chopped

1 teaspoon finely chopped garlic
6 tablespoons vinegar
6 tablespoons water
1 teaspoon salt
1 tablespoon vegetable oil

Combine the peppers, onion, and garlic in a bowl. Bring the vinegar, water and salt to the boil and pour over the pepper mixture, stirring to mix well. Allow to cool then trickle the oil so that it floats on the surface of the sauce. The sauce will keep for 3 or 4 weeks if covered and refrigerated, but it is best eaten fresh as an accompaniment to any meat or fish dish.

A small amount will enliven a bland soup or plain vegetable.

mango or green pawpaw chutney   *st kitts*

2 lb. hard, green (unripe) mangoes, or 2 lb. unripe pawpaw
8 oz. sultanas, coarsely chopped
4 oz. cashew nuts, coarsely chopped

2 oz. fresh ginger root, finely chopped
3 cloves garlic, minced
2 fresh hot red peppers, chopped
1 lb. light brown sugar
3/4 pint malt vinegar
Salt to taste

Peel the mangoes or pawpaw and cut into 1-inch cubes. Put into a heavy saucepan with all the other ingredients, mix thoroughly and simmer, stirring from time to time, until the mixture has thickened, about half an hour. Pour into sterilized jars. Makes about 2 1-pint jars.

Use with curries and cold meats.

mango sauce   *st kitts*

3 cups chopped half-ripe   ⅛ teaspoon ground ginger
   mangoes   ⅛ teaspoon ground cinnamon
1 cup water   Pinch of salt
1 cup sugar

Put the mangoes and water in a saucepan and cook, covered, until the mangoes are soft. Add the sugar, ginger, cinnamon and pinch of salt and cook, uncovered, stirring from time to time for 10 minutes longer. Or until the sauce is thick and well blended.

This sauce is good with meat, or served with biscuits as a dessert.

lemon butter sauce   *u.s. virgin islands*

½ lb. unsalted butter   1 tablespoon lemon juice
½ teaspoon salt

In a double boiler, over hot water but off the heat, stir the butter with a wooden spoon until it is creamy. Add the salt, continue stirring, and gradually add a tablespoon of lemon juice. Serve at once with St Croix fish pudding.

mango chutney   *jamaica*

3 lb. hard, green (unripe) mangoes, preferably a fleshy type

2 tablespoons salt

½ lb. ripe tamarinds (see Glossary)

¾ pint vinegar, preferably Pickapeppa cane vinegar, otherwise malt vinegar

1½ lb. West Indian brown sugar, or any light brown sugar

4 tablespoons peeled and chopped fresh ginger root

3 oz. seedless raisins

1 teaspoon ground allspice

1 oz. hot dried red peppers, seeded and roughly crumbled

Peel the mangoes and cut the flesh off the seeds into pieces about 1-by-2 inches. Mix with the salt and set aside for 2 hours. Pick the shell off the tamarinds, or use tamarind pulp, if available. Cover with 6 tablespoons boiling water, allow to stand for about half an hour then force the pulp through a sieve. Discard the seeds. Drain the mangoes thoroughly, discard liquid and put into a large, heavy saucepan with the other ingredients and simmer, stirring from time to time, until the mixture is thick and the mangoes are tender, about half an hour. The mango pieces should not disintegrate. Pour into sterilized jars. Makes about 3 1-pint jars.

Use with curries and cold meats.

nicole scott's sauce ti-malice   *haiti*

Hot Sauce

6 tablespoons vinegar, preferably cane vinegar

3 tablespoons lime, or lemon, juice

½ tablespoon salt

1 medium onion, finely chopped

1 carrot, scraped and very finely diced

4 oz. finely chopped cabbage

3 radishes, finely chopped
1 clove garlic, crushed
Salt, freshly ground pepper
  to taste
1 tablespoon tomato paste

1 fresh hot pepper, seeded
  and crushed, or 1 teaspoon
  hot pepper sauce
2 tablespoons olive, or salad,
  oil

Combine all the ingredients in a bowl and allow to stand for 1 hour before using. Serve with Griots de Porc, or any meat, or suckling pig.

pepper wine   *jamaica*

6 whole fresh hot red peppers

1 pint light rum, or dry
  sherry

Put the whole peppers into a glass jar and pour in the rum or sherry. Cover tightly with the lid and allow to stand 10 days before using. Use a few drops in soups or sauce. Pepper Vinegar is made in the same way. Makes about 1 pint.

If fresh peppers are not available, whole, hot dried peppers may be used.

mojo para puerco asado   *dominican republic*

Sauce for Roast Suckling Pig

8 tablespoons peanut oil
4 or 5 spring onions, finely
  chopped
6 cloves garlic, crushed
1 teaspoon fresh hot red or
  green pepper, seeded and
  chopped

6 tablespoons vinegar,
  preferably cane or malt
6 tablespoons Seville orange
  juice
Salt, freshly ground pepper

Heat the oil in a saucepan, add the spring onions and garlic and sauté until the spring onions are tender, but not browned. Add the rest of the ingredients and simmer gently for 2 or 3 minutes. Serve with the suckling pig.

If liked, pour all the fat from the pan in which the pig was roasted, deglaze the pan with the orange juice, scraping to take up all the brown bits, and add this to the sauce.

Orange juice may be used if Seville orange juice is not available.

mrs lilian johnston's chilli sauce   *st kitts*

6 lb. tomatoes, peeled and finely chopped
1 lb. onions, finely chopped
½ lb. sugar
2 tablespoons salt

1 pint malt vinegar
1 tablespoon seeded and finely chopped hot peppers, preferably red

Combine all the ingredients in a large pan and bring to the boil. Lower the heat and cook, stirring, until the mixture is quite thick. Pour into sterilized jars and seal. Makes about 3 pints.

mango relish

These fresh mango chutneys are closely related and obviously derive from an Indian original. They are good with curry and make an excellent accompaniment to boiled, baked or grilled fish or meat, especially cold meat. The Rougail de Mangues Vertes was traditionally served as an hors d'œuvre in Martinique and Guadeloupe but unfortunately it seems to have lost much of its popularity. This is a pity, as it makes an unusual and refreshing beginning to a meal.

mrs bessie byam's mango relish   *trinidad*

2 hard, green (unripe)
  mangoes, weighing 1 lb.
  each
1 teaspoon finely chopped
  garlic

1 teaspoon salt
1 teaspoon fresh hot red or
  green pepper, seeded and
  finely chopped
1 tablespoon olive oil

Peel the mangoes and grate down to the seeds, or cut off the flesh and chop fine. Add the garlic, salt, and hot pepper, mixing thoroughly. Place in clean jar, and top with the oil. Cover tightly and refrigerate until ready to use. This relish will keep for several days, but is essentially meant to be eaten quite soon after it is made.

Traditionally eaten with Rice and Peas, it is good with curry and with any plainly cooked fish or meat, especially cold meat.

rougail de mangues
vertes   *martinique–guadeloupe*

Green Mango Relish

2 hard, green (unripe)
  mangoes, weighing 1 lb.
  each
2 teaspoons grated onion
½ teaspoon finely chopped
  fresh hot red pepper, or

cayenne pepper to taste
1 tablespoon peanut oil
Salt, freshly ground pepper
  to taste
Chopped parsley

Peel the mangoes, chop flesh coarsely and put through a sieve. Add the grated onion, hot pepper, salt and pepper to taste, and the oil. Garnish with parsley.

In the past this fresh chutney was served as an hors d'œuvre. It is also good with curry, or fish, or with meat, especially cold meat.

salsa criolla cocida   *dominican republic*

Cooked Tomato Sauce, Creole Style

3 tablespoons vegetable or
  olive oil
1 medium onion, finely
  chopped
1 large tomato, peeled and
  chopped

1 fresh hot pepper, seeded
  and finely chopped
Salt, freshly ground pepper
1 tablespoon vinegar

Heat the oil in a small saucepan and sauté the onion until tender but not browned. Add the tomato, hot pepper, salt and pepper to taste and cook, stirring, for about 5 minutes or until well blended and fairly thick. Stir in the vinegar, mixing thoroughly. Serve with any meat or fish.

salsa criolla cruda   *dominican republic*

Uncooked Tomato Sauce, Creole Style

1 medium onion, finely
  chopped
1 large tomato, peeled and
  chopped
1 hot green pepper, seeded
  and finely chopped

2 cloves garlic, minced
1 tablespoon chopped parsley,
  or fresh green coriander
Salt, freshly ground pepper
9 tablespoons olive oil
3 tablespoons vinegar

Combine all the ingredients in a bowl and allow to stand for about 15 minutes before using for the flavour to develop. Serve with any meat or fish, or with eggs. It is especially good with grilled lobsters or spiny (rock) lobsters.

salsa de tomate   *dominican republic*

Tomato Sauce

3 lb. tomatoes, peeled, seeded
   and chopped
6 tablespoons olive oil
Bay leaf

1 teaspoon sugar
Salt, freshly ground pepper
2 cloves garlic, minced

Put the tomatoes in a heavy saucepan and cook over low heat,
stirring from time to time with a wooden spoon until some of the
liquid has evaporated and the mixture is getting thick. Stir in
the oil, and add the remaining ingredients. Cook, stirring, for 5
minutes. Cool and use in soups, casseroles, with fish and shellfish
or stirred into cooked beans.

    This sauce will keep, refrigerated, for several weeks and is
extremely useful to have on hand.

salsa roja para frijoles negros   *cuba*

Sweet Pepper Sauce for Black Beans

This is an exceptionally good sweet pepper and tomato sauce
dating back to the beginning of this century. Traditionally it is
served with Cuban black beans, but may be used with any meat
or fish.

⅜ pint olive oil
¾ lb. tomatoes, peeled and
   chopped
2 cloves garlic, crushed
6 grinds black pepper, or
   ¼ teaspoon
½ teaspoon Spanish (hot)
   paprika, or cayenne

¼ teaspoon orégano
½ teaspoon sugar
Salt to taste
⅛ pint tomato purée
½ lb. pimentos, chopped and
   the liquid from the tin
3 tablespoons cane vinegar

Heat the oil in a saucepan and add the tomatoes. Cook, stirring with a wooden spoon until the tomatoes have disintegrated, about 5 minutes. Add all the rest of the ingredients, except the vinegar, and cook, stirring from time to time, over low heat until the sauce is thick. Remove from the heat and stir in the vinegar.

sauce piquante   *st martin*

Hot Sauce

2 tablespoons capers
2 tablespoons chopped
  gherkins
1 clove garlic, finely chopped
1 fresh hot red pepper,
  seeded and finely chopped

2 tablespoons chopped parsley
Salt, freshly ground pepper
  to taste
9 tablespoons olive oil,
  preferably French
3 tablespoons red wine vinegar

Mix all the ingredients together thoroughly. Serve with cold meats, hors d'œuvres, or with plainly cooked meats, fish and shellfish.

sauce vinaigrette   *french islands*

French Dressing

3 tablespoons cane or white
  wine vinegar, or lime, or
  lemon juice, or a mixture
  of both
Salt
Freshly ground pepper

Pinch sugar
½ teaspoon Dijon mustard
  (optional)
9 tablespoons olive, or salad
  oil

Combine the vinegar or juice, salt and pepper to taste, and the sugar in a bowl, together with the mustard, if liked. Beat with

a fork until the salt has dissolved. Beat in the oil to blend
thoroughly.

salsa tártara   *dominican republic*

Tartare Sauce

½ pint mayonnaise
2 tablespoons finely chopped
   capers
4 oz. finely chopped pickled
   cucumbers
1 tablespoon finely chopped
   onion
1 tablespoon chopped chives

1 tablespoon finely chopped
   parsley
1 hard-boiled egg, finely
   chopped
4 oz. finely chopped black
   olives
1 tablespoon prepared
   mustard
Salt, freshly ground pepper

Mix all the ingredients together. Serve with Camarones Rellenos
(see Index) and with fried fish and shellfish.

sauce créole   *martinique*

Creole Sauce

This sauce is used for lobsters and crayfish, and any plainly
cooked fish.

¼ pint tomato purée
1 fresh hot green pepper,
   seeded and chopped
1 medium onion, finely
   chopped

1 tablespoon finely chopped
   celery
Salt, freshly ground pepper
   to taste

2 spring onions, finely
   chopped and using both
   green and white parts

1 tablespoon thinly sliced
   pimento-stuffed olives

3 tablespoons lime juice

Combine all the ingredients, stirring to mix well. Serve at once, or refrigerate until ready to use. The sauce will keep for about a week refrigerated.

breads, puddings
and desserts

arrowroot custard

2 tablespoons arrowroot
¾ pint evaporated milk
2 oz. sugar

½ teaspoon vanilla
3 eggs, well beaten

Mix the arrowroot and the milk together in a saucepan, add the sugar, and cook, stirring constantly, with a wooden spoon, over low heat until the mixture is thickened. Add the vanilla and the eggs and continue cooking, stirring constantly, over very low heat for about 5 minutes longer. Cool. Refrigerate before serving with stewed fruit, fruit pies, sliced mangoes, or any dessert in place of cream.

bakes

Fried Biscuits

½ lb. plain flour
2 teaspoons baking powder
½ teaspoon salt
2 teaspoons sugar

2 tablespoons lard
3 tablespoons water
Oil for frying

Sift the flour, baking powder, salt and sugar together into a bowl. Rub in the lard until the mixture is crumbly. Add the water and stir to make a soft dough. Knead lightly on a floured board, adding a little more flour if necessary. Pinch off pieces of dough (about 2 tablespoons each) and roll into balls. Flatten into circles about ½-inch thick. Fry in a little hot oil in a large, heavy frying pan until golden on both sides, or bake on a hot, greased griddle. Makes about 10. Serve warm as bread.

baked bananas flambée   *antigua*

4 large bananas, peeled and
   sliced lengthwise
4 oz. brown sugar
3 tablespoons lime juice

6 tablespoons light rum
1 teaspoon ground allspice
2 oz. unsalted butter

Arrange the bananas in a well-buttered shallow fireproof serving dish. Sprinkle with the sugar, lime juice, half of the rum and the allspice. Dot with the butter. Bake in a 400°F (gas 6) oven for 15 minutes, basting 2 or 3 times during the cooking. At the moment of serving, heat the other half of the rum, pour over the bananas and set alight. Serves 4.

banana bread   *jamaica*

4 oz. unsalted butter
4 oz. sugar
1 egg
8 oz. plain flour
1 tablespoon baking powder
½ teaspoon salt
½ teaspoon nutmeg

2 large, ripe bananas (about
   1 lb.)
1 teaspoon vanilla
3 oz. seedless raisins
4 tablespoons coarsely chopped
   pecans

Cream butter and sugar together in a mixing bowl until light and fluffy. Add the egg and beat thoroughly. Sift the flour, baking powder, salt and nutmeg into another bowl. Mash the bananas and add the vanilla. Add the sifted ingredients and the banana alternately to the egg-butter-sugar mixture, beating after each addition until thoroughly blended. Toss the raisins with a teaspoon of flour and add them, with the pecans, to the batter, mixing well. Pour into a greased 9-by-5-inch loaf tin. Bake in a 350°F (gas 4) oven for about 1 hour, or until a cake tester comes out clean.

banane céleste   *martinique*

6 oz. cream cheese
2 oz. brown sugar
¾ teaspoon cinnamon

4 large ripe bananas, peeled
  and halved lengthwise
4 tablespoons unsalted butter
3 tablespoons double cream

Mix the cream cheese, sugar and ½ teaspoon of the cinnamon together until well blended. Set aside. Heat the butter in a heavy skillet and sauté the banana halves until they are lightly browned on both sides. Lay 4 of the halves in a buttered shallow fire-proof serving dish. Spread half the cream cheese mixture on the bananas and top with the remaining 4 banana halves. Spread them with the rest of the cream cheese mixture. Pour the cream over them. Bake in a 350°F (gas 4) oven for about 15 minutes, or until the cream cheese mixture is golden brown. Sprinkle with the remaining ¼ teaspoon of cinnamon and serve immediately. Serves 4.

banana whip and fruit cream   *anguilla*

Many dishes can be quite accurately assigned to individual islands, but others have spread to so many islands that their actual birthplace is lost. Banana Whip and Fruit Cream could be attributed in a general sort of way to the English-speaking islands.

4 large ripe bananas
2 oz. sugar, or to taste
6 tablespoons orange juice

3 tablespoons light rum
3 egg whites
Pinch salt

Peel the bananas and mash them with the sugar, orange juice and rum, adding more sugar if liked. Beat the egg whites with the salt until they stand in peaks. Fold the whites into the banana mixture, lightly but thoroughly. Chill for several hours in the refrigerator until lightly set. Serve with Fruit Cream. Serves 6.

FRUIT CREAM

4 egg yolks
3 tablespoons sugar

⅜ pint orange juice

Beat the egg yolks with the sugar until pale yellow. Transfer to a heavy saucepan, add the orange juice and cook over low heat, beating constantly with a wire whisk until the mixture begins to foam up. Remove immediately from the heat as the mixture must not be allowed to boil. Chill for several hours before using. Serve with Banana Whip. Serves 6.

Fruit Cream may be used instead of whipped cream, or custard, on puddings, or stewed fruits such as guavas. Other fruit juices may be used to flavour Fruit Cream. Adjust the amount of sugar to taste.

beignets de banane   *martinique*

Banana Fritters

3 large ripe bananas
4 tablespoons dark rum

2 tablespoons sugar
1 teaspoon vanilla

BATTER

½ lb. plain flour
1 tablespoon sugar
½ teaspoon salt
1 teaspoon baking powder
1 tablespoon melted
   unsalted butter

1 egg
¼ pint milk
1 tablespoon rum
Vegetable oil for deep frying
Vanilla sugar flavoured with
   ground cinnamon

Peel the bananas and cut into halves lengthwise; cut each half into 4 equal pieces. Place in a bowl. Combine the rum, sugar and vanilla and pour over the banana slices. Leave for 1 hour, turning the pieces occasionally.

To make the batter, sift the flour, sugar, salt and baking powder together, into a mixing bowl. Add the butter, egg, milk and rum, mixing to a smooth paste. Let the batter stand until the bananas are ready. Dip the banana pieces in the batter, and fry in deep oil (375°F on a frying thermometer) until they are golden brown all over. Drain on paper towels. Sprinkle with the vanilla sugar. Serves 4 to 6.

To make vanilla sugar, drop a vanilla bean, 1 to 2 inches long, into a jar of sugar. Keep the jar tightly closed and add more sugar from time to time as it is used, until the bean has lost all flavour. Add ground cinnamon to taste to the vanilla sugar before sprinkling it on the beignets.

bienmesabe   *puerto rico*

Coconut Cream Sauce

This is a sweeter, less rich, version of the Cuban dessert sauce, Coquimol. It crops up in various versions wherever Spanish is spoken.

1 lb. sugar
⅜ pint water
⅜ pint coconut milk (see
  Index)

6 egg yolks
Slices of sponge cake, or lady
  fingers
Sherry (optional)

Boil the sugar and water together until it forms a syrup at the thread stage. Remove from the heat, stir the coconut milk into the syrup, mixing thoroughly. Beat the egg yolks and add them to the mixture, stirring constantly over gentle heat until thickened. Do not let it boil. To serve, pour over sponge cake or lady fingers. If liked, the cake may be sprinkled with sherry before the sauce is poured on.

boija   *st croix*

Coconut Corn Bread

½ oz. packet active dry
  yeast
¾ lb. flour
½ lb. corn meal
¼ lb. finely grated coconut
2 large ripe bananas, mashed

¼ lb. unsalted butter,
  melted and cooled
¼ lb. sugar
½ teaspoon ground allspice
1 teaspoon salt
Water to mix

Dissolve the yeast in a cup of lukewarm water. Pour into a mixing bowl and add half the flour to make a sponge. Cover with a cloth and leave in a warm place to rise until double in bulk, about 1½ hours. Add all the rest of the ingredients and enough water, about ¼ pint, to make a stiff batter, beating thoroughly with a wooden spoon to incorporate the sponge evenly. Pour into 2 greased 9-by-5-by-3-inch loaf tins. Cover loosely with a cloth and leave in a warm place to rise until double in bulk, about ½ hour. Bake in a 350°F (gas 4) oven for 45 minutes to 1 hour, or until the bread begins to shrink from the sides of the pan, and the top is lightly browned. Let cool few minutes in tin. Then turn out on cake rack to complete cooling.

boniatillo   *cuba*

Sweet Potato Paste

This is made with boniatos, the white sweet potato, either the pink or white skinned variety.

1 lb. sweet potatoes, peeled and sliced	Peel of 1 lime
¾ lb. sugar	2-inch stick of cinnamon
6 tablespoons water	3 egg yolks, beaten
	3 tablespoons sherry

Boil the sweet potatoes in water to cover until tender, about 25 minutes. Drain and mash. In the meantime make a syrup with the sugar, water, lime peel and cinnamon. Boil in a heavy saucepan until it reaches the soft ball stage (250°F on a sugar thermometer). Remove the peel and cinnamon and mix the syrup with the sweet potatoes. Cook in a heavy saucepan over low heat, stirring constantly until the mixture forms a thick paste. Off the heat, stir in the egg yolks and mix well. Return to the heat and cook, stirring, for 2 or 3 minutes. Remove from heat and add sherry. Cool. Serve as a dessert with a sauce, or with cream, or use as a base in other desserts such as Sweet Potato Cake. Makes about 3 cups.

cafiroleta   *cuba*

Mix equal quantities of Boniatillo (Sweet Potato Paste) and Coquimol (Coconut Cream Sauce) together and serve as a dessert.

carrot dumplings   *montserrat*

3 oz. flour   1½ oz. unsalted butter
½ teaspoon salt   ·   2oz. finely grated carrot
1 teaspoon baking powder

Sift the flour, salt, and baking powder into a bowl. Rub in the
butter with the fingertips until the mixture is crumbly. Add the
carrot, and enough cold water to make a fairly stiff dough. Turn
out onto a floured board and knead lightly. Form into balls about
1½ inches in diameter. Drop them into soup and simmer for
15 minutes, or cook separately in boiling salted water. Makes
about 12 dumplings.

coconut bread   ·   *trinidad*

¾ lb. plain flour   1 egg, well beaten
1 tablespoon baking powder   ⅜ pint evaporated milk
1 teaspoon salt   1 teaspoon vanilla
½ lb. sugar   4 oz. unsalted butter,
½ lb. finely grated fresh   melted and cooled
  coconut   Sugar

Sift the flour, baking powder, and salt together. Mix in the sugar
and coconut. Add the egg, milk, vanilla and butter, mixing
lightly but thoroughly. Divide the mixture between 2 greased
9-by-5-inch loaf tins. Fill each about ⅔ full. Sprinkle with sugar
and bake in a 350°F (gas 4) oven for about 55 minutes, or until
a cake tester comes out clean. Let loaves cool partially in tins.
Then turn out on cake rack.

coconut milk sherbet   *barbados*

1 medium sized coconut   3 tablespoons water
  (about 1½ lb.)   Pinch cream of tartar
¾ pint warm milk   2 drops almond extract
½ lb. sugar

Puncture 2 of the eyes of the coconut and drain out the coconut water. Split the shell and take out the meat. Pare the brown skin from a piece of coconut about 4 inches square and grate it on the coarse side of a hand grater. Spread the coconut on a baking sheet or shallow baking pan and toast in a 325°F (gas 3) oven for about 15 minutes, or until lightly browned. Remove from oven and set aside.

Finely grate the rest of the coconut, unpeeled, in the usual way for making coconut milk, or reduce in an electric blender with the warm milk. Squeeze through a kitchen towel to extract all the liquid. Set aside.

In a small, heavy saucepan combine the sugar, water and cream of tartar and cook, stirring from time to time, until the sugar is dissolved and the syrup clear. Combine the syrup, almond extract, coconut milk, and toasted coconut in a large bowl, stirring to mix well. Pour into 2 ice cube trays with the dividers removed. Freeze for 3 to 4 hours, stirring every half hour to break up the solid particles that form on the bottom and sides of the trays. The finished sherbet should have a fine, snowy texture. Serve in parfait glasses or dessert dishes.

coconut pie   *st kitts*

2 large eggs   2 oz. freshly grated coconut,
2 oz. sugar   or tinned shredded moist
6 tablespoons evaporated milk   coconut

6 tablespoons coconut milk (see Index)

1 tablespoon unsalted butter, melted

8-inch pie shell, unbaked

Beat the eggs and sugar together until light and fluffy. Add the grated coconut, the evaporated milk and coconut milk and butter. Pour into the pie shell. Bake in a 450°F (gas 8) oven for 10 minutes, then reduce the heat to 350°F (gas 4) and bake for 25 to 30 minutes longer, or until the custard is set and the pastry is lightly browned. Serves 4.

coconut soufflé   *jamaica*

1 envelope (1 tablespoon) unflavoured gelatine

4 eggs, separated

2 oz. sugar

⅜ pint coconut cream

4 oz. finely grated fresh coconut

Grated rind 1 lime

1 oz. coarsely grated fresh coconut

Put 3 tablespoons cold water into a small, heavy saucepan, sprinkle the gelatine on top of the water and let it soften for a few minutes. Place over very low heat and, stirring constantly with a wooden spoon, dissolve the gelatine. Set aside.

Put the egg yolks into the top of a double boiler, away from heat, and add the sugar, beating constantly until the yolks are lemon coloured and form a ribbon. Heat the coconut cream separately. Set the egg yolks over hot water and low heat and pour in the coconut cream, beating constantly. Stir until the mixture forms a custard thick enough to coat the spoon. Remove from the heat and stir in the finely grated coconut, lime rind, and gelatine. Cool.

Beat the egg whites until stiff and fold into the cooled custard. Pour into a 1½-pint soufflé dish and refrigerate for several hours, or until firm. Meanwhile, spread the coarsely grated coconut on a baking sheet and toast for 10 minutes in a 325°F (gas 3) oven, or until light brown. Cool. Sprinkle over the soufflé and serve. Serves 6.

coco quemado   *cuba*

Coconut Pudding

1 lb. sugar
⅜ pint water
1 lb. grated coconut

4 egg yolks, lightly beaten
1 teaspoon ground cinnamon
6 tablespoons dry sherry

Cook the sugar and water together to form a syrup at the thread stage. Add the coconut, then stir in the egg yolks. Add the cinnamon and sherry and cook over low heat, stirring constantly with a wooden spoon, until the mixture is thick.

Pour into a flame-proof serving dish. Put under the grill to brown the top. Serve with plain or whipped cream. Serves 6.

coquimol   *cuba*

Coconut Cream Sauce

This is very similar to the Puerto Rican coconut sauce Bien-mesabe though rather richer.

Water from 1 coconut
½ lb. sugar
¾ pint rich coconut milk
   made from 1 coconut
and ⅜ pint single cream (see
   Index)

6 egg yolks
1 teaspoon vanilla
2 tablespoons light rum
   (optional)

Make the coconut water up to ⅜ pint, adding plain water if necessary. Combine the coconut water and sugar in a saucepan and cook, stirring, until the sugar is dissolved. Continue cooking over brisk heat until the syrup reaches the soft ball stage, or 230°F on a sugar thermometer. Remove from the heat and pour in the coconut milk, stirring constantly. Beat the egg yolks lightly. Stir about ½ cup of the hot syrup into the eggs, then pour this into the syrup stirring constantly with a wooden spoon. Cook over low heat, stirring, for about 5 minutes, or until the sauce has thickened. Remove from the heat, cool slightly, and stir in the vanilla and the rum, if liked.

Serve over cake, or instead of whipped cream with desserts such as Gâteau de Patate.

cold rum soufflé   *jamaica*

This is a domestic version of the very good cold rum soufflé developed by the chef at the Jamaica Inn, Ocho Rios. In my experience, it is important to use Appleton Estate rum for the right flavour. However, this is a matter of taste, and any good island rum may be substituted.

1 tablespoon cornflour	1 envelope (1 tablespoon)
2 tablespoons cold water	unflavoured gelatine
⅜ pint single cream	½ teaspoon vanilla
4 eggs, separated	6 tablespoons Appleton Estate
¼ lb. sugar	rum, or other island rum
	Pinch salt

Mix the cornflour with the water and stir into the cream and cook, stirring constantly, over low heat until thickened. Set aside. Beat the egg yolks with the sugar until they are lemon coloured and form a ribbon. Sprinkle the gelatine on ¼ cup cold water to soften. Add the gelatine and the egg mixture to the cream mixture and cook, stirring over very low heat for 5 minutes. Remove from the heat, add the vanilla and rum, stirring to blend well. Add the salt to the egg whites and beat until they stand in peaks. Fold into the yolk mixture. Pour into a 2½-pint soufflé dish, or glass serving bowl, and chill in the refrigerator until set. Serves 6.

corn meal pone   *trinidad and barbados*

½ lb. pumpkin, peeled
½ lb. finely grated fresh
  coconut
2 oz. sugar
1 teaspoon ground allspice

½ teaspoon salt
2 oz. seedless raisins
4 oz. corn meal
1 oz. butter, melted
Milk to mix

Grate the raw pumpkin and mix with the coconut, sugar, all-spice, salt, raisins and corn meal. Stir in the butter. Add enough milk to make a fairly stiff batter, and beat for a minute or two. Pour into a shallow, greased baking pan and bake in a 350°F (gas 4) oven for about half an hour, or until a cake tester comes out clean. This can be eaten as a sweet bread, or as a pudding. Serves 6.

dal puri   *trinidad*

Split Pea Stuffed Bread

4 oz. split peas
1 tablespoon massala (curry
  powder)
1 teaspoon ground cumin
Salt, freshly ground pepper
1 small onion, finely chopped

1 clove garlic, crushed
½ lb. plain flour
1 teaspoon baking powder
1 tablespoon vegetable oil
Extra ghee or oil for frying
  puris

Soak the peas overnight and drain unless they are the quick-cooking variety, in which case omit this step. Put the peas into a saucepan with enough water to cover and stir in the massala (curry powder). Simmer, covered, until tender. Add the cumin, salt and freshly ground pepper to taste, the onion and garlic, and stir to mix well. The mixture should be fairly dry. Set aside.

Sift the flour with baking powder and ½ teaspoon of salt. Add the oil to ½ cup of water and stir into the flour to make a stiff dough. Add a little more water if necessary, but keep the dough stiff, not soft. Knead thoroughly, cover with a cloth and allow to stand for 1 hour. Knead again and divide into 4 equal sized balls. Allow to rest for 10 minutes, then roll out lightly. Put ¼ of the split pea mixture in the centre of each circle of dough, moisten the edges with water and gather up the dough to cover the split peas, sealing it firmly. Roll the filled puris out very carefully to ¼-inch thickness. This is rather tricky as the stuffing mixture bursts out if the dough is rolled too heavily. Using a pastry brush, paint the puri with ghee or oil and cook on a hot, greased griddle, turning frequently and brushing with more ghee or oil. Cook until lightly browned and puffy, about 10 minutes. Eat as a snack, or as an accompaniment to a main dish. Makes 4.

daube de banane   *martinique*

Banana Pudding

2 oz. unsalted butter
6 large bananas, peeled and
   halved lengthwise

⅜ pint sugar-cane syrup (see
   Glossary, under Cane syrup)
⅜ pint sweet red wine
½ teaspoon cinnamon

Heat the butter in a flameproof serving dish and sauté the bananas until they are lightly browned on both sides. Combine the cane syrup, wine, and cinnamon in a saucepan and heat through, stirring to mix well. Pour over the bananas and simmer over very low heat for 15 minutes. Serves 6.

dumplins   *antigua*

Dumplings in Antigua are familiarly known as dumplins.

½ lb. plain flour   1 oz. unsalted butter
1 tablespoon baking powder   ½ teaspoon salt

Sift the flour, salt and baking powder into a bowl. Rub in the butter with the fingertips until the mixture is crumbly. Add enough cold water to make a fairly stiff dough. Turn out on to a flour board and knead until smooth. Shape into balls about 1½ inches in diameter, and flatten. Drop into boiling salted water to cover and cook for about 10 minutes. Makes about 18 dumplins. The dumplins may be dropped into a soup or stew instead of being cooked separately.

flan de coco   *puerto rico*

Coconut Custard

14 oz. sugar   ⅜ pint coconut milk (see
6 eggs, lightly beaten   Index)
¾ pint evaporated milk or   4 oz. freshly grated coconut
    half milk, half double cream

Put ½ lb. of the sugar into a small, heavy saucepan and set it over a medium heat. Cook, stirring with a wooden spoon until the sugar caramelizes. Have ready a 3-pint porcelain mould warmed with boiling water, and dried. Pour in the caramel, turning the mould so that the caramel coats the bottom and an inch or so of the sides. Set aside.

Add the remaining sugar to the eggs. Pour the evaporated milk and coconut milk into a saucepan, bring to scalding point and slowly pour into the egg mixture, stirring with a wooden spoon or wire whisk. Add the coconut and pour into the caramelized mould. Set the mould in a pan of hot water in a 350°F (gas 4) oven and bake for 1 hour, or until a toothpick inserted into the custard comes out clean. Cool thoroughly and unmould onto a serving platter. If any caramel is left in the mould, add a little hot water and set the mould on an asbestos mat over medium heat until the caramel dissolves. Pour over the custard. Serves 6 to 8.

floating islands   *jamaica*

This is a popular dessert that crops up on a number of islands. Both Jamaica and Barbados think of it as local. It is a very old recipe.

3 eggs, separated
2 oz. sugar
¾ pint single cream
1 teaspoon vanilla
3 tablespoons guava jelly

6 tablespoons double cream
3 tablespoons light Jamaica
   rum, such as Appleton
   Estate
1 tablespoon sugar

Combine the egg yolks and sugar in the top of a double boiler away from any heat and beat until the yolks are light and lemon coloured. Scald the single cream and pour into the egg mixture in a steady stream, beating constantly. Place over water in lower half of boiler and cook over gentle heat, stirring constantly, until the mixture thickens and coats the spoon. Do not let it boil. Cool, stir in the vanilla, pour into a serving dish and refrigerate.

Let the guava jelly stand at room temperature. Beat lightly with a fork to soften. Beat the egg whites until they stand in stiff peaks. Fold in the guava jelly. Drop by spoonfuls onto the custard to make the islands. Whip the double cream with the sugar. Add the rum when the cream is stiff and whip for a few seconds longer. Serve separately, or spoon round the outer edge of the custard. Serves 6.

floats   *trinidad*

Fried Yeast Biscuits

These fried biscuits are an essential part of the traditional Trinidadian dish, Accra (Saltfish Cakes) and Floats.

3 tablespoons lukewarm water   1 teaspoon sugar
¼ oz. active dry yeast   4 oz. lard, chilled and cut
14 oz. flour   into ¼-inch dice
1 teaspoon salt   ¾ pint vegetable oil

Pour the water into a small bowl and sprinkle the yeast over it. Let it stand for a few minutes, then stir to dissolve. Set aside in a warm, draught-free place. Sift the flour, salt and sugar together into a bowl. Rub the lard into the flour until the mixture is crumbly. Add the yeast and enough lukewarm water to make a fairly soft dough. Knead on a lightly floured board until the dough is smooth and elastic, about 5 minutes. Return to the bowl, cover and leave in a warm, draught-free place until it has doubled in bulk, about 1 hour. Pinch off pieces of the dough and roll into small balls about 1½ inches in diameter. Arrange on a baking sheet and leave in a warm draught-free place until they have doubled in bulk, about 45 minutes to an hour. Then roll the balls out thin. Heat the oil in a large, heavy frying pan and fry the floats until they are golden brown, about 3 minutes on each side. Drain on paper towels. Serve warm with Accra (see Index). They may also be served with any other codfish cakes, or as a bread, since they are quite delicious. Makes about 18.

figues bananes fourrées   *haiti*

Stuffed Bananas

In the French-speaking islands the bananas known as figues are simply our dessert bananas as distinct from the plantain known as banane. The banane must be cooked before it can be eaten. In addition to figues, there are a great many varieties of eating banana less suited to this sort of presentation.

2 tablespoons seedless raisins	3 oz. icing sugar
3 tablespoons dark rum	3 tablespoons coarsely
3 very large bananas	chopped peanuts
3 tablespoons lemon juice	12 glacé cherries
4 oz. unsalted butter	

Put the raisins to soak in 2 tablespoons of the rum. Peel the bananas and cut into halves lengthwise, then crosswise. Sprinkle with the lemon juice to prevent them turning brown. Cream the butter with the sugar until it is very pale and smooth. Beat in the remaining tablespoon of rum. Scoop out a cavity about $\frac{1}{4}$ inch deep the length of each half banana and stuff with the rum butter cream. Sprinkle with the peanuts, garnish with the raisins and any rum they have not absorbed, and decorate with the glacé cherries. Refrigerate for 2 or 3 hours before serving. Serves 6.

gâteau patate   *martinique*

Sweet Potato Cake

2 lb. sweet potatoes	Grated rind 1 lime
1 oz. unsalted butter	1 tablespoon lime juice
6 oz. dark brown sugar	$\frac{1}{2}$ teaspoon each cinnamon
3 tablespoons dark, island rum	and nutmeg, ground
4 eggs	$\frac{1}{2}$ teaspoon salt
6 tablespoons milk	2 teaspoons baking powder

Peel and slice the sweet potatoes and cook with enough water to cover until tender, about 25 minutes. Drain and mash. While still warm mix in the butter, sugar and rum. Beat in the eggs, one at a time. Then add the milk, grated rind and lime juice. Sift together the cinnamon, nutmeg, salt and baking powder and mix thoroughly into the sweet potatoes.

Pour into a greased 9-by-5 loaf pan. Bake for about 1 hour in a 350°F (gas 4) oven or until a cake tester comes out clean. Let cool few minutes in the pan then turn onto cake rack to cool.

A very similar cake bread is also found in Trinidad, usually with the addition to the batter of 2 oz. of raisins.

gâteau de patate   *haiti*

Sweet Potato Cake

2 lb. sweet potatoes
1 large banana
2 oz. butter, melted and
   cooled
3 eggs, well beaten
½ lb. sugar

⅜ pint evaporated milk
2 oz. seedless raisins
4 tablespoons molasses
¼ teaspoon each ground
   nutmeg and cinnamon
½ teaspoon vanilla

Peel and slice the sweet potatoes and cook in water to cover until tender, about 25 minutes. Drain and mash. Peel and mash the banana and add to the sweet potatoes. Add all the other ingredients, mixing thoroughly. Pour into a greased 9-by-5 loaf pan and bake in the centre of a 350°F (gas 4) oven for 1½ hours. Let cool for a few minutes in the pan then turn onto cake rack to cool.

This is a cross between a pudding and a bread and is delicious for tea time. Served with rum-flavoured whipped cream or with a rich Coconut Cream, it makes a splendid dessert. A little rum may be poured over the cake at serving time with advantage.

gingerbread   *jamaica*

½ lb. plain flour
1 tablespoon baking powder
½ teaspoon baking soda
1 teaspoon allspice, ground
½ teaspoon salt
8 oz. unsalted butter
4 oz. dark brown sugar
⅜ pint molasses

⅜ pint evaporated milk or
    half milk, half double
    cream
2 eggs, well beaten
1 oz. freshly grated ginger
    root, or 2 teaspoons
    ground Jamaica ginger
3 oz. finely chopped
    crystallized ginger

Sift the flour, baking powder, soda, allspice and salt together.
Melt the butter, cool, and mix with the sugar, molasses, milk
and eggs. Add to the flour, blending thoroughly. Fold both the
grated and the crystallized ginger into the mixture. Pour into
a greased 9-by-5-inch loaf pan and bake in a 350°F (gas 4) oven
for about 35 minutes, or until a cake tester comes out clean. If
using ground ginger instead of freshly grated ginger, sift with
the dry ingredients.

ginger mousse   *jamaica*

This mousse is frequently credited to Trinidad but I am inclined
to think it is Jamaican in origin, especially as Jamaican ginger is
justly famous.

1 envelope (1 tablespoon)
    unflavoured gelatine
3 tablespoons cold water
¾ pint evaporated milk or
    half double cream, half
    milk
4 eggs, separated

4 oz. sugar
Pinch salt
6 tablespoons rum, preferably
    a light Jamaican rum
6 oz. finely chopped
    crystallized ginger

Soften the gelatine in the water. Scald the milk and stir in the gelatine to dissolve. Remove from heat. Beat the egg yolks with the sugar until they are pale yellow and form a ribbon. Pour the egg mixture into the milk, stirring constantly with a wooden spoon. Cook, stirring, over very low heat until the custard is thick enough to coat the spoon. Remove from the heat. Beat the egg whites with a pinch of salt until they stand in peaks. Add the rum and the ginger to the cooled custard, mixing well. Stir in a quarter of the egg whites, then fold in the rest gently but thoroughly. Pour into a serving bowl and refrigerate until set. Serves 6.

gratin d'ananas au rhum   *martinique*

Pineapple Gratin with Rum

½ lb. sugar
4 egg yolks from large eggs
2 whole large eggs
¼ lb. plain flour
¾ pint milk
1 teaspoon vanilla
⅜ pint double cream

6 tablespoons dark rum
¾ lb. coarsely chopped pineapple
4 tablespoons toasted slivered almonds
6 oz. sifted icing sugar

Make a thick crème pâtissière: place the sugar and egg yolks in a heavy saucepan and beat until the mixture is pale yellow and forms a ribbon. Beat in the 2 whole eggs, then the flour. Place over very low heat and cook, stirring until the mixture is lukewarm. Meanwhile bring the milk to the boil. Pour it into the egg mixture, stirring vigorously with a wire whisk. Continue to cook stirring, for about 3 minutes, or until the mixture is thick and smooth. Remove from the heat and stir in the vanilla, add the cream and the rum. Strain into a bowl.

Butter a gratin dish (shallow ovenware) and pour in half the cream. Cover with the pineapple and top with the rest of the cream. Sprinkle with the almonds and the icing sugar and put under a grill for a minute or two to brown the top. Serves 6 to 8.

guava pie   *jamaica*

2 tins (34 oz. each) guava
  shells
6 tablespoons lime, or lemon,
  juice
1 tablespoon arrowroot

1 9-inch baked pie shell
  using short-crust pastry
  (see recipe for Mango Pie)
½ pint double cream

Drain the liquid from the guava shells, measure, and pour into a small saucepan. Set the shells aside. Bring the guava juice to the boil and reduce to about ¼ pint. Add the lime juice. Dissolve the arrowroot in a little cold water, stir into the guava juice and cook over low heat, stirring constantly, until the mixture thickens lightly. Remove from the heat.

Spread a thin layer of this glaze over the bottom of the pie crust. Arrange the guava shells, cut side down, in the pie crust in decorative circles. Pour the rest of the glaze over them and cool to room temperature. Whip the cream and serve separately with the pie. Serves 6.

ice creams

Ice cream is extremely popular throughout the islands and good use is made of the fruits that occur in lavish profusion. These recipes, with the exception of Avocado Ice Cream which is from Jamaica, are all from Grenada and are made on the basis of an egg custard.

BASIC CUSTARD FOR ICE CREAM

4 eggs	¾ pint milk
4 oz. sugar	½ teaspoon vanilla

Beat the eggs lightly with the sugar. Scald the milk and stir into the eggs. Cook the egg mixture in the top of a double boiler over hot water, stirring constantly until the mixture coats the spoon. Cool. Add the vanilla. With the addition of fruit pulp, this makes enough ice cream for 6 to 8 servings.

avocado ice cream

Peel and mash 2 medium-sized avocado pears with 2 oz. sugar and a squeeze of lime juice. Mix with the Basic Custard. Turn into a freezing tray and freeze to a mush. Remove from refrigerator, beat well and return to freezing compartment.

banana ice cream

Peel 3 fully ripe bananas and mash. Mix with the Basic Custard. Freeze as above.

coconut ice cream

Add ⅜ pint coconut milk and ⅜ pint double cream to the Basic Custard. Freeze as above.

Top ice cream with grated coconut (toasted with sugar in a 350°F (gas 4) oven for 15 minutes and cooled before using).

guava ice cream

Mix 1 cup stewed sweetened guava purée with Basic Custard. Freeze as above.

mango ice cream

Mix 1 cup mango pulp with 2 oz. of sugar. Mix thoroughly with Basic Custard. Freeze as above.

pawpaw ice cream

Mix 1 cup of mashed pawpaw (papaya) with 2 oz. sugar and 1 tablespoon lime juice. Mix thoroughly with Basic Custard. Freeze as above.

pineapple ice cream

Mix 1 cup crushed pineapple with 2 oz. sugar. Mix thoroughly with Basic Custard. Freeze as above.

soursop ice cream

Mix ¾ pint of soursop (see Glossary) juice with ⅜ pint of double cream. Add 4 oz. sugar, stir well and freeze as above. No custard is used in this recipe, just the soursop juice, cream and sugar.

le gâteau martiniquais   *martinique*

Martinique Sweet Potato Cake

The sweet potatoes used in this cake are the white type, either
red or white skinned, called boniatos. They are true sweet
potatoes, but are less sweet and have firmer flesh than the
orange sweet potato, known as Louisiana yam, which may also
be used. The term yam is mistakenly used, since yams and sweet
potatoes come from entirely different botanical families. If the
Louisiana yam is used, the cake will need longer cooking time.

2 lb. sweet potatoes	Pinch salt
10 oz. sugar	3 eggs, well beaten
2 oz. unsalted butter	2 tablespoons dark rum,
¾ pint coconut cream (see	preferably Martinique
Index)	*rhum vieux*

Peel and slice the sweet potatoes, and put on to cook with enough
cold water to cover in a large saucepan. Cook, covered, until the
sweet potatoes are tender, about 20 minutes. Drain very
thoroughly. Return to the saucepan and mash with the sugar,
butter, coconut cream and salt. Beat in the eggs. Pour into a
buttered 9-inch round cake pan and bake in a 400°F (gas 6)
oven until a cake tester comes out clean, about 2 hours. Remove
from the oven and pour the rum over the cake. Allow to stand
about 5 minutes in the cake pan then turn out to cool. When
cool, refrigerate.

GLAÇAGE AU CHOCOLAT

Chocolate-Butter Icing

3 oz. semi-sweet	3 tablespoons dark rum,
chocolate	preferably Martinique
	rhum vieux
	4 oz. unsalted butter

To make the icing, put the chocolate into the top of a double boiler, over hot water, with the rum, and cook, stirring, until the chocolate is smooth. Remove from the heat, but do not take the chocolate off the hot water. Using a wire whisk, beat in the butter, a tablespoon at a time. Place the mixture over cold water, and continue to beat until it is cool. Allow to stand until it is thick. Spread over the cake, frosting top and sides. Return to the refrigerator until ready to serve. Serves 6 to 8.

In Martinique the cake is sometimes made without any baking. In this case it is essential to use the white (boniato) sweet potato. When the sweet potato is cooked, it should be drained, mashed and then dried slightly over low heat. Omit the eggs, and use only ⅜ pint of the very richest coconut cream. Combine with mashed potatoes. Pour into a buttered mould. Do not douse with rum. Chill thoroughly until the cake is set. (It is helpful to line the mould with buttered waxed paper.)

Turn cake out, frost and return to the refrigerator until immediately before serving.

lime pie   *st kitts*

2 tablespoons cornflour
¾ pint water
½ oz. unsalted butter
2 eggs, well beaten
½ pint strained fresh lime
  juice

2 tablespoons finely grated
  lime rind
½ lb. sugar
9-inch baked pie shell

Mix the cornflour to a paste with a little of the water. Add the rest of the water and pour into a saucepan. Cook, stirring with a wooden spoon, over low heat until thickened. Stir in the butter. Remove from the heat and cool slightly. Stir in the eggs, the lime juice and rind, and the sugar. Cook, stirring, over very low heat for about 5 minutes, or until the mixture has thickened.

Pour into the pie shell and chill. Serve with whipped cream, or Arrowroot Custard. Serves 6.

If liked the pie may be topped with meringue.

FOR MERINGUE

3 egg whites   Pinch salt
3 tablespoons sugar

Beat egg whites, sugar and salt together until the whites stand in peaks. Drop by spoonfuls to cover the pie filling. Bake in a 325°F (gas 3) oven for 15 minutes, or until the meringue is delicately browned.

lime soufflé   *barbados*

1 envelope (1 tablespoon)   4 eggs, separated
  unflavoured gelatine   ¾ lb. sugar
⅜ pint strained fresh lime   4 tablespoons finely grated
  juice   lime rind
1 tablespoon cornflour   Pinch salt
3 tablespoons water   2 oz. coarsely grated fresh
⅜ pint evaporated milk or   coconut, or tinned shredded
  use half milk, half double   moist coconut
  cream

Soften the gelatine in the lime juice and set aside. Mix the cornflour with the water. Pour the milk into a saucepan and stir the cornflour into it. Cook over low heat, stirring constantly with a wooden spoon, until the mixture is smooth and thickened. Beat the eggs yolks until blended, then beat in the sugar gradually Stir into the milk mixture and cook, stirring constantly, until the custard is thick, about 5 minutes. Stir in the gelatine and lime juice, and cook just long enough to dissolve the gelatine. Stir in 3 tablespoons of the grated rind. Cool. Beat the egg whites with the salt until they stand in peaks. Fold gently into the custard. Pour into a $2\frac{1}{2}$-pint soufflé mould or glass serving dish, and chill in the refrigerator until set.

Before serving, spread the coconut in a baking pan and toast it in a 325°F (gas 3) oven, for 10 to 15 minutes, or until light brown. Cook, and sprinkle on the soufflé with the remaining tablespoon of lime rind. Serves 6.

lime soufflé   *tobago*

$1\frac{1}{2}$ oz. unsalted butter
3 tablespoons plain flour
6 tablespoons evaporated milk
6 oz. sugar
6 tablespoons strained fresh
  lime juice

3 tablespoons finely grated
  lime rind
4 eggs, separated and 1 extra
  egg white
Pinch salt

Heat the butter in a saucepan, add the flour and cook, stirring with a wooden spoon, for 1 or 2 minutes without letting the mixture take on any colour. Add the milk, and sugar, and cook, stirring, for 3 or 4 minutes longer. Stir in the lime juice and rind, and mix well. Allow to cool for a few minutes then beat in the egg yolks, one by one. Beat the egg whites with the salt until they stand in peaks. Stir 2 tablespoons of the beaten whites into the soufflé mixture, then gently fold in the rest of egg whites. Pour into a buttered $2\frac{1}{2}$-pint soufflé mould. Bake in a 375°F (gas 5) oven for 30 to 35 minutes or until done. Serve immediately. Serves 6.

mango sherbet   *jamaica*

1 envelope (1 tablespoon)   4 oz. sugar
    unflavoured gelatine   3 tablespoons lime juice
3 cups sieved mango purée

Sprinkle the gelatine on 4 tablespoons cold water, then dissolve,
stirring, over low heat. Cool. Mix mango purée, sugar, lime juice
and gelatine. Chill until the mixture is syrupy. Beat until light
and fluffy. Serve with whipped cream, or ice cream. Serves 6.

mango cream   *jamaica*

1 envelope (1 tablespoon)   4 oz. sugar
    unflavoured gelatine   1 tablespoon lime juice
2 cups mango purée   ⅜ pint double cream

Sprinkle the gelatine on 4 tablespoons cold water, then dissolve,
stirring, over low heat. Cool. Mix the mango purée, sugar, lime
juice and gelatine. Whip the cream until stiff, then fold lightly
but thoroughly into the mango mixture. Pour into a mould
rinsed out with cold water. Refrigerate until set. Unmould and
serve plain, or garnished with slices of mango. Serves 6.

mango ice cream   *jamaica*

1 large, fleshy mango   6 tablespoons water
    weighing about 1½ lb.   3 tablespoons lime juice
4 oz. sugar   ⅜ pint double cream

Peel the mango, cut off the flesh and chop fine. Make a syrup
with the sugar and water simmered together for 5 minutes.

Cool. Add to the mango with the lime juice, mixing thoroughly. Whip the cream until stiff and fold into the mango mixture. Freeze in refrigerator ice trays with the cube dividers removed, at the coldest temperature available. Stir after 1 hour, and again at the end of the second hour. The ice cream should be ready in about 2½ hours from beginning of freezing. Makes 2 ice trays, 6 or more servings.

mango fool   *english-speaking islands*

3 cups mango purée, sieved
1 tablespoon lime juice
4 oz. sugar

1 pint stiffly whipped cream, chilled

Season the mango purée with sugar and lime juice. Chill thoroughly. Just before serving fold in the whipped cream. Blend lightly so that the mixture is not quite uniform in appearance, but has discernable streaks of cream and mango. Serves 6.

If liked the cream may be flavoured with 3 tablespoons of light rum.

mango pie   *english-speaking islands*

SHORT CRUST PASTRY FOR 9-INCH PIE PLATE

6 oz. plain flour
1 tablespoon sugar
¼ teaspoon salt
3 oz. unsalted butter, chilled
   and cut into small pieces

1 oz. lard, chilled and cut
   into small pieces
3 tablespoons cold water

Sift the flour, sugar and salt together into a large bowl. Rub the fat into the flour with the fingertips until the mixture is crumbly.

Sprinkle water over the mixture and mix lightly to a stiffish dough. Gather into a ball, wrap in waxed paper and chill until firm enough to roll out. Turn on to a floured board and roll out into a circle large enough to line the pie plate. Brush the pie plate with melted butter. Roll the pastry round the rolling pin and unroll it into the pie plate. Press the pastry lightly into the sides of the pan, and over the rim. Trim away any excess, and crimp the edges with a fork or the fingers. Prick the bottom with a fork. Bake shell on the centre shelf of an oven preheated to 350°F (gas 4) for 25 minutes, or until golden brown. If air bubbles form, prick bottom of shell 2 or 3 times during the first 10 minutes of baking. Cool before filling.

FILLING FOR PIE

Large, fleshy mango,
    weighing about 1 ½ lb.
3 tablespoons lime juice

4 oz. sugar
3 tablespoons water
1 tablespoon arrowroot

Carefully peel the mango. Feel with the tip of a small, sharp knife where the seed is, and cut off 2 slices lengthwise, down each side of the mango as close to the seed as possible. Cut each slice into lengthwise strips about ¼ inch thick, sprinkle with a little of the lime juice and set aside. Cut all the remaining flesh off the seed. There should be about 1 cup of pulp. Put the pulp into a saucepan with the sugar, remaining lime juice and water and cook until soft, about 10 minutes. Rub through a sieve, return to the saucepan and stir in the arrowroot mixed with a little cold water, and cook until thickened, stirring constantly. Cool slightly. Arrange the mango slices in the baked pastry shell in an overlapping pattern, using the shorter pieces to fill in at the sides. Spoon the purée over these pieces evenly. Chill well before serving. Serve plain, or with custard, whipped cream, or ice cream to taste. Serves 6.

mango ice   *jamaica*

2 cups sieved mango purée   6 tablespoons water
2 tablespoons lime juice   1 egg white
2 oz. sugar

Mix the mango purée with the lime juice. Simmer the sugar and
water together for 5 minutes to make a syrup. Cool. Add to the
mango purée, mixing thoroughly. Beat the egg white until it
stands in peaks. Fold into the mango mixture. Freeze until firm,
about 3 hours in refrigerator ice trays. Every half hour during
the freezing process, stir the mixture, scraping into the centre
the ice crystals that form around the edge of the tray. The
finished ice should have a snowy texture. Makes 2 ice trays, 6 or
more servings.

mango mousse   *barbados*

Ripe mangoes, weighing   1 envelope (1 tablespoon)
   about 4 lb.   unflavoured gelatine
6 tablespoons lime juice   2 egg whites
4 oz. granulated sugar   Pinch of salt
                                  6 tablespoons double cream

Peel the mangoes, cut the flesh off the seeds, and purée in an
electric blender with the lime juice, being careful not to overblend. There will be 5 cups of purée. Stir in the sugar. Dissolve
the gelatine in 3 tablespoons hot water, cool, and stir into the
mango purée. Beat the egg whites with the salt until they stand
in peaks. Whip the cream until it is stiff. Fold the cream into the
egg whites, then fold this mixture gently into the mango purée.
Pour into a large serving dish, or into individual dishes, and
refrigerate for 2 to 3 hours, or until set. Serves 6 to 8.

mousse à l'ananas   *martinique*

Pineapple Mousse

¾ pint unsweetened   6 tablespoons cornflour
   pineapple juice   6 egg whites
½ lb. sugar, or less to taste   Pinch salt

Pour the pineapple juice into a saucepan, and add the sugar.
Use a little of the juice to dissolve the cornflour, then add the
cornflour to the saucepan and cook, stirring constantly with a
wooden spoon over low heat for 5 minutes. Cool. Beat the egg
whites with the salt until they stand in peaks. Fold into the
mixture, gently but thoroughly. Turn into a serving dish and
refrigerate. Serve with Crème Anglaise.

CRÈME ANGLAISE

Custard Sauce

6 egg yolks   1 teaspoon vanilla
2 oz. sugar   ¼ lb. coarsely chopped
⅛ teaspoon salt   pineapple
¾ pint single cream

In the top of a double boiler, but not over any heat, beat the egg
yolks, sugar, and salt together until the mixture is pale yellow
and forms a ribbon. Scald the cream and pour it slowly into the
egg mixture, stirring constantly with a wooden spoon or wire
whisk. Pour hot, not boiling, water into the lower part of the
double boiler. Replace the top part with the custard and cook,
stirring constantly over very low heat so that the water does not
boil, until the mixture thickens and coats the spoon. Remove
from the heat and stir until slightly cooled. Strain, and add the
vanilla and pineapple. Chill and serve as a sauce with the mousse.
Serves 6 to 8.

mrs roy lyons' mango cheese   *jamaica*

Jamaicans insist that you must use No. 11 mangoes for this recipe to succeed. I have tried it with several types of mango and report success. However, if it is overcooked the mango paste turns into what Jamaicans graphically call tie-teeth.

Juicy-type mangoes   Lime juice (optional)
Sugar

Peel the mangoes, cut off the flesh and push through a sieve to remove any stringy part. To each cup of purée add 1 cup of sugar and 1 teaspoon lime juice, if liked. Cook in a heavy saucepan over medium heat, stirring constantly with a wooden spoon. When the bubbles grow smaller and a spoon drawn across the bottom of the pan leaves a clean wake, the mango should be tested: drop a little onto an ice cube, if it sets, turn the mango cheese into a damp mould and when cool, turn out. In Latin America this is eaten with fresh cheese and crackers. It may be eaten by itself or with plain cake or cookies.

orange bread   *barbados*

½ lb. plain flour
4 teaspoons baking powder
4 oz. sugar
½ teaspoon salt

1 tablespoon grated orange rind
1 egg, well beaten
⅜ pint orange juice
2 oz. unsalted butter, melted

Sift the flour, baking powder, sugar, salt and orange rind together. Mix the egg with the orange juice and butter and fold into the flour. Pour the batter into a greased 9-by-5 loaf tin and bake in a 350°F (gas 4) oven, for 30 minutes, or until a cake tester comes out clean.

pan de maíz   *dominican republic*

Corn Bread

10 oz. yellow corn meal
6 oz. plain flour
3 tablespoons baking powder*
1 teaspoon salt
8 oz. unsalted butter
½ lb. finely grated fresh
   coconut

½ teaspoon aniseed
   (optional)
6 tablespoons double cream
6 tablespoons coconut milk
   (see Index)
4 eggs, well beaten

Sift the dry ingredients together. Cream the butter until light
and fluffy and gradually blend into the corn meal and flour. Add
the coconut and the aniseed, if liked. Add the cream, coconut
milk, and the eggs. Mix well, beating for a minute or two.
Grease two 9-by-5 loaf tins. Spoon the mixture, which should be
very soft, into the tins. Bake in the centre of a 350°F (gas 4) oven
for 30 minutes, or until the bread shrinks slightly from the sides
of the tin and is golden brown. This is very good sliced, toasted
and buttered. Makes 2 loaves.

pain de patates douces   *haiti*

Sweet Potato Bread

2 lb. sweet potatoes
4 oz. unsalted butter,
   melted and cooled
¼ pint each milk and
   coconut milk (see Index)
⅜ pint molasses
1 large banana, mashed

½ teaspoon each ground
   cinnamon and nutmeg
½ teaspoon salt
1 teaspoon vanilla
Grated rind of 1 lime
3 oz. raisins (optional)
4 oz. sugar

*This amount of baking powder may look alarming but it is needed
as the corn meal is very dense in texture.

Peel the sweet potatoes, chop coarsely and grate in a blender, bit by bit, to a medium consistency. Put into a large mixing bowl and add all the other ingredients, mixing thoroughly. Pour into a greased rectangular baking dish. Bake in a 400°F (gas 6) oven for about 45 minutes. Serve at room temperature from the baking dish. Makes 6 to 8 servings.

pan dulce de maíz   *dominican republic*

Sweet Corn Bread

¾ lb. yellow corn meal
¼ lb. plain flour
3 tablespoons baking powder*
½ teaspoon each ground cinnamon, nutmeg and cloves
¼ lb. sugar
1 teaspoon salt
3 oz. each of butter and lard

6 tablespoons each milk and coconut milk (see Index)
4 eggs, well beaten
Grated rind of 1 lime, or lemon
½ lb. finely grated fresh coconut
½ lb. mixed fruits and peels (glacé cake mix)

Sift all the dry ingredients, including the spices, together.

Cream the butter and lard until light and fluffy and add to the corn meal mixture. Add the milk, coconut milk, eggs and grated rind. Mix in the grated coconut and the fruits and peels, lightly floured. Mix well and pour into 2 greased 9-by-5 loaf tins. Bake for about 35 minutes in the centre of a 350°F (gas 4) oven, or until a cake tester comes out clean.

* This amount of baking powder may look alarming but is needed as the corn meal is very dense in texture.

pastel de batata

cuba

Sweet Potato Cake

4 oz. unsalted butter
2 cups sweet potato paste
(Boniatillo, see Index)
½ teaspoon vanilla

2 eggs, separated
¼ lb. flour
2 teaspoons baking powder
Pinch of salt

Melt the butter, and beat it into the sweet potato paste. Add the vanilla. Beat the egg yolks thoroughly and add. Sift the flour with the baking powder and add. Beat the egg whites with a pinch of salt until stiff and fold into the potato mixture gently but thoroughly. Pour into a buttered 3-pint soufflé dish, and bake in a 350°F (gas 4) oven for about 45 minutes, or until a cake tester comes out clean. This can be served as a sweet bread, or with rum-flavoured whipped cream as a dessert. Makes 6 to 8 servings.

piña con ron

puerto rico

Pineapple with Rum

I first encountered this way of serving pineapple in Puerto Rico, but later met with it in other islands. In Martinique *rhum vieux* is poured over the fruit with a generous, unmeasured hand, giving the pineapple a very heady flavour. The lighter Puerto Rican rum is also extremely pleasant.

1 small, ripe pineapple   Rum

Cut the pineapple lengthwise into thirds, slicing through the leaves, which should be left on. Carefully cut the flesh from each shell in 1 piece. Cut off the core by slicing lengthwise. Halve the flesh lengthwise then cut crosswise into bite-size pieces. Replace in the pineapple shells. Pour on rum to taste. Serves 3.

pitch lake pudding   *barbados*

This Bajan pudding, which sometimes appears as Mousse An-
tillaise, is said to have been inspired by Trinidad's Pitch Lake, a
seepage of natural asphalt. It makes an exceptionally good party
dessert. The recipe can be successfully doubled.

4 oz. unsweetened cocoa	5 eggs, separated
2 tablespoons instant espresso coffee	3 tablespoons dark rum
	Pinch of salt
8 oz. caster sugar	½ pint double cream

Place the cocoa in the top of a double boiler over hot water.
Dissolve the coffee in ¼ pint boiling water. Add the sugar and
stir until dissolved. Stir this mixture gradually into the cocoa and
cook, stirring with a wooden spoon over low heat for 5 minutes.
Beat in the egg yolks, one at a time, beating vigorously after
each addition. Remove from the heat and stir in the rum. Add
the salt to the egg whites and beat until they stand in stiff peaks
on the beater when it is lifted from the bowl. Fold into the cocoa
mixture gently but thoroughly. Pour into a 1 ½-pint soufflé dish,
or glass serving dish, and refrigerate overnight, or for several
hours.

To serve, beat the cream until stiff and spread it over the
mousse. The cream may be flavoured and sweetened if liked, in
which case add 1 tablespoon caster sugar and 1 tablespoon dark
rum. Serves 6.

pudding au fruit à pain   *martinique*

Breadfruit Pudding

½ tin (26 oz.) breadfruit	2 oz. unsalted butter, melted and cooled
4 oz. sugar	

Grated rind of 1 lime, or
lemon
2 tablespoons plain flour
3 tablespoons Martinique
rhum vieux

½ teaspoon vanilla
¾ pint milk
2 large eggs

Drain the breadfruit, divide in 2 equal parts. Store the second half with the tinned liquid in a covered container in the refrigerator. It will keep for a week or two. Mash the breadfruit until smooth. Add the sugar, butter, lime rind, and flour, mixing well. Stir in the rum, vanilla, milk and eggs, beating until the mixture is smooth. Pour into a buttered mould or baking dish and cook for 1½ hours in a 350° (gas 4) oven, or until a toothpick inserted into the pudding comes out clean. Serve at room temperature with rum sauce, or any dessert sauce. Serves 6.

If using fresh breadfruit, peel, remove the core and cook 1 lb. of the breadfruit in boiling salted water until tender, about 20 minutes. Drain and use as tinned breadfruit.

I like to pour a jigger of *rhum vieux* over the pudding while it is still warm, then turn it out onto a serving platter, and when it is quite cold, mask it with double cream whipped with a tablespoon of sugar and a tablespoon of *rhum vieux*. It may be refrigerated. It is also delicious served with a very heavy Coconut Cream flavoured with *rhum vieux* and a little sugar.

pumpkin buns   *trinidad*

½ lb. plain flour
½ teaspoon salt
1 teaspoon ground allspice
1 teaspoon ground ginger
3 oz. seedless raisins
½ oz. active dry yeast
6 tablespoons lukewarm water

2 oz. sugar
½ lb. cooked mashed West
Indian pumpkin
1 oz. unsalted butter
2 eggs, well beaten
Grated rind of 1 lime

Sift the flour with the salt, allspice, and ginger into a mixing bowl. Add the raisins. Sprinkle the yeast on the lukewarm water and stir in the sugar. Set aside until it bubbles. Add the butter to the pumpkin while it is still warm, and stir to blend well. Make a well in the flour mixture and add the yeast, pumpkin, eggs and grated rind. Mix to a smooth dough, cover and set in a warm, draught-free place until doubled in bulk, about half an hour. Shape into 12 buns and place on a greased baking sheet. Leave to rise again in a warm draught-free place. Bake in a 400°F (gas 6) oven for about 15 minutes or until done. Serve warm or at room temperature.

pumpkin tea bread   *trinidad*

½ lb. plain flour
1 tablespoon baking powder
½ teaspoon salt
4 oz. unsalted butter
6 oz. sugar
1 egg, well beaten

1 teaspoon Angostura bitters
½ lb. cooked mashed West
  Indian pumpkin
3 oz. glacé fruit mix, or
  seedless raisins

Sift the flour with the baking powder and salt into a bowl. In a separate bowl cream the butter and sugar until the mixture is light and fluffy. Add the egg and Angostura bitters, mixing well, then beat in the pumpkin and the flour alternately until the batter is smooth. Toss the glacé fruits with a tablespoon of flour and stir into the batter. Pour into a buttered 9-by-5-inch loaf pan and bake in the middle of a 375°F (gas 5) oven for about 30 minutes, or until a cake tester comes out clean.

roti   *trinidad*

Bread

Roti simply means bread, and this is the term most often used in Trinidad for parathas, which is what these are. They are of Indian origin, but like everything else in the Caribbean, have evolved from the original. One 12-inch roti makes a magnificent lunch when a generous dollop of curried chicken, kid, shrimp or potatoes is placed in the centre, and the bread folded over it like an envelope. It can be eaten with a knife and fork; fingers however, are more fun. The 8-inch roti is served as a bread with curries. I have two versions of roti, one a little more elaborate than the other, both very good.

½ lb. plain flour
1 teaspoon baking powder
1 teaspoon salt

1½ oz. butter, or vegetable
  shortening
Ghee (see Index)
Extra flour

Sift the flour, baking powder and salt into a bowl. Rub in the butter or shortening with the fingertips until the fat is in small flakes. Pour 3 tablespoons cold water over the flour and mix to make a fairly stiff dough. Add more water, 1 tablespoon at a time, until the dough holds together but is not sticky. Knead until smooth. Cover, and leave in a warm place for half an hour. Knead again for 3 or 4 minutes then divide into 4 equal balls. Roll out on a floured board into 12- or 8-inch rounds. Brush lightly all over with ghee, then sprinkle with flour. Fold in half, then in half again, to form a 4-layered quarter circle. Cover and leave for half an hour. Then shape roughly into a circle with the hands, and roll out on to a floured board into 12- or 8-inch rounds. Heat a cast-iron frying pan or griddle so that a little flour sprinkled on it will brown instantly, or a drop of water will sputter. Place 1 of the roti in the pan or on the griddle and cook for about a minute. Turn, and spread with a thin layer of ghee. Cook for 2 minutes, then spread again with ghee. Cook for 1 minute longer then turn. Cook for about a minute then remove from pan to a board. Hit with a wooden mallet all over until it is flaky. Wrap in a towel and keep warm until the other roti are cooked. Serve at once. Serves 4.

½ lb. plain flour
¼ teaspoon baking soda
½ teaspoon salt

Milk, or water to mix
Ghee (see Index) or
   vegetable oil

Sift the flour, baking soda, and salt into a bowl. Add enough milk or water to mix to a stiff dough. Knead the dough thoroughly on a lightly floured board. Form into 4 balls and roll out into 8-inch circles. Brush all over with ghee or vegetable oil and fold into a ball again. Cover and allow to stand for about 15 minutes. Roll out again into 8-inch circles. Heat a cast-iron frying pan or griddle until a drop of water will sputter when dropped on it, or a little flour will brown instantly. Cook the roti for about 1 minute, turn, spread with ghee or vegetable oil and cook, turning frequently until the roti is baked. Remove from the pan and clap with both hands until pliable. Wrap in a towel to keep warm until the other roti are cooked. Serve at once. Serves 4.

surullitos   *puerto rico*

Corn Sticks

¾ pint water
1 teaspoon salt
6 oz. yellow corn meal
Vegetable oil or lard for
   frying

4 oz. grated Edam or mild
Cheddar cheese, which are
the nearest equivalents to
the local cheese known as
native cheese

Combine the water and salt in a saucepan and bring to the boil. Pour in the corn meal in a steady stream, and cook, stirring for about 5 minutes, or until the mixture is thick and smooth. Remove from the heat and stir in the cheese, mixing well. Cool.

Take out by spoonfuls and form into cigar-shaped cylinders about 3 inches long and 1 inch in diameter. Heat oil or lard in a large, heavy frying pan and fry the corn sticks until golden brown all over. Drain on paper towels and keep warm until the mixture is used up. Serve warm as bread, or as an accompaniment to drinks. Makes about 24.

sweet cassava bread   *st kitts*

½ lb. finely grated cassava   ¼ lb. freshly grated coconut
1 teaspoon salt   ¼ lb. brown sugar

Mix the cassava and salt. Place in a damp kitchen towel or cloth, and wring out all the liquid. (The liquid can be used to make cassareep.) Spread half the cassava meal in the bottom of a small iron or other heavy pan and pat down firmly. Cover with the coconut and the brown sugar. Add the rest of the cassava and pat down lightly. Bake in a 350°F (gas 4) oven until lightly browned, about 20 minutes. Makes 6 servings.

sweet potato and coconut bread   *barbados*

1 lb. white sweet potatoes   4 tablespoons lime juice
4 oz. finely grated fresh   2 eggs, well beaten
  coconut   1 ½ oz. seedless raisins
1 oz. unsalted butter   1 ½ oz. chopped crystallized
1 teaspoon ground allspice   ginger
1 teaspoon baking powder   1 ½ oz. mixed fruits and
½ teaspoon salt   peels (glacé cake mix)
¼ pint orange juice   3 tablespoons dark rum

Peel and grate the sweet potatoes. Mix with the coconut in a large bowl. Soften the butter and beat in. Add the allspice, baking powder and salt to the orange and lime juice and add, stirring to mix thoroughly. Add the eggs, raisins, ginger and mixed fruits and peels, again stirring to mix thoroughly. Pour into a greased baking dish or loaf tin and bake in a 350°F (gas 4) oven for 1 hour, or until a cake tester comes out clean. Pour the rum over the loaf while it is still hot. Serve warm, as a pudding, from the baking dish with whipped cream, or turn out of loaf tin, slice and serve with butter as a sweet bread. Serves 6.

tarta de batata   *dominican republic*

Sweet Potato Tart

⅝ pint coconut milk (see Index)

1 lb. cooked, mashed sweet potato

½ teaspoon ground nutmeg

1 teaspoon ground cinnamon

1 oz. unsalted butter, melted and cooled

2 oz. caster sugar

Grated rind 1 lime

4 eggs, lightly beaten

1 unbaked 9-inch pastry shell

1 teaspoon sugar

½ pint double cream

1 tablespoon light rum, such as Appleton Estate or Mount Gay

Mix the coconut milk and sweet potato thoroughly in a bowl with the nutmeg, cinnamon, butter, sugar and lime rind. Fold in the eggs. Pour the mixture into the pastry shell and bake in a 400°F (gas 6) oven for 30 minutes or until set.

Add the sugar to the cream and beat until the cream is stiff. Add the rum, all at once, and beat for a minute or two longer. Transfer to a serving bowl. Serve the tart chilled, or at room temperature, accompanied by the bowl of cream. Serves 6.

tarta de ciruelas pasas   *dominican republic*

Prune Tart

1 lb. pitted prunes
1 oz. plain flour
½ lb. sugar
¼ teaspoon salt

½ teaspoon ground cinnamon
⅜ pint double cream
1 unbaked 9-inch pastry shell

Set aside 18 of the prunes. Finely chop the rest. Sift together the flour, sugar, salt and cinnamon. Stir in the cream. Add the chopped prunes and mix well. Turn into the unbaked pie shell. Decorate in a circle around the pie filling with the reserved whole prunes.

Bake in a 400°F (gas 6) oven for 35 to 40 minutes, or until set. Serve with whipped cream, if liked. Serves 6.

tere lomba's budin de pan   *puerto rico*

Tere Lomba's Bread Pudding

1 lb. day-old loaf sandwich
   bread
1 pint milk
5 eggs, well beaten
½ lb. sugar
1 teaspoon ground cinnamon

¼ teaspoon ground nutmeg
4 oz. unsalted butter, melted
3 tablespoons rum
1 lb. pasta de guayaba
   (guava paste), cut into
   ¼-inch dice

Remove the crusts from the bread and cut it into cubes, place in a bowl and pour the milk over it. Allow to stand for 15 minutes. Stir in the eggs, sugar, cinnamon, nutmeg, butter and rum, mixing thoroughly. Fold in the guava dice. Pour the pudding into a caramelized 2½-pint mould. Stand the mould in a baking pan containing 1 inch of water. Bake in a 350°F (gas 4) oven for about 1 hour and 45 minutes, or until a cake tester comes out clean. Serves 6.

To caramelize the mould see Index for Flan de Coco (Coconut Custard).

wilma's sweet cassava bread   *st lucia*

½ lb. cassava meal   4 oz. grated coconut
2 oz. brown sugar

Mix the cassava meal, sugar and coconut thoroughly. If the cassava and coconut are freshly grated no liquid is needed. Otherwise the mixture should be moistened with enough water to make it handleable. Grease a heavy, 10-inch skillet and when it is hot enough for a drop of cold water to sputter, add the cassava mixture, patting it down evenly. Cook over fairly brisk heat for about 1½ minutes, turn and cook other side, until lightly browned. This is pleasant by itself or with stewed fruit. Serves 2 to 4.

banana daiquiri

cuba

2 oz. light rum
½ oz. banana liqueur
½ oz. lime juice

½ small banana, peeled and
   coarsely chopped
½ cup crushed ice

Combine all the ingredients in an electric blender, and blend at high speed until smooth and frothy. Pour into a champagne glass. Serves 1.

batido de piña

puerto rico

Fresh Pineapple Drink

4 oz. light rum
3 oz. fresh pineapple,
   coarsely chopped

Caster sugar to taste
½ cup finely crushed ice
Sprig fresh mint

Combine the rum and pineapple in an electric blender and blend on high speed until the pineapple is completely pulverized and the drink smooth. Taste, and blend in some sugar if necessary.

Put the ice into a goblet and pour in the liquor. Stir to mix. Decorate with the sprig of mint. Serves 1.

blue mountain cocktail   *jamaica*

1½ oz. light Jamaica rum   2 tablespoons orange juice
¾ oz. vodka   1 tablespoon lime juice
¾ oz. Tia Maria   3 or 4 ice cubes

Combine all the ingredients in a cocktail shaker and shake
vigorously. Pour, unstrained, into glass. Serves 1.

cuban cocktail   *cuba*

2 oz. light rum   1 tablespoon lime juice
¾ oz. apricot brandy   3 or 4 ice cubes

Combine the ingredients in a cocktail shaker and shake vigorously. Serve strained or unstrained. Serves 1.

cuban special   *cuba*

2 oz. light rum   3 or 4 ice cubes
1 teaspoon Curaçao   Stick pineapple
1 tablespoon pineapple juice   Maraschino cherry
1 tablespoon lime juice

Combine the rum, Curaçao, pineapple and lime juices, and the
ice cubes in a cocktail shaker and shake vigorously. Serve strained
or unstrained and decorated with fruit. Serves 1.

curaçao special

½ oz. light rum
½ oz. dark rum
½ oz. 151% proof rum
½ oz. sweet vermouth
½ oz. Curaçao
1 oz. orange juice

½ teaspoon lime juice
½ teaspoon grenadine
½ cup finely crushed ice
1 tablespoon dry red wine
Slice of orange
Maraschino cherry

Combine the rums, vermouth, Curaçao, orange and lime juice and grenadine in a mixing glass and stir to mix well. Put the ice into a goblet and pour the liquor over it. Stir. Carefully pour the red wine on top. Garnish with orange slice and cherry. Serves 1.

ginger beer

This is a popular Christmas drink.

1 teaspoon active dry yeast
2 teaspoons plain flour
2 oz. fresh ginger root, or
　　use ground ginger
6 pints boiling water

1½ lb. sugar
6 tablespoons lime juice
2 teaspoons grated lime rind
Slice toast

Mix the yeast and flour with 3 tablespoons lukewarm water, cover and leave in a warm place until it is bubbly. Peel the fresh ginger root and crush with the flat side of a cleaver. Put into a large bowl and pour on the boiling water. Cool. Add the sugar, lime juice and rind, and stir to mix thoroughly. Spread the yeast on the slice of toast and add. Cover and stand in a warm place for 24 hours. Remove the toast. Strain, bottle and cork tightly. Wait 2 days before using. Serve in small tumblers, with or without ice cubes. Makes about 16 servings.

ginger beer   *trinidad*

This drink is popular throughout the English-speaking islands, especially at Christmas time. The crystal clear ginger beer makes a pretty contrast to the pink of Sorrel Drink, also popular at Christmas.

1 oz. fresh ginger root, or
  use 1 tablespoon ground
  ginger
4 tablespoons lime juice

Peel 1 lime
½ lb. sugar
1½ pints boiling water
1 teaspoon active dry yeast

Peel the ginger root and crush it lightly with the flat side of a cleaver. Combine the ginger, lime juice, peel and sugar in a large bowl and pour the boiling water over them. Put the yeast into a small bowl with 3 tablespoons lukewarm water and let it stand for a few minutes, then stir to dissolve it completely. Let it stand in warm, draught-free place for about 5 minutes, or until it begins to bubble. Add it to the ginger mixture, and stir thoroughly. Cover the bowl and leave in a warm, draught-free place for a week, stirring every second day. Strain through a fine sieve, bottle, and let the beer stand at room temperature for 3 or 4 days longer. Chill, and serve, with or without ice, in tumblers. A little rum may be added to the ginger beer, if liked. Makes 1½ pints.

daiquiri   *cuba*

2 oz. light rum
2 tablespoons lime juice

1 teaspoon caster sugar
3 or 4 ice cubes

Combine all the ingredients in a cocktail shaker, and shake vigorously. Strain into a thoroughly chilled cocktail glass. Serves 1.

el jíbaro

1 ½ oz. orange juice   1 oz. 151% proof rum
1 ½ oz. lemon juice   Dash of Grand Marnier
1 ¼ oz. dark rum   Lime slice
2 or 3 cubes ice   Mint leaves

Combine the orange and lemon juice, the dark rum and the ice
cubes in a cocktail shaker and shake vigorously. Strain into a
tumbler and add the 151% proof rum and Grand Marnier.
Garnish with the lime slice and mint leaves. Serves 1.

frozen daiquiri   *cuba*

3 oz. light rum   2 teaspoons caster sugar
2 tablespoons lime juice   2 cups finely crushed ice

Place all the ingredients in an electric blender and blend on high
speed until the contents have the consistency of snow. Serve
immediately in a thoroughly chilled saucer champagne glass,
with short drinking straws. Serves 1.

hartley augiste's rum punch   *dominica*

Dominica produces some glorious rum. The tiny mountainous
island lying between Martinique and Guadeloupe also produces
glorious limes, and is in fact the home of Rose's Lime Juice. The
combination of rum and lime produces the best rum punch I have
ever had.

2 oz. Dominica rum, or use a light rum from Martinique or Guadeloupe
½ oz. lime juice
3 teaspoons simple syrup (see Index)

2 or 3 dashes Angostura bitters
3 or 4 ice cubes
Maraschino cherry

Combine the rum, lime juice, simple syrup, bitters and ice in a cocktail shaker and shake vigorously. Strain over ice cubes in a small tumbler. Garnish with the cherry. Serves 1.

hot buttered rum   *jamaica*

Cinnamon stick
2 oz. light Jamaica rum
¼ oz. unsalted butter

6 oz. boiling cider, or apple juice
Nutmeg

Put the cinnamon stick into an 8 oz. mug. Add the rum and butter and pour on the hot cider. Stir and grate a little nutmeg on top. Serves 1.

kibra hacha   *curaçao*

This drink is named after the tree which grows in Curaçao. All the branches lean to one side. The significance of the name applied to the drink escapes me.

1½ oz. light rum
½ oz. Curaçao
1 teaspoon lime juice

2 dashes Angostura bitters
3 or 4 ice cubes

Combine the rum, Curaçao, lime juice, and bitters in a mixing glass and stir well. Pour over the ice cubes in a glass. Serves 1.

leo byam's cream punch   *trinidad*

Creole Eggnog

A friend, Leo Byam, gave me this excellent recipe for the traditional holiday eggnog. It is supposed to keep, if refrigerated, but I have never found that anyone gave it a chance.

6 medium eggs	1 teaspoon vanilla
2 8 oz. tins sweetened condensed milk	Dash Angostura bitters
Grated peel 1 lime, or lemon	1 pint Trinidad rum, or more to taste

Beat the eggs slightly in a large bowl. Add all the other ingredients, except the rum, and mix well. Add the rum, mixing thoroughly. Serve over crushed ice in punch cups. Makes 6 to 12 servings.

mangoade   *jamaica*

2 cups coarsely chopped ripe mango	1 teaspoon grated orange rind
2 oz. sugar, or to taste	¾ pint orange juice
¾ pint water	¼ pint lime juice

Rub the mango through a sieve. Combine the sugar, water and orange rind in a saucepan and heat, stirring, until the sugar has dissolved. Cool and add to the mango purée and fruit juices. Refrigerate. Serve in tall glasses over ice cubes. Serves 6.

mango daiquiri　　　　　　　*cuba*

4 oz. light rum
1 oz. Curaçao
½ cup finely chopped fresh
　mango

2 tablespoons lime juice
1 tablespoon caster sugar
2 cups finely crushed ice

Place all the ingredients in an electric blender and blend at high speed until the contents have the consistency of snow. Pour into 2 thoroughly chilled champagne glasses and serve with short drinking straws. Serves 2.

noël's planter's punch
from mandeville　　　*jamaica*

1 ½ oz. dark Jamaican rum
¾ oz. lime juice
3 oz. orange juice

½ cup crushed ice
Maraschino cherry

Combine all the ingredients in a cocktail shaker and shake vigorously. Strain into a tumbler and garnish with the cherry. Serves 1.

peach daiquiri　　　　　　*cuba*

2 oz. light rum
½ medium-sized ripe fresh
　peach, peeled and coarsely
　chopped

1 tablespoon caster sugar
1 cup finely crushed ice

Combine all the ingredients in an electric blender and blend at high speed for about 30 seconds. Pour into a thoroughly chilled champagne glass and serve with short drinking straws. Serves 1.

peanut punch   *trinidad*

2 tablespoons cornflour   6 tablespoons peanut butter
¼ pint water   Sugar to taste
¾ pint milk

Mix the cornflour and water in a small saucepan. Add the milk,
peanut butter and sugar, to taste. Cook, stirring with a whisk,
over moderate heat until thickened and thoroughly mixed. Cool
and refrigerate. Serve in tumblers, with or without ice. Serves 2.

Though this is traditionally served as a soft drink, many
Trinidadians find it improved, as indeed I do, by the addition of
a good Trinidadian or similar rum. Add 4 oz. rum to the above
recipe and serve in tumblers with ice cubes.

pineapple daiquiri   *cuba*

2 oz. light rum   1 tablespoon lime juice
½ oz. Cointreau   Caster sugar
¼ pint pineapple juice   Ice cubes

Combine the rum, Cointreau, pineapple and lime juice in an
electric blender and blend quickly at high speed. Taste and
blend in a little caster sugar, if necessary. Fill a glass with ice
cubes and pour in the daiquiri. Serves 1.

planter's punch   *all islands*

1½ oz. light rum   1 teaspoon lime juice
1½ oz. orange juice   4 ice cubes

Combine the rum, orange juice and lime juice in a cocktail shaker with 3 of the ice cubes and shake vigorously. Place the remaining ice cube in a glass and strain the punch over it. Stir and serve. Serves 1.

planter's punch   *jamaica*

2 tablespoons lime juice
2 tablespoons simple syrup
  (see Index)
3 oz. dark Jamaica rum

Dash Angostura bitters
½ cup finely crushed ice
Maraschino cherry

Combine the lime juice, syrup, rum, bitters and crushed ice in a cocktail shaker and shake vigorously. Pour, unstrained, into a small tumbler. Decorate with the cherry. Serves 1.

planter's punch   *puerto rico*

2 tablespoons fresh lime juice
2 teaspoons caster sugar
1½ oz. dark Puerto Rican
  rum
½ teaspoon Angostura bitters
½ cup crushed ice

Ice cubes
Carbonated water
1 to 2 tablespoons 151%
  proof rum
Pineapple stick, slice of
  orange, maraschino cherry

Combine the lime juice, sugar, rum, bitters and crushed ice in a cocktail shaker and shake vigorously. Pour, unstrained, into a tumbler. Add ice cubes or a little carbonated water to taste. Invert a teaspoon in the glass and carefully pour in the 151% proof rum so that it floats on top of the drink. Garnish with the pineapple stick, slice of orange and cherry. Serves 1.

piña colada   *puerto rico*

4 oz. pineapple juice   ½ cup crushed ice
2 oz. coconut cream   Pineapple stick
2 oz. golden rum   Maraschino cherry

Place all the ingredients, except the pineapple stick and cherry,
in an electric blender, and blend for a few seconds. Pour,
unstrained, into a tumbler and decorate with the pineapple
stick and cherry. Serves 1.

pineappleade   *st kitts*

1 medium-sized pineapple   1 lb. sugar
¼ pint lime juice   3 pints water

Peel the pineapple and grate fruit finely. Place in a bowl and
pour the lime juice over it. Boil the sugar with ¾ pint of the
water for 4 minutes, then pour over the fruit. Add the remaining
water, and stir to mix well. Let it stand for 1 hour. Strain,
pressing the fruit down into the sieve to extract all the juice.
Serve in tumblers with crushed ice, or add 1½ to 2 oz. rum to
each serving. Makes about 3 pints.

punch au lait de coco   *martinique*

Rum and Coconut Milk Punch

1½ oz. white rum, preferably   ⅛ teaspoon vanilla
   Martinique *rhum blanc*   4 oz. coconut milk
½ oz. jus de canne   ½ cup finely crushed ice
   (cane syrup, see Glossary)   Nutmeg

Combine the rum, cane syrup, vanilla, coconut milk and ice in a cocktail shaker and shake vigorously. Pour, unstrained, into a goblet. Grate a little nutmeg on top. Serves 1.

If liked, the drink may be strained. Sweetened coconut milk, sold in tins, may be used for this drink, in which case, omit the cane syrup.

punch blanc   *martinique–guadeloupe*
White Punch

This aperitif, perhaps the most popular in Martinique and Guadeloupe, is also known as Punch au Petit Citron Vert (punch with small green lime), usually shortened to Petit Punch, Little Punch. It is made with the local rhum agricole, a very gentle white rum, and jus de canne – pure cane syrup, which is now available from the islands, sometimes labelled cane juice. If it is not available, simple syrup (see Index) is the best substitute, though it lacks the special flavour.

½ oz. cane syrup   1 or 2 ice cubes
1½ oz. white rum   Water
Small piece green lime peel

Pour the cane syrup and rum into a small glass, twist the peel to release the oil and drop it in, add an ice cube or two and water to taste. Stir gently. Serves 1.

A more traditional way to drink the Petit Punch is to mix the syrup and rum together with the peel, but without ice, and drink this neat, followed by a glass of iced water.

punch vieux   *martinique–guadeloupe*

Old Punch

This is made with the smooth, dark, aged rum known as vieux (old, aged).

½ oz. cane syrup
1 ¼ oz. *rhum vieux*

2 or 3 ice cubes
Water

Pour the cane syrup and rum into a small glass, add an ice cube or two and water to taste. Stir gently. Serves 1.

Traditionally ice is seldom served with a vieux, however a newer fashion is to serve the drink poured over 3 or 4 ice cubes, with or without the jus de canne (cane syrup).

refresco de coco y piña   *dominican republic*

Coconut and Pineapple Drink

¾ pint coconut milk (see Index)
10 oz. coarsely chopped pineapple

2 tablespoons caster sugar
1 drop almond extract

Combine the coconut milk, pineapple, sugar and almond extract in an electric blender and blend at high speed until the mixture is very smooth and the pineapple completely pulverized.

Strain through a fine sieve, pour into a jug and refrigerate until thoroughly chilled. Serve in tumblers with or without ice cubes according to taste. Serves 3 to 4.

This may be served with the addition of 1 ½ oz. of light rum per serving, over 2 or 3 ice cubes. Serves 6.

refresco de lechosa   *dominican republic*
Milk and Papaya Drink

1 small ripe papaya, weighing
    about 12 oz.
6 tablespoons coconut milk, or
    milk (see Index)
3 tablespoons lime juice

½ teaspoon grated lime rind
2 oz. caster sugar
1 teaspoon vanilla
½ cup finely crushed ice
Lime slices for garnish

Peel the papaya, cut in half and remove the black seeds, and
chop fruit coarsely. Combine the papaya, coconut milk, lime juice
and rind, sugar, vanilla and ice in an electric blender and blend
at high speed until the mixture is smooth and thick. Serve in
chilled tumblers, garnished with lime slices. Serves 3 to 4.

rum cocktail   *english-speaking islands*

2 oz. light or dark rum,
    according to taste
2 oz. milk
½ cup finely crushed ice

2 dashes Angostura bitters
1 teaspoon caster sugar, if
    liked
Nutmeg or ground cinnamon

Combine the rum, milk, crushed ice, Angostura bitters and
sugar in a mixing glass and swizzle to a foam. Pour into a glass
and grate a little fresh nutmeg on top, or sprinkle with cinnamon.
Serves 1.

rum flip   *english-speaking islands*

4 oz. light Jamaican,
   Trinidadian, or Bajan rum
1 egg, lightly beaten
1 teaspoon caster sugar

2 dashes Angostura bitters
½ cup finely crushed ice
Nutmeg

Combine the rum, egg, sugar, bitters and ice in a cocktail shaker and shake vigorously. Pour, unstrained, into a small tumbler. Sprinkle with a little grated nutmeg. Serves 1.

rum float   *english-speaking islands*

1 oz. simple syrup (see Index)
1 oz. ice water
2 oz. light or dark rum,
   according to taste

Dash Angostura bitters
Pinch cinnamon
Small piece lime rind

Pour the simple syrup and ice water into a glass. Stir to mix. Float the rum on top by tilting the glass a little and trickling the rum down the side. Trickle the bitters down the side in the same way. Sprinkle the surface with the cinnamon and gently lay the lime rind on top. Serves 1.

rum neat   *english-speaking islands*

This is regarded as a splendid pick-up after a day's hard work.

2 to 3 oz. good, full-bodied
   rum

Cold water

Pour the rum into a cocktail glass and sip slowly. Then drink the same amount of cold water. Serves 1.

rum punch   *antigua*

This is one of my favourite rum punches.

1 oz. lime juice   2 oz. light rum,
1 oz. orange juice   preferably local, or from
1 oz. pineapple juice   Barbados or Trinidad
1 oz. grenadine   3 or 4 ice cubes
                                    Nutmeg

Combine the juices, grenadine, rum and ice cubes in a cocktail
shaker and shake vigorously. Strain into a small tumbler and
grate a little nutmeg on the top. Serves 1.

rum punch   *barbados*

This punch follows a very old formula that is still popular both
in the island and in England. It is charming in its simplicity and
leaves the choice of rum, light or dark, up to the drinker.

One of sour – 1 oz. lime juice   Three of strong – 3 oz. rum,
Two of sweet – 2 oz. simple   preferably Bajan rum
  syrup (see opposite)   Four of weak – 4 oz. water

Pour all the ingredients into a mixing glass and stir well. Chill,
pour into a tumbler and serve with a dash of Angostura bitters
and a grating of nutmeg. If liked, garnish with a sprig of mint,
or a lime leaf. Serves 1.

rum sour   *jamaica*

1½ oz. light Jamaica rum   1 teaspoon caster sugar, or
¾ oz. lime juice   to taste
1 cup crushed ice   Slice of orange

Combine the rum, lime juice, sugar and ice in a cocktail shaker and shake vigorously. Strain into a sour glass and decorate with the slice of orange. Serves 1.

shrub   *martinique–guadeloupe*

4 Seville oranges   A bottle *rhum vieux* from
4 oz. granulated sugar   Martinique or Guadeloupe,
3 tablespoons water   or use any dark rum

Using a vegetable peeler, peel the skins off the oranges as thinly as possible. Boil the sugar with the water until the sugar is dissolved. Pour out a little of the rum to make room for the syrup and orange peel. Add the syrup and peel to the rum bottle, re-cork and leave for 2 weeks.

Strain and rebottle. Serve as a liqueur.

simple syrup

Sugar does not dissolve readily in alcohol, and for this reason caster sugar is specified in drinks. Simple syrup gives a much smoother drink and is very easy to make.

1 lb. granulated sugar   ¾ pint cold water

Combine the sugar and water in a bowl. Stir from time to time until the sugar is dissolved. Use in drinks instead of sugar; ½ oz. (1 tablespoon) simple syrup equals 1½ teaspoons sugar.

sorrel cocktail   *trinidad*

2 or 3 ice cubes
1 ½ oz. light Trinidad
   rum

3 oz. Sorrel Drink (see below)
Squeeze lime juice

Put the ice cubes into a glass. Add the rum and sorrel drink. Add
a squeeze of lime juice and stir. Serves 1.

sorrel drink   *trinidad*

This is made from the sepals of an annual plant called rosella or
sorrel (see Glossary). Traditionally a Christmas drink in Trinidad,
when the sorrel sepals are at their best. The drink can also be
made with dried sorrel, or sorrel syrup.

If you use syrup follow the instructions on the bottle.

1 oz. dried sorrel sepals
3-inch piece stick cinnamon
Piece dried orange peel,
   about 3-by-1-inch
6 cloves
1 lb. sugar
3 pints boiling water

6 tablespoons medium dark
   rum, preferably Trinidad
   rum, or use Appleton
   Estate or Mount Gay
1 teaspoon ground cinnamon
   (optional)
¼ teaspoon ground cloves
   (optional)

Put the sorrel, cinnamon, orange peel, cloves and sugar into a
large jar or crock and pour the boiling water over them. Cool,
cover loosely, and leave for 2 or 3 days at room temperature.
Strain, add the rum, cinnamon and cloves and leave for another
2 days. Strain through a fine sieve lined with cheesecloth and
serve in chilled glasses, with or without ice cubes. If preferred,
the drink may be used after the first 2 or 3 days. Simply strain
and add the rum, or not, as liked. Makes about 3 pints.

spanish town   *jamaica*

2 oz. light Jamaica rum   ½ cup finely crushed ice
1 teaspoon Curaçao   Nutmeg

Combine the rum, Curaçao and ice in a cocktail shaker and shake
vigorously. Pour, unstrained, into a small glass and grate a little
nutmeg on top. Serves 1.

stuyvesant cooler   *curaçao*

½ cup crushed ice   2 tablespoons lime juice
1 ½ oz. light rum   Slice orange
1 ½ oz. Curaçao   Maraschino cherry

Put the crushed ice into a goblet. Pour in the rum, Curaçao and
lime juice. Stir to mix. Decorate with the orange slice and cherry.
Serves 1.

tamarinade   *jamaica*

6 whole tamarinds, shelled   2 oz. sugar
¾ pint water

Soak the tamarinds in the water for 30 minutes. Add the sugar,
stir to dissolve and let stand 5 minutes longer. Strain and chill
thoroughly. Serve over ice cubes in small tumblers. Serves 2.

Ackee, akee, achee. This is the fruit of a West African tree, *Blighia sapida*, named in honour of Captain Bligh who introduced it to Jamaica. A handsome evergreen, it bears a fruit whose scarlet shell and shiny black seeds alone would make the tree worth cultivating for its decorative aspect. The edible parts, sometimes called vegetable brains, is the aril, which looks like a small brain, or scrambled eggs, according to the eye of the viewer. It has a delicate flavour and is best known in the Jamaican dish Saltfish and Ackee. Tinned ackees from Jamaica are quite widely available in Indian and other speciality food shops.

Akkra. Originally a West African fritter made from black-eyed peas (they are the samsa of Upper Volta), they are called calas in the Dutch Islands, and are popular in Jamaica, as akkra where soy beans are also used. The name, changed to accra, is also used for fritters made of a heavy batter into which other ingredients are mixed, the most popular being salt cod. These are called stamp and go in Jamaica, acrats de morue in Martinique and Guadeloupe and bacalaitos in Puerto Rico. In Haiti the name changes to marinades. The recipes differ sufficiently from island to island to make necessary the inclusion here of a wide selection.

Allspice, pimento, Jamaica pepper. The poivre de la Jamaïque, or toute-épice of the French Islands, the pimienta de Jamaica or pimienta gorda of the Spanish-speaking islands, is the dark-brown berry of an evergreen tree, which the Spaniards found growing all over Jamaica when they first arrived in the Caribbean. When dried, the berries, which closely resemble peppercorns, have the combined flavour of nutmeg, cinnamon and clove. The Spaniards were no botanists and seem to have called everything pimienta, or pepper. The allspice tree is a bay, belonging to the myrtle family. Allspice is available wherever spices are sold.

Annatto, annotto. These are the seeds of a small, flowering tree of tropical America, *Bixa orellana*. The Spanish name achiote is sometimes corrupted to achote. The seeds are also known as bija or bijol in some of the Spanish-speaking islands. In the French and Dutch islands they are called roucou. In the West Indies the orange pulp surrounding the seed is used to colour and flavour food, usually in the form of aceite or manteca de achiote (annatto oil or lard). In Latin America, especially in south-eastern Mexico and Guatemala, the whole seed is ground and used as a spice. Annatto is not available in Britain and is therefore omitted from the recipes.

Arrowroot. Mostly imported from St Vincent, is a white starchy powder made from the underground rhizome of the *Maranta arundinacea* It is very popular as a thickening agent in Caribbean sauces and gravies to which it gives a light and delicate quality. It is also used in desserts and in the making of cakes and biscuits. It is widely available.

Aubergine. Also called garden egg, eggplant, or melongene in some of the English-speaking islands. It is known in the Spanish-speaking islands as berenjena, and in the French-speaking islands as aubergine and bélangère, the latter being a very large variety.

Avocado. *Persea americana,* first cultivated in Mexico as far back as 7000 B.C. but now grown in most tropical and semi-tropical countries. They are usually marketed unripe, when they are hard to the touch, and should be kept until the flesh yields when a gentle pressure is applied.

Banana and **banana leaves.** Bananas both green and ripe are used a great deal in West Indian cooking. They are used in appetizers, as a starchy vegetable when green, and in desserts. When plantains are not available, bananas make a good substitute. Banana leaves which can be 10 feet long and 2 feet wide, are used for wrapping such foods as conkies from Barbados and pasteles from Puerto Rico. Kitchen parchment and aluminum foil make adequate substitutes but do not add the delicate flavour that banana leaves give.

Banane Pesé. Pressed plantain. *See Tostones de plátano.*

Bay rum. *Pimenta acris,* is an evergreen tree native to West Africa and closely related to the West Indian, principally Jamaican, tree which produces allspice, and the West African tree which produces melegueta pepper. All these grow in the West Indies and some confusion arises between bay rum berries and leaves, known in the French islands as bois d'inde, and melegueta pepper known also as Guinea pepper or grains of paradise. Bay rum berries and melegueta peppercorns can be used interchangeably. There is no substitute.

Beans. English-speaking islanders use the terms peas and beans interchangeably, as do all English-speaking communities. However, their usage differs slightly from most others. Kidney beans in Jamaica are called peas. In Trinidad pigeon peas are often simply referred to as peas, in the way we use the term peas to mean green peas. The French islands use the term pois, peas, for the beans, such as kidney beans, that originate in Mexico. Cuba follows Mexican usage and calls its beans frijoles. Puerto Rico is more apt to use the term habichuelas, while in the Dominican Republic both terms are used, though habichuelas occurs more frequently than frijoles. The only types of bean not available are the pois de bois of Guadeloupe, called Pois d'Angole in Martinique, which closely resemble pigeon peas.

Breadfruit. These are large green fruits, usually about 10 inches round, which hang lantern-like from handsome trees. *Artocarpus communis*, with large, dark-green, deeply indented leaves. Cultivated since time immemorial in the south Pacific, the trees were introduced to the West Indies by Captain Bligh in 1792. Breadfruit are sometimes available in shops and markets selling tropical produce. However, tinned breadfruit makes an excellent substitute. Breadfruit are not edible until cooked, when the flesh, yellowish-white, is a little like a rather dense potato. It can be used in place of any starchy vegetable, rice or pasta, to accompany a main dish. It makes a fine soup.

Calabaza. Known as West Indian or green pumpkin, they are available in markets specializing in West Indian produce. The pumpkins, not to be confused with pie pumpkin, come in a variety of sizes and shapes, usually large, and are generally not sold whole, but by the wedge. The yellow flesh has a delicate flavour and is used mainly in soups and as a vegetable.

Callaloo, calaloo, callilu, calalou, callau. The principal ingredient in, and the name of, what is probably the most famous of all the island soups. The term applies to the leaves of two distinct types of plant which are used interchangeably. The first are the elephant-ear leaves of the diverse group of tropical plants with edible tubers classified as taro, but known in the Caribbean under a wide variety of names (*see Taro*). The other is Chinese spinach, *Amaranthus gangeticus*, sometimes sold as yin-choi or hon-toi-moi in Chinese shops, and as hiyu in Japanese shops. It is widely cultivated in India and Ceylon where it is known as bhaji, so that one finds it called both bhaji and callaloo in many West Indian markets, especially in Jamaica and Trinidad, where there is a sizeable Indian population. It can also be bought tinned from shops selling West Indian produce.

Cane syrup. This is pure cane juice and is sometimes sold in health food shops. It is sometimes labelled cane juice. In the French islands, where it is used a great deal in rum drinks, it is called jus de canne. When it is not available use simple syrup (see Index).

Cassareep. This is the boiled down juice squeezed from grated cassava root, and when flavoured with cinnamon, cloves and brown sugar is the essential ingredient in Pepperpot, an Amerindian stew originating in Guyana and popular in Trinidad, Barbados and other islands. Bottled cassareep is sold in West Indian shops.

Cassava. *Manihot utilissima*, also called manioc, mandioca, yucca or yuca, is a tropical vegetable with a long tuberous root at least 2 inches in diameter and from 8 to 10 inches long. It is covered with a brown bark-like rather hairy skin, and the flesh is white and very hard. It can be cooked and eaten as a starchy vegetable. Cassava meal or flour for making bread or cakes, is obtained by washing, peeling and grating cassava, pressing out the juice, and drying the meal. It can be bought ready made as cassava or manioc meal. Tapioca and cassareep are both made from cassava. There are two varieties of the plant, bitter and sweet. Bitter cassava is poisonous until cooked. In the French islands cassava meal is often called farine, a shortened form of farine de manioc.

Chayote, cho-cho, christophene. The Spanish, English and French names for a tropical squash, *Sechium edule*, originally from Mexico, but now widely grown in tropical regions throughout the world. The skin is rather prickly and there is a single, edible seed. Fresh and canned cho-cho are available from shops selling West Indian produce.

Chicharrones. These are fried pork cracklings.

Chive. *Allium schoenoprasum*, the smallest and mildest of the onion family, is much used in island cooking, especially in islands where the French have been. Known in English as chive, cive or sometimes simply herb, in French as ciboulette and oignon pays and in Spanish as cebollino, the chives of the West Indies are more fully flavoured than ours, and may be a different species. Long-established chives grown outdoors seem to acquire a flavour closer to that of the Caribbean herb. Spring onions, using both white and green parts, also approximate the flavour.

Chorizo. A Spanish sausage used in the Spanish-speaking islands. Lightly smoked, and made from coarsely chopped pork, seasoned with hot peppers and garlic. It is available from delicatessens.

Conch. A large Antillean marine mollusc of the gastropod class, 9 inches to a foot long, with a heavy spiral shell yellow shading to pink inside. The flesh is usually tenderized by pounding, before the mollusc is cooked. It is widely used in island cooking, in soups, stews and salads. The Carib name is lambi or lambie, and is used in many islands, both French and English. The Spanish name is concha, and the French conque. The English conch is pronounced conk as in the French. No recipes are included in the book since conch is virtually unobtainable outside the Caribbean and there are no suitable substitutes.

Coriander. *Coriandrum sativum*, or Chinese parsley, also known as culantro, culantrillo, cilantro (Spanish), coriandre (French), yuen-sai (Chinese), and koyendoro (Japanese), is an annual herb originally from the Mediterranean area but now cultivated throughout the world. The green leaves, which rather resemble parsley, are used a great deal in the cooking of the Spanish-speaking islands. The seeds which can be bought packaged from supermarket spice shelves, are widely used in curries. Fresh coriander is usually sold with its roots on. They should not be removed, and the plants should not be washed before storing. They should be wrapped in paper towels and placed in the refrigerator in a plastic bag, or put into a glass jar with cover. They should be washed and soaked for a few minutes in cold water just before using.

Court bouillon. In the French islands this term is used to describe a fish poached in a special manner, and does not mean the classic poaching liquid of French cookery.

Crapaud. The French word used to describe the very large frogs found on the islands of Dominica and Montserrat. They are also known as mountain chicken.

Crayfish, crawfish. The sea crayfish, or spiny or rock lobster, of the islands, which has meat in the tail and lacks the large claws of the lobster. It is often called lobster in the English-speaking islands and is langosta in Spanish, langouste in French.

Créole, criolla. These are terms not easy to define. Créole and criolla dishes are the culinary result of the meeting of the techniques and raw materials of France and Spain, Africa and America, in the kitchen. Créole applies to the cuisines of Louisiana and the Gulf States, as well as to the French-speaking West Indies, while criolla applies to the Spanish-speaking West Indies and all of Latin America.

Curaçao. An orange liqueur made in the Dutch island of Curaçao from the peel of the bitter oranges that grow there.

Dal. The Hindi name for all the legumes. In Trinidad, however, dal, sometimes spelled dahl, usually means split peas. Gram, or channa, dal is chick pea.

Escabeche. The Spanish for pickled, and is used to describe a method of cooking fish, poultry and game in which the food is cooked in oil and vinegar, or cooked and then pickled in an oil and vinegar marinade. In Jamaica escabeche has been transformed into escovitch and caveached fish.

Ginger root. In its fresh form it is popular in West Indian cookery. The root, usually about 3 inches long, is gnarled with a brown skin and moist, yellow flesh. Placed in a plastic bag, it will keep, refrigerated, for several weeks. It may be peeled and put in a jar of sherry, or salted water. Ground ginger may be used as a substitute, though the flavour is less pungent.

Guava. The fruit of an evergreen tree native to tropical America. Guavas are usually about 5 or 6 inches in diameter with pale yellow skins and pink or white flesh. They may be eaten raw, but are also made into a paste, into jams and jellies, and are stewed. Cooked and with the seeds removed, the shells are sold tinned.

Gungo peas. *See Pigeon Peas.*

Hearts of palm. The tender hearts of palm trees, sold tinned in slightly salted water. They are used fresh in the islands in salads and as a vegetable. The tinned product is an excellent substitute. Called palmito in the Spanish-speaking islands, it is known in the French islands as chou palmiste, chou coco, and chou glouglou, according to the type of palm from which it comes.

Keshy yena. A baked Edam or Gouda cheese with a variety of fillings. It originates in Curaçao and the name, which derives from the Spanish queso (cheese) and relleno (stuffed) is in Papiamento, the patois of the Netherlands Antilles that is a mixture of Portuguese, Spanish, Dutch, English and African words. Curiously enough the dish has been adopted by Chiapas and Yucatán in Mexico, where it was probably introduced some time in the last century by Dutch and German coffee men. It is called queso relleno there.

Mango. The fruit of an evergreen tree native to Asia, but now cultivated in tropical and semi-tropical regions throughout the world. All mangoes are green when unripe, and vary in colour when ripe from green-skinned to a deep rose red. The flesh varies from a light yellow to a deep orange yellow. Mangoes are ripe when the flesh yields to gentle pressure. They range in weight from about 10 ounces to about 1½ pounds. They are used a great deal in island cooking, the hard, unripe mango for chutney and relishes, while ripe mangoes may be eaten by themselves, or made into jam, pies, ice cream and drinks.

Melegueta pepper, Guinea pepper, grains of paradise. These are the small brown berries of the West African tree, *Amomum melegueta.*

Mountain chicken. *See Crapaud.*

Okra. This was introduced into the islands from Africa, though it is of tropical Asian origin. It has a great many names. In English it may be okra, or ochro, ladyfingers, or bamie. In the Spanish-speaking islands variants stem from the standard Spanish, quimbombó. In Cuba and Puerto Rico, it is quingombó, and in the Dominican Republic it is quimbombó or molondrón. In the French-speaking islands it is gombo.

Papaya, pawpaw. *Carica papaya,* is the fruit of a woody, herbaceous plant that looks like a tree and is native to tropical America. It is hard and green when unripe, but changes to yellow or orange when ripe, and the fruit varies greatly in size from 6 inches to well over 1 foot. The immature fruit is used as a vegetable in island cooking. Green papaya is also used to make a chutney or relish, and makes a main dish when stuffed. Ripe, it is eaten as a melon, or in fruit salad. It is known as pawpaw in the English-speaking islands, as papaya in most

Spanish-speaking islands, with the exception of Cuba where it is called fruta bomba and the Dominican Republic where it is called lechosa. In the French islands it is papaye. Tins of ripe papaya are quite widely available.

Peppers. All peppers, both hot and sweet, originated in Mexico but have spread so widely all over the world that they are an accepted part of all kitchens. In the islands one finds the usual sweet green or red (ripe) bell peppers and the red pimento. Any sweet pepper may be used in place of these. The hot peppers of the Caribbean have a very distinctive and splendid flavour, and are sometimes available crushed and bottled in vinegar. They are worth searching for in shops selling tropical foods. There is an island hot-pepper sauce from Jamaica, Pickapeppa Hot Pepper Sauce, that is widely available. If found fresh they may be used to make Pepper Wine or Pepper Vinegar, preserving their distinctive flavour. Otherwise, any hot pepper may be used, fresh, tinned or bottled.

Pigeon peas. These are of African origin and are popular in West Indian cooking, both dried and fresh. They have a number of names: in Jamaica they are known as gungo, gunga or goon-goo peas, while Trinidad recognizes them as pigeon peas, gungo peas and arhar dahl. The Spanish-speaking islands call them gandules. They are available dried or tinned in many oriental grocers.

Plantain, plátano (Spanish), **banane** (French). A large member of the banana family, and must be cooked before eating. It is widely used in West Indian cooking, both green, ripe, and semi-ripe, as an appetizer, in soups, as a starchy vegetable, and as a dessert.

Rosella. *Hibiscus sabdariffa*, a tropical plant grown for its fleshy red sepals which are used to make drinks, jam and jelly. It is available in the islands, fresh at Christmas time, but all year round in its dried form. It is also known as sorrel, and flor de Jamaica. Sorrel syrup is available in tropical food shops and can be used instead of the fresh or dried sepals.

Salt codfish. This is very popular in all the islands. In the English-speaking islands it is usually called simply saltfish, and sometimes fish other than cod are used. In the Spanish-speaking islands it is bacalao, and in French morue.

Seville orange. Also called sour and bigarade orange. It is grown extensively in Spain, and throughout the West Indies. It is large, with a rough reddish-orange skin. The pulp is too acid to be eaten raw. The juice is used a great deal in meat and poultry dishes in the Caribbean, particularly in the Spanish-speaking islands. The oranges are also used to make marmalade, and can sometimes be found in some fruit shops in the winter. The juice freezes successfully. A mixture of lime or lemon, and sweet orange juice can be used as a substitute but lacks the distinctive and pleasant flavour of the bitter orange.

Shrob, shrub. A liqueur made in the French islands, from rum and the peel of bitter oranges.

Sofrito. A basic tomato sauce originally used in Spanish cooking. The Puerto Rican version differs quite considerably from the Spanish and is essential to the cooking of the island. It is also used on other Spanish-speaking islands. It can be made in quantity and stored in the refrigerator where it will keep for some weeks. See Index for recipe.

Soursop. This is the spiny dark green fruit of a tropical American tree, *Annona muricata*. The edible pulp is tart and delicately flavoured. It is used mainly for drinks, ices and sherbets. It is guanábana in Spanish and corossol in French. It can be bought in tins.

Sweet potato. *Ipomoea batata*, is originally from tropical America though its exact birth place is not known. Skin colour is reddish brown, pink or white, and the flesh ranges from deep orange through yellow to white. Some confusion arises about sweet potatoes since those with moist orange-yellow flesh and reddish brown skin are also known as Louisiana yams. Yams, however, are from an entirely different botanical group, the *Dioscoreas*. Two other sweet potatoes are available, both far less sweet than the Louisiana yam. One has fairly dry mealy flesh which is yellowish in colour. The boniato, which is brown or pink skinned with white flesh, is only very slightly sweet. This is the preferred sweet potato of the islands, and the one most widely available in England.

Tamarind. *Tamarindus indica*, a large tropical tree whose seed pods contain a brown acid pulp, used principally in curries. The pulp may be bought in special food shops, especially those selling Indian foods.

Taro. Great confusion reigns among this group of tropical root vegetables but if one bears in mind that, shape and name apart, they all taste much the same, the confusion clears up. Taro belongs to the arum family and is known in Jamaica, Barbados, and Trinidad as coco, eddo and baddo, the leaves being called callaloo. A closely related group, the malangas, cultivated in many of the islands, are found in markets as malanga, dasheen, tanier, tannia, and yautía. Their leaves are also known as callaloo. The roots which come in a wide range of sizes have rather rough brown skin and flesh which ranges from white to yellowish to grey-white and purplish. Any recipe for potatoes can be used for these tubers. If taro is not available use yam or sweet potato (boniato) or even ordinary potato.

Tostones de Plátano. More often than not simply called tostones, are slices of green plantain partly fried, then flattened and fried until crusty and brown on both sides. Popular in the Spanish-speaking islands, as an accompaniment to both meat and fish dishes, they are also served as an accompaniment to drinks. They are known as banane pesé (pressed plantain) in Haiti and always accompany griots, grillots.

Yams. These are the edible tubers of a number of plants of the *Dioscorea* family. They come in a great variety of sizes and shapes and may weigh as much as 100 pounds each though most are about the size of a large potato and weigh 1 pound or less. The flesh is white or yellow and has a very pleasant rather nutlike flavour, and a texture rather like potatoes. They may be cooked according to any potato recipe. They are widely used in West Indian cooking and are available in most markets selling tropical foods. Yams should not be confused with the incorrectly named Louisiana yam, the orange-fleshed sweet potato, as they belong to entirely different botanical families.

Yard-long beans. *Vigna sesquipedalis*, also known as Chinese beans, asparagus beans and, in the Netherlands Antilles, as boonchi, are originally from tropical Asia, and can sometimes be found in oriental food shops. The beans, which have a very delicate flavour somewhat akin to green beans, grow to a length of up to 4 feet, but are only about ½ inch round. They are flexible enough to wrap around the skewered meat and vegetables in the Aruba dish, Lambchi and Boonchi.

importers and suppliers

Enco Products Ltd
71–5 Fortress Road
London NW5 1AU

This firm imports all West Indian foods. If
you have difficulty finding any ingredients
they will give you the name of your nearest
stockist.

index

MORE ABOUT PENGUINS AND PELICANS

Penguinews, which appears every month, contains details of all the new books issued by Penguins as they are published. From time to time it is supplemented by *Penguins in Print*, which is our complete list of almost 5,000 titles.

A specimen copy of *Penguinews* will be sent to you free on request. Please write to Dept EP, Penguin Books Ltd, Harmondsworth, Middlesex, for your copy.

In the U.S.A.: For a complete list of books available from Penguins in the United States write to Dept CS, Penguin Books, 625 Madison Avenue, New York, New York 10022.

In Canada: For a complete list of books available from Penguins in Canada write to Penguin Books Canada Ltd, 41 Steelcase Road West, Markham, Ontario.

A PENGUIN HANDBOOK

A BOOK OF MIDDLE-EASTERN FOOD

Claudia Roden

This cook's tour of the Middle East contains more than 500 recipes from many countries including Syria, the Lebanon, Egypt, Iran, Turkey, Greece, Iraq, Saudi Arabia, the Yemen, the Sudan, Algeria, Tunisia, and Morocco.

'The cuisine of the Middle East has, for some mysterious reason, remained practically unexplored, but now that we can buy most of the ingredients here, we have an opportunity – encouraged by Claudia Roden – to try it for ourselves. This is a book for those wishing to widen their cookery knowledge and add new variety to the dinner table. Particularly good are the set-the-scene introductions to each recipe, and the section on origins and influences. And the dietary laws are useful for those who entertain overseas visitors. It makes fascinating reading' – *Good Housekeeping*

'This book is absolutely gripping – which is the way a cookery book should be' – Caroline Conran in the *Sunday Times*

A PENGUIN HANDBOOK

MEDITERRANEAN FOOD

Elizabeth David

This book is based on a collection of recipes made by the
author when she lived in France, Italy, the Greek Islands,
and Egypt, doing her own cooking and obtaining her
information at first hand. In these pages will be found
recipes, and practical ones, evoking all the colour and sun of
the Mediterranean; dishes with such exciting and
unfamiliar names as the *Soupe au Pistou*, the *Pebronata* of
Corsica, or the *Skordaliá* of the Greeks. The book includes
recipes from Spain, Provence, Greece, Italy and the
Middle East, making use of ingredients from all over the
Mediterranean now available in England. The majority of
the dishes however do not require exotic ingredients, being
made with everyday vegetables, herbs, fish, and poultry,
but treated in unfamiliar ways.

'In *Mediterranean Food* Mrs David proves herself a
gastronome of rare integrity . . . She refuses to make
ignoble compromises with expediency. And in this, surely,
she is very right . . . Above all, she has the happy knack of
giving just as much detail as the average cook finds
desirable; she presumes neither on our knowledge nor our
ignorance' – Elizabeth Nicholas in the *Sunday Times*